A PARENT'S GUIDE TO

RAISING GRIEVING CHILDREN

A PARENT'S GUIDE TO

RAISING GRIEVING CHILDREN

Rebuilding Your Family after the Death of a Loved One

Phyllis R. Silverman
Madelyn Kelly

OXFORD

UNIVERSITY PRESS

2009

OXFORD
UNIVERSITY PRESS

Oxford University Press, Inc., publishes works that further
Oxford University's objective of excellence
in research, scholarship, and education.

Oxford   New York
Auckland   Cape Town   Dar es Salaam   Hong Kong   Karachi
Kuala Lumpur   Madrid   Melbourne   Mexico City   Nairobi
New Delhi   Shanghai   Taipei   Toronto

With offices in
Argentina   Austria   Brazil   Chile   Czech Republic   France   Greece
Guatemala   Hungary   Italy   Japan   Poland   Portugal   Singapore
South Korea   Switzerland   Thailand   Turkey   Ukraine   Vietnam

Copyright © 2009 by Oxford University Press, Inc.

Published by Oxford University Press, Inc.
198 Madison Avenue, New York, New York 10016
www.oup.com

Oxford is a registered trademark of Oxford University Press

Library of Congress Cataloging-in-Publication Data

Silverman, Phyllis R.
A parent's guide to raising grieving children: rebuilding your family after
the death of a loved one / Phyllis R. Silverman and Madelyn Kelly.
p.   cm.
ISBN 978-0-19-532884-4
1. Grief in children.   2. Bereavement in children.   3. Parenting.
4. Child rearing.   I. Kelly, Madelyn.   II. Title.
BF723.G75S55 2009
155.9'37083—dc22
2008044055

1   3   5   7   9   8   6   4   2

Printed in the United States of America

To Eloise Cole, 1942–2005, who never stopped giving until there was no more time.

—PRS

For Tom and Jack, who are the reason why.
And for Mike: always with us; always missed.

—MSK

Acknowledgments

This book would not exist without the bravery and honesty of the many widows, widowers, and children who shared with us their darkest memories, their saddest thoughts, their tentative steps, and their emerging hopes. They did it for you, to accompany you and guide you through this terrible journey of loss.

Readers often ask if what we say is supported by research. Phyllis has been talking to grieving parents and children for decades, including her pivotal role as project director and co-principal investigator of the Harvard/MGH Child Bereavement study. Parents who lost a spouse and children who lost a parent were eager to tell her their stories, both to honor the person who died and to let others benefit from their experience. Part of our understanding of grief and its impact on children comes from this important research.

Phyllis has also spoken to families and colleagues at centers for grieving children all over the United States. Donna Schurmann, director of the Dougy Center in Portland, Oregon is a friend who has always supported her work.

Program Director Donna Scharff and Executive Director Barbara Clarke at The Children's Room in Arlington, Massachusetts couldn't have been more helpful and encouraging throughout this long project. Members of the Parent Council and the Teen Age Theatre Group also willingly added their experiences. Madelyn found solidarity and support in The Children's Room's Thursday "B" group, along with new perspectives and numerous personal stories that helped shape this book.

We promised anonymity to all who told their tales; therefore, we do not name them here.

In this journey, Phyllis met Eloise Cole, a bereaved parent who founded NEW SONG, a bereavement center in Phoenix, Arizona. She was excited about this book but did not live to see its birth. We thank the Alon Family for sharing the pain of watching their daughter Yael die, and for encouraging her friends to talk to Phyllis about what that death meant to them. Tina Chery, whose son was the victim of an accidental neighborhood shooting, found a way to be part of the solution, not part of the problem. Special thanks go to Phyllis's daughter, Gila Silverman, who wrote with much feeling about the meaning of her friend's suicide.

Three of Madelyn's friends contributed their own stories of great grief and great wisdom to this book, along with endless guidance and support for her: Susan Moran, the merry widow, full of compassion, empathy, and real humor; and Pam Walter and Mary Ann McGann, both of whom learned the hardest way about the lifelong impact of losing a parent.

The anonymity we promised, in the end, meant little to these friends. They saw this book as a tribute to their lost loved ones, and as a way of honoring their lives by helping others.

We were blessed with wonderful editors at Oxford University Press. Maura Roessner was patient and generous and put up with an awful lot of second (and third) guessing. Mallory Jensen was able to ferret out ideas that weren't fully thought through and phrases that were less than felicitous, and was always available to us. Maura and Mallory, you always made us feel like you were on our side, and that we were in this together. Thank you.

Our greatest appreciation goes to our families. This book took a long time to get done, and Phyllis thanks her husband Sam for his patience, for his encouragement, and for his delight in finally seeing it finished.

Madelyn's sons Tom and Jack Kelly provide love and encouragement to their mom every day; they bravely shared their feelings and perceptions about their terrible loss for this book. Madelyn is deeply grateful to Tom and Jack and to those who mourn alongside them: to Mike's family—Tom and Marguerite Kelly, Katy Kelly and Steve Bottorff, Meg and Tony Rizzoli, and Nell and Dennis Conroy—who have nothing in common with any of the bad in-laws in the book; and to her family—Anita and Irwin Greenberg, Cheryl Greenberg and Dan Lloyd—who stepped into the breach with her, and never left.

PHYLLIS ROLFE SILVERMAN
MADELYN KELLY

Contents

A PARENT'S GUIDE TO

RAISING GRIEVING CHILDREN

1

Road Map for a Long Journey

I feel like a complete zombie. I'm trying to figure out how to keep my kids' lives from falling apart, and I can't even get dinner on the table.

A widower, three weeks after the death of his wife

It's been a year since my daughter died, and my seven-year-old is still a complete mess. He doesn't pay attention at school, talks back to his teachers, gets into fights. Shouldn't he be over it by now?

A mother of three

Every now and then I get a flashback and remember that he died. By now, I've almost adapted to it, so it feels like everybody lives this way.

A nine-year-old boy, five years after his father's death

We are truly sorry you need this book, because reading this means that something tragic has happened in your family. Someone you love has died, or is going to die.

Perhaps the best word for what you and your children feel is anguish. You feel naked. No matter who is around you, even if you are surrounded by friends and relatives, you feel deeply, fundamentally, existentially, alone.

How can your family survive this crisis? There are times when it will feel impossible, and you'll have no idea how to proceed. It will be all you can do to put one foot in front of the other and get through the day. You'll all have to make changes in your routines, in relationships, in work or school, and, most importantly, in your sense of how you fit in the world. But you will adapt. You will survive. Your family will go on. You will know happiness and joy and love again; you will lead rich and rewarding lives; and you will find ways to keep the person who died in your hearts. Your lives won't be the same, but neither must they be diminished. It won't be easy, but it is possible, and with this book, we are here to help, offering you a road map of what lies ahead, assisted by the painfully acquired wisdom of many people who have navigated this way before.

All around you there will be people who don't know what you're feeling, wanting to help but not knowing what to do or what to say. Friends and relatives, too often, will mouth well-meaning but ultimately useless platitudes like "this too shall pass," or "it was meant to be," and, all too soon, the unwittingly cruel "you need to get on with your life." This widow says she walked around in a daze for months, wondering how everyone else's lives could just go on as before, when hers was so altered:

> It drives me crazy when people come up to me and say "how are you?" I mean, how am I supposed to answer? "My whole world has come apart, thanks for asking." I usually just say, "Fine, thanks, how are you?" And then I hear them saying, "Isn't it amazing how well she's doing?"

This book is different. We really do know how you are. We know that there's no getting over the loss of a loved one. We understand your worries about how your children are going to make it through this: your fears about them acting out or not talking about what they're feeling; your questions about how they're doing in school and in their relationships with friends; your concerns about whether their sense of themselves will develop as it should. And we understand your questions about how *you* are going to make it through this: mourning and examining your relationship with the person who died, wondering who you will be without that person in your life; struggling with your house, work, and money; worrying about how to manage your family.

YOU DON'T HAVE TO DO THIS ALONE

We aren't going to tell you how you should be feeling, what you should be doing, or how to behave. We know that no two people grieve in the same way or deal with their grief in the same way. We will give you advice, though, and try to point you in directions that might help you and your family through this time. Not through this time as if it has an end, but through this time when you feel utterly lost and hopeless, as though you're on a mountain path with hidden switchbacks and a sheer precipice to your side. And through the later time as well, the better days ahead, when you have made accommodations to the loss and your family life is humming along again, but the person who died is still gone and you all have to continue to live with that knowledge, trying to chart the rest of your lives going forward, but always with that absence within.

Part of how we do this is through the words of fellow travelers—scores of children and adults who've lost their parents, siblings, spouses, children, or friends—all of them eager to share their stories in order to give you the kind of support they often couldn't find themselves. There's great relief to be had in hearing from others who have been in your shoes. In interviews and bereavement group discussions, we've seen widows and widowers discover with amazement and relief that theirs aren't the only children who suddenly insist upon sleeping in their parent's bed; we've listened to bereaved children debate how to answer when people ask how many brothers and sisters they have; we've learned from discussions about visiting cemeteries, getting health insurance, mowing the lawn, dating (both parents and children), and dealing with friends, teachers, and others who don't understand; we've watched people whose spouses have died from drug or alcohol abuse discuss how and when to tell their children the truth about their parent; and we've heard from bereaved adults who are utterly unable to get beyond their own grief, to reach out to their children.

Without hearing from these people, you might not know what grieving children look like. Are they like John Kennedy Jr. saluting his father's coffin? Batman or Harry Potter, avenging their parents' deaths? Real children are not superheroes. They might not even look upset—they don't often cry, especially not in public; they're neither ashen nor visibly shaken. You'll see them playing, watching TV, looking unaffected. But inside, they're a mess. Everything they knew about the world has just been proved wrong, or everything they feared has just been proved right. They have no idea what will happen next.

Others will look at them, adults and children alike, and not understand what's happening behind the facade. They'll ask them how they feel; they'll challenge the way they're acting; they'll analyze their behavior; they'll tell them to "get over it." This boy is fed up with all the bad advice:

> People tell kids it's OK to be mad at the person who died. Why would I be mad at my dad? They say it's OK to be mad at God. Why would I be mad at God? I don't think God decides who dies. So a word of advice to adults; if you sense that a child is mad at someone, then tell them it's OK to be mad, but don't tell them it just for future reference, because then they feel that they should be mad at those people, not just that they can.

WHY WE WROTE THIS BOOK

We come at this book from two perspectives: the clinical and the personal. Phyllis Rolfe Silverman has been studying grief for most of her professional life, in an extraordinary, groundbreaking career of working with bereaved families. She learned early that if she was to understand this very real and human experience, the bereaved themselves would be her teacher. She explains how this came about:

> I was doing the finishing work on my Ph.D. dissertation when I was offered a position that would focus on the needs of the widowed. This led to what became known as the Widow-to-Widow program. At a meeting with the widows who would implement the program, I shared with them what the professional literature in the late 1960s said about grief: that the crisis would be resolved within six weeks. These women just laughed and said that wasn't at all what it was like to lose a spouse. So I asked them what it really was like, and I listened to what they said, and I've been trying to listen ever since.

> What they told me was that it takes at least two years to get your head screwed on so that you can turn around and consider that there will be a future. They talked about how they felt something was wrong with them for not feeling better as quickly as everyone expected them to. And they said they couldn't go back and pick up their lives as other people told them they should. I learned then, and I continue to learn, that my best teachers are people who have lived through their grief and are willing to share with me and others what they have learned.

When Phyllis began her research on how the death of a loved one affects children, she was surprised to hear virtually every newly bereaved parent ask her the same question: Will my children be OK? They were looking for reassurance that their children would not be emotionally damaged for life. As one parent explained her thinking:

> I worry that my children will never have a full life now. They've never existed without their father, and I'm afraid they won't know that they can exist without him now.

After years of research and countless hours of conversation with bereaved children and parents, Phyllis has learned that most children's lives will not be irrevocably damaged as a result of a death in the family. Their lives will never be the same, but that doesn't mean they're doomed to a lesser existence; in fact, the experience will help many gain a sensitivity to others and a zest for making the most of their lives that goes well beyond their peers'. What's more, Phyllis discovered that a crucial determinant in helping children cope with the death is your ability to be there for them, to recognize them as mourners, and to give them support and care as they deal with all the emotions and changes they're coming up against. It's hard to believe this when you're experiencing acute grief, but your children can, and will, have full and fulfilling lives, even in the wake of this catastrophic loss.

That message was of particular interest to Madelyn Kelly, a journalist whose husband, Michael, was killed while reporting on the war in Iraq. Their two young sons, Tom and Jack, describe what it was like for them to lose a parent:

My father died in Iraq when I was only six years old. That is one reason I would like to be like him so much. That morning my mom woke me up at 7:00 and told me the terrible news. I cried for hours. All day, more and more people came to my house. People liked my dad so much that they drove in from western Massachusetts, New York, and Washington, D.C., the day he died, and hundreds came in from as far as Ohio, California, and Washington State for his funeral. When I went back to school the next week it was hard for me, because everyone kept on saying sorry to me, which reminded me that he was dead. For years, I couldn't believe that he was dead. Although I haven't, never will, and never want to get over it, I now try to believe that he's still alive, but I know that somewhere deep inside me, I know he's dead. Although I can never solve this problem, I've come as close to solving it as I ever will. I try to do what he would want me to do if he was alive. *Tom, at age ten.*

Maybe my life is a little lonelier now that my father's dead. I wish I had gotten to know him a little better, because I was only three when he died. On the other hand, when you do get to know somebody well, when they die, it might be a little harder on you. *Jack, at age nine.*

Madelyn read about Phyllis's research while looking for ways to understand what her children were going through and to help them cope with their loss. That led her family to a bereavement center where Phyllis is a board member, called The Children's Room, Center for Grieving Children and Teenagers. Several years and hundreds of conversations with bereaved families later, both at The Children's Room and with other widows and widowers she got to know, it led her to work with Phyllis on putting what they've learned into this book.

The people quoted in these chapters provide an unequaled opportunity to get into the heads and hearts of the bereaved. You'll hear from children, parents, and grandparents, people who are probably at the lowest points of their lives, trying to put words to their experience. Reading this book allows you, in a way, to be a fly on the wall, to hear how other people deal with death and the many issues it brings with it. And it puts you in the company of those who understand the special pain and confusion of raising children after a loss.

What this book does not give is easy answers. There's no right way to do things, no one-size-fits-all advice, though there are some behaviors and attitudes that can make your adjustments less or more difficult. On the most basic level, bereaved children need to know that their grief is legitimate, to learn a vocabulary that helps them describe and accommodate the changes in their lives, to be involved in the family's new directions, and to find a way to continue a connection to the person who died. These are serious, challenging, decades-long struggles, and your children need to know they're not facing them alone.

In general, we have found that families that are child-centered, meaning that they're focused on their children's grief and needs, have an easier time navigating this dark passage. As hard as it may be to accomplish when you're feeling so raw and desperate yourself, your children will have a much easier time if you make their well-being the focus of your family's rebuilding.

Your children need care, continuity, and connection. Care involves giving them the love and attention they need no matter what, as well as meeting basic needs, from food and clothing to emotional support and spiritual guidance, despite your own great sorrow. You provide a sense of continuity when you reassure your children that tomorrow will happen, and your family will carry on. It will look different and feel different, but you have a past and future together and that will never change. Connection means recognizing your children as mourners, involving them in rituals, and helping them find a way to keep the person who died present in their lives, especially as time passes.

This rebuilding is an uneven, arduous process that can feel futile at times. But what we know from the research is that this child-centered approach is the best bet for your family, and the best hope for your children's future. This young woman's father died when she was eleven years old. Now a college senior, she reflects on what she's learned since then, with a decade's worth of clarity:

I can't say what my life would have been like if my father had lived. I know it was different. But it was not bad, and I see it as quite good now.

HOW TO READ THIS BOOK

You and your children are facing an altered existence, and it will take years to integrate your old life and your new one. This book is here to help you do that, each step of the way. We'll take you from diagnosis (when applicable) through the first days after death, and well into the years afterward. We will show you how your children's developmental ages affect their ability to understand and respond to what is happening, we'll give you ideas about how and where to get help, and we'll look at ways to keep your connections to the person who died.

This book is designed so that you can read as much as you need to, as much as you can handle, at any given time. Most of you won't read it from cover to cover, nor do you need to (we certainly hope nobody has to deal with the death of a spouse, a child, and a friend, all at the same time). Instead, we encourage you to start by reading the sections that apply to everyone: Chapter 1, Chapter 2 (which looks at how children understand death at different ages), and Chapter 8 (where to look for, and get, help of all kinds), and then whichever of the other chapters apply to your family at this time. Chapter 3 is for those who have learned that someone in the family is facing death. Chapter 4 covers the period immediately following the death, from telling your children, through the funeral, and back to school and work. Chapter 5 looks in depth at how the death of a parent affects children; Chapter 6 looks at the effect of a sibling's death; Chapter 7 at the death of a friend. Chapter 9 is a chapter that can be read time and again for ideas on how to keep the person who died alive in your hearts. And Chapter 10 explores the bereaved family over the passage of time, looking at how family members may be moving at separate paces as they make their own accommodations to the death.

You might read the book all at once, looking for some previews of what lies ahead, or you might read some of it now and then not pick it up again for a few months, following your family's path through life after a death. Whatever works for you. There will be sections where it's painful to read what your children are going through, or where it's upsetting to read something you wished you had known at the time, and there will be pages where you're grateful for an idea or suggestion, relieved to learn you've made the right choice, and calmed by the knowledge that you are not going through this alone.

We try whenever possible to get around the inadequacies and imprecision of language, but sometimes that's impossible. There are times when we use more generic language than we want to, because there's no way to encompass all we want to say otherwise. For example, in English, you can't use the singular "child" without having to sooner or later describe that child as a "he" or a "she." As a result, for the most part, we cheat that by using the plural "children."

We also use an imprecise phrase when we talk about the death of "a loved one." We know that that's not always the way to describe family members who die—we have talked to widows and widowers of violent abusers, alcoholics, addicts, embezzlers, and other criminals; a number of those parents we spoke to were divorced or separated from the person when they died. But they all still worry about their children and how to help them with this death, because the loss of a parent is something to deal with, no matter who that parent was. Many children are unaware of their parents' flaws and grieve the death even if their surviving parent is relieved by it. When children do have unhappy memories of the person who died, they still mourn the death and regret that they will never be able to confront the person, to get what's too glibly called "closure." No matter what the relationship, they will have to develop a workable construct of the person who died. There are things you can do to help that happen, and we discuss them along the way.

Finally, while most of the book is written as if it's being read by those raising bereaved children, we know that some people who have just experienced a great loss are unable, in the beginning, to sit down and read about death. They'll need friends and relatives to read this book for them, or the parts of the book that are appropriate to their situation, and pass on the relevant stories, information, and advice. To those friends and family who are looking for something to do to help, this is one of the best gifts you can give—the gift of understanding; the gift of experience; the gift of advice that really works.

SOME WORDS OF ADVICE

Throughout this book, you'll hear grieving adults and children tell their stories, so you can learn from their experiences, and from their mistakes. We also asked the children for specific advice they might have for others in their situation. Here's a sample of some of the things they want you to know:

Two years after her mother died, this fifteen-year-old girl emphasizes the importance of talking to someone who has been through the same ordeal:

I would tell a kid whose parent died, it happened to me so I know how you feel. It's all right to think about it, to be sad and to cry—but you have to get on with it. It doesn't help to keep it bottled up. Try to be open with friends. It doesn't get better right away, but it does get better with time. I would tell an adult, if you want to help, you should ask if the kid wants to talk and what she wants to talk about—don't just start off.

This young boy's brother died in an accident. He wants you to know how insecure that makes him feel:

Wherever you go, there's no place that is completely safe.

This girl thinks it's important to reassure your children that their new and scary feelings are normal:

After it happened I was afraid my mother and brother would die. Sometimes I'd wake up early in the morning, lie on the couch outside my mother's room and wait for her to get up to be sure she didn't die. It helped to learn that other children felt this same way after their parent died.

This sixth-grade boy wants people to stop saying things he doesn't know how to respond to:

People will sometimes do things like say "I'm so sorry," and what do you say? I'd like to say it's OK, but it's not.

A third-grade boy says he feels very much alone:

I wish someone else in my class only had one parent. Death is different than divorce because with divorce you can see them sometimes. But even if you don't, you know they're still alive or they could have an effect on the world. When they die, you know you won't see them again.

A seventeen-year-old boy says, two years after his father's death:

It's difficult but you can overcome it. Keep the same things you thought were important. Don't deal with anything too quickly. Takes time to get used to the death. Don't fight it. People should listen more than talk.

His sister, two years younger, describes how communicating helps everyone:

Talk about it with friends and relatives. There are a lot of people that can help and they'll get over the shock.

A thirteen-year-old boy agrees that talking is the best way to cope with a death:

Talk to other people—about your feelings and the person who died. I did it and it was helpful; otherwise it gets built up inside.

Advice from an eleven-year-old:

No two situations are the same. No one will ever understand how you felt and you won't understand how they felt but it's good to talk about it to family members and others who knew the person who died.

A college sophomore shares her thoughts, ten years after her father died:

Please involve the children; they need to know what is happening. Comfort them. It is difficult for them to talk about their feelings, but they need to know that they are important and that their grief is appropriate.

A twelve-year-old girl offers reassurance to others, two years after her father died:

It's OK, 'cause I've been through it. You know you have to go on with your life and not feel sorry for yourself.

A high school senior passes along the wisdom she's gained through her experience:

The person who died would not want you to ruin your life. You just have to keep living, move on. I want to experience life as much as I can. I do not want to die. I know that life is too precious, and I need to take care. I have more respect for life and in some ways I am more mature.

And a young adult provides a glimpse of how children look back on their loss:

My life is different because my father died, not necessarily good or bad. Different.

These children share their advice in the hope that it will help you and your children to bear the unbearable loss. Our hope is that reading this book will let you understand each family member's thoughts and concerns, while giving you ideas about how to address them.

We wish you comfort and sustenance in these formidable days ahead, as well as the knowledge that you are not alone.

2

What Death Means to Children

How do you tell your children their father died? When they went to sleep, everything was fine. I woke them up and told them Daddy didn't feel good. I asked a neighbor to stay with them and I took my husband to the hospital. He was dead before I knew what happened. Fortunately, there was a chaplain on duty. I asked him if he could come home with me. I had no idea how to explain all of this to my children—they were six, eleven, and fourteen, and they were waiting at home for me to tell them what the doctor said had made Daddy sick. The chaplain agreed, but he couldn't promise that he had all the right words, either. It didn't occur to me that maybe there was no right way. When we got there, I can't remember what happened. The children were there, my neighbor was there, and there was a lot of crying. I usually like things quiet and orderly; I rarely show my feelings, but I guess this was the time when it felt OK that there was what felt like an explosion.

A mother of three, several months after her husband's death

Telling your children that someone they love has died may be the hardest thing you'll ever do. You are already shattered by the news yourself, and now you have to be the one to blow apart your children's known universe. You want to cushion the blow, make it more bearable, but there are no magic words; there's no way to make it easy on them or you. And no matter what you say or how you say it, your children might not even fully comprehend the meaning. Very young children don't even know that people can die; older children don't know what to do when someone does die. This girl was eight when her father died after an illness:

We all knew he was going to die, but when it happened, I had no idea that he wouldn't be there tomorrow. I couldn't imagine what it meant. It took a while before I understood that he wasn't coming back.

With all that you're going through at this moment, it may seem like an insurmountable effort to step back and think about child development and how that relates to your children's understanding of death. Yet it is essential to remember that your children are going to be scared, confused, and lost, and they'll need your help to make sense of what's going on around them. Being aware of the various developmental factors—neurological, psychological, emotional—that go into how your children think and act might help you find more appropriate words to make it easier for them to understand what you are telling them, and for you to understand their response.

AGE MATTERS

Your children's reactions to the news that a loved one has died will depend on their individual styles of behavior, their age, and their understanding of what death means. This may be the first time they have come face to face with death, or they may be so young that they don't even know what death is. Their responses will also be colored, in part, by your own reaction to what's happened. Death will leave you pained, stunned, angry, and disbelieving, just like they are, and they'll be looking to see how you respond as guidance for how to deal with those feelings. This young widow describes her shock when her husband died after a long illness:

> I know it intellectually, but emotionally, I can't really believe it. I go toward it and quickly retreat. It doesn't seem possible.

Another distraught widow, a day after her husband's sudden death, exclaims:

> I can't and I won't believe he is really gone!

The finality of death is similarly staggering to children. A fifteen-year-old girl describes her dislocation from reality:

> After they told me my father had died, I had to go outside to see if the sun was still shining. It didn't seem possible.

While everyone has a difficult time understanding what has happened, adults at least know, at some level, what death means. You know that death is final, that there is no returning from the grave, that you cannot go up to heaven to visit, and that all of us will die someday. You may not believe it's really happened; you might feel as if your world has come crumbling down on you; but you know that there will be a tomorrow, and that in spite of your wishes to the contrary, your loved one will not be there.

Children know nothing of the sort. Their reactions will evolve and change as they grow and mature, but when they're first hearing about the death, if children are to grasp what is happening, they have to be told in language they can understand. A young widow tells us:

> I tried to explain that when a person dies they can't come alive again. I didn't use the word sleep. I thought that for a three-year-old, she might not want to go to sleep again.

That widow understood immediately how important it is to be sensitive to the language you use in telling your children what happened. Euphemisms for death, like "passed away" or "has gone to be with God" can be tempting because they sound less harsh, but children need clearer, more straightforward language and explanations.

As your children try to make sense out of what you're telling them, it might seem as if they have not even heard what you said. They might go out and play, acting as if nothing has happened. Conversely, they might crawl into bed and demand that you join them for comfort and reassurance. Your children are struggling to make sense out of this shattering news, and they are hardly equipped to do so.

Even when they are visibly upset, most children can't stay in that moment for long and will soon be ready to move on to do something else. When you see how easy it is to distract them, you might assume that this means they're not truly upset by the death. However, it seems that in their confusion and despair, children seek places where they have some certainty, where they are familiar with the rules. In the words of one teenager:

> When I got the news, I didn't say a word. I took my bike out and went to my friend's house. He went with me and we rode along the beach, a place my mother loved and where I go all the time to enjoy the atmosphere. I told my friend the news that my mother was killed in an accident. We didn't say much, but he was there for me. Watching the ocean quieted me a bit. Finally I realized my father would be worried; he didn't know where I was. And we rode back home.

While you have many difficult tasks to perform shortly after getting the bad news, people to call and arrangements to make, your children often don't have active roles to play at this time. For that reason, too, they might go to the part of their world that is comfortable and familiar. There's only so much they can take in at one time. One mother notes her child's contradictory behavior, just half an hour after hearing of her father's death:

> My daughter got all excited when my parents arrived at the hospital. She ran to them and said, "I am not sad anymore, now that you are here." They offered to take her for ice cream. I smiled because I knew that in five minutes she would be sad again. She is, after all, only six, and for the moment she was quite able to forget why we were there. It's sort of like she has one feeling at a time and that's all she can handle. But I wasn't fooling myself. She was very aware that her father had just died. She was there to say good-bye. But what dead means to her is not at all clear. I'm not sure how much she could take in about what we all lost at that moment and that it was forever.

If you have children who are at different developmental stages, you'll have to adjust your words and explanations accordingly. The ways they digest the news can spin older and younger children in opposite directions. One mother recalls, months after the death:

> After we told the children that our ten-year-old had died, our four-year-old son kept asking if God would take care of his brother, and our fifteen-year-old daughter kept asking, if there is a God, how could he let this happen to her brother? She kept yelling at her brother to stop asking such stupid questions. We had no easy answers.

A four-year-old is concrete and specific and sees the world in terms of needs; therefore, this boy worries about who will take care of his brother, as he would worry about who would take care of him. At fifteen, his sister can see more of the fullness of what has happened. She understands the finality of death. While someone her age might ordinarily be able to grasp the limited scope of her younger brother's understanding and keep her from yelling at him, her own stress got in the way this time. Or maybe it just felt better for her to have someone to lash out at.

The differences in these children's perceptions of God also make a good snapshot of how developmental age plays out in reaction to a death. Very young children, like the four-year-old above, tend to see God as a specific being whose job is to take care of people. He would, therefore, take care of the loved one who died. An older child may become angry at God for having taken the loved one away. Adolescents, like the fifteen-year-old, can turn that anger into a more philosophical challenge: maybe there is no God, because if there were, why would He let their loved one die? These differences exist not only at the time of impact. The four-year-old may become angry at God in a few years—and then, a few years later still, may question His very existence. In each of these stages, each time that child considers the question, the reality of the death may feel brand-new: fresh, raw, and excruciating. One widow describes the ongoing pain:

> My daughter was doing really well, three years after her father died. She had friends, was doing well in school, had stopped wanting to be near me all the time to make sure I was OK. Then, just after she turned fifteen, she suddenly got all upset, almost as upset as she was when he died. When I finally got her to talk about it, she said she was sad because her father wouldn't be able to walk her down the aisle. It's like she'd never figured that out before, that some day she'd get married, and he wouldn't be there.

This teenager is just developing what one widow calls "the anticipation of future loss." Adults understand it immediately after the death; they know that their loved one will not be there at the recital or the first date or the big game or graduation, and that plays into their grief from the start. But young children can't look that far ahead, so they have to experience the loss again and again as they reach each of these milestones. Sometimes you can prepare them before a momentous event, so the absence doesn't take them by surprise. One widow says:

> The morning of my daughter's middle school graduation, I said, "Let's take a moment to think about how proud Daddy would be right now." I think it helped her to not obsess about it when she was on stage.

A widower takes a different approach:

> Before any significant event, I find a casual way to tell a story about their mother—it doesn't have to be related to the day—it's usually something light and silly. But I find that having a minute to think about mom makes it easier for them later in the day.

You can tailor your method to fit the way your children like to talk about the person who died; some prefer a straight-ahead mention while others like a more oblique approach. Some may prefer to not talk about the person at all.

Your children will have to make a lot of these sorts of accommodations to their loss as they grow and as they actively grapple with the fact that someone very important in their life is dead, and this means the person is no longer present in their lives. Where did he go? Where did she disappear to? What happens now?

What follows are children's responses by age group around the time they learned of the death. Many of the specific situations described will be dealt with in greater detail in subsequent chapters; here, they are meant as examples of developmental stages, to give you some insight into what your children can hear, and understand, at different ages.

PRESCHOOL-AGE CHILDREN: A LIMITED CONCEPT OF DEATH

Very young children generally experience the death of a parent as the loss of someone who takes cares of them and gives order to their world. Young children have little real understanding of how death differs from going away. The line between themselves and others is still very hazy, and their sense of self still depends on the presence or feedback of others to make them feel safe and whole. Young preschoolers need a concrete person to love them and maintain their sense of well-being. They know, on some level, that they cannot survive on their own. Children who lose a parent at this young age lose someone who holds them together, directs them in the world, gives them things, plays with them, feeds them, and gives them approval and love. Their inner core knows no way of holding itself together without the parent.

Very young children do not have words to express or to help them make sense of what they have lost. They may be able to use a word like "dead," but even then, it is rarely clear what it means to them. One father took his eighteen-month-old daughter to see her mother, who had died at home. She looked at her mother in her bed and said "Mommy all gone," but that's the kind of language a toddler uses for just about anything that's disappeared: juice or cookies or toys or friends after a party; there's no clear understanding of the permanence or the magnitude. At her mother's funeral, it was obvious that the toddler and her four-year-old sister could not really make sense out of what they were seeing. Their father remembers:

At the funeral, the children, with their young cousins, four and five years old, repeatedly ran up to the coffin and kissed their mother/aunt, looking back as they ran away. Each time they did this they seemed very disappointed. It finally became clear to those of us watching that they were trying to see if, like Snow White, their mother would wake up with a kiss. I didn't want to interfere, but finally my sister tried to explain that their mother's death was not the same as what had happened to Snow White. They were forlorn and retreated quietly as they tried to understand this new information.

After the death, preschoolers know something is missing, but most often they expect that the loved one will come back, as if their being gone is time-limited, much like when that juice is "all gone" and another cup of juice replaces it. One mother recalls:

My two-year-old would get excited when a man entered the house, until he realized that it wasn't his father. There was no way to really explain "dead." I could see the disappointment in his face. I held him and tried to make him feel safe.

Children at this age respond to the angst and tension and sadness around them. They need to be held, to be comforted, and to play with people they know and trust. They can be distracted by things they like to do. Even if they cannot articulate what is missing, they might call out, over and over again, for the person who has died, and ask when he is coming back. This is what a three-year-old girl asked shortly after being told her mother had died:

So, tomorrow morning mommy will be here? When is mommy coming back?

They may cling to the person caring for them as if they, the children, are in danger. They may be afraid to sleep alone in their bed and need to sleep in or next to your bed.

Your preschoolers won't really understand that the dead cannot see, hear, move, or come back to life, or that everyone dies eventually. They may cry and say they are sad as they watch others around them expressing their sadness. But whereas in the past, tears may have summoned you to soothe them and make it all better, bereaved youngsters suddenly learn that this is something you can't make better. You might be able to give them comfort, but their tears won't bring back the person who died.

The younger children are, the less likely they are to understand that death is final and universal. They can explain that the dead can't come out of the grave because of the heavy stone on top of them, but they still think the dead can return. Since they see the world as revolving around themselves and have a sense of their own omnipotence, they also may think that the dead can come back to life if they wish it, or they may believe that wishing will undo what has happened. Clara was four when her father died. A short while afterward, she was alone in her backyard, where there was a ladder. As she remembers years later, that gave her an idea:

> I managed to get the ladder against a large tree in the backyard. Don't ask me how. I decided that I would climb the ladder and then the tree and get to heaven to visit my father. It is a good thing my mother came out of the house. I was halfway up the ladder. I came down when she yelled at me. Amazing that I didn't fall. I don't know what could have happened. The ladder was pretty wobbly as I recall and I was a bit frightened when I looked down. But I was pretty angry when my mother stopped me, because, as I remember, I wanted to get up there to visit.

At this age, children think very concretely and have a limited sense of time. They mostly live in the here and now. If told that someone is in heaven, they will imagine that as a physical place, much like the world they see around them, with God as a parent surrogate who takes care of the dead. A four-year-old worries about his sister who died:

> Can Jody have a peanut butter and jelly sandwich for lunch when she gets hungry in heaven?

Your preschooler's tenuous grasp of the concept of death may reveal itself in different ways. A four-year-old had words for what had happened to his father:

> My daddy is dead; he got sick and didn't get better.

But he couldn't go any further with the thought; and he could not explain what it all meant. For a long time he kept asking why his father didn't call him, as he did whenever he went away on a trip. This confusion makes a lot of sense if you consider that by the time they are three years old, most children have learned that when people go away, they can be relied upon to return. When this turns out to not be true, it shakes their trust and their sense of how the world works. One widow explains:

> We always used to say "Daddy and Mommy always come back" to reassure our toddlers when we went out without them. But then Daddy didn't come back one day, and I could never use that phrase again. It took more than a year before my four-year-old would let me out of his sight without becoming extremely anxious.

Your children are anxious because they can't fathom how someone they love can just disappear from their lives. Children at this age, still believing in the magical power of their own thinking, may believe that death was caused by their bad behavior or something they said or did not say. A five-year-old girl thinks she knows what happened:

> I had a fight with my sister last night and then she died.

You need to tell young children very clearly, with appropriate vocabulary, that their parent or sibling did not voluntarily go away. They died. They did not want to leave, and the death was in no way connected to anything the child did. But even with those words, your children's misery won't be easily assuaged. A mother whose husband was murdered explained to their five-year-old that Daddy was dead and wouldn't be coming home. Nevertheless, it was too much for the boy to handle:

> Every time someone mentioned my husband's name, my son ran under his bed. It was like he understood more than I realized and was hiding from what was going on. I understood his feelings; I wanted to run away, too.

The concept of death is confusing and mystifying for everyone, but especially for those who lack a frame of reference for catastrophe. With so much to synthesize and then resynthesize in the years ahead, don't expect this to be a short-term crisis. People who don't know better may tell you that children get over a loss quickly, and you'll want so badly for that to be true that you might believe it. But don't be deceived: this is far from over. Four-year-old Jenny sat and wailed at her mother's funeral, making some adults ask why someone didn't take her outside. But Jenny was crying because she knew it was her mother in the coffin, and she'd been told she would not see her mother again. Her only comfort was in staying close to her father. When they got back from the cemetery, and the saddest moments had passed, she lost her somber mood. Her father relates:

> She went out to play with friends' children afterward and I heard her laughing. I knew she would be all right.

We all want desperately for our children to be "all right," but one light moment with friends does not signify the end of despair. Your children may be very young, but they are full-fledged mourners. There are going to be many hard days and weeks and months ahead; even years. Your children are learning one of life's hardest lessons before they're even able to take care of themselves. Whether it is a parent or a sibling who has died, your children still depend on others to care for them, to frame their world, and provide feedback about who they are. They need to feel that they are not alone.

ELEMENTARY SCHOOL-AGE CHILDREN: A GROWING UNDERSTANDING OF DEATH

As children approach school age, they begin to understand the concept of death. They'll have some idea that it is a permanent state, but the particulars will remain elusive. This woman's six-year-old hoped to make sense of things by asking for details after her father died suddenly:

> She asked me a lot of questions about what happened. Where is he? Is he coming back? Did he take anything with him? Did he have any clothes on?

By the time children are in school, they begin to understand that the dead do not move, do not breathe, do not see, and cannot come out of the grave. At the same time, though, they also believe that the person who died is watching them, and they like that idea. They begin to learn that people die from illness, accidents, war, and even murder. They can begin to distinguish between what is in their imagination and what is real. The remnants of magical thinking, however, remain, as reflected in the words of an articulate seven-year-old:

> I had a fight with my father the night before he had a heart attack and died. I thought that's what killed him. Nothing my mother said could change my mind. My mother finally took me to the family doctor. I've known him since I was a baby. I really like him. He explained how the heart worked, took out a model and explained in plain English what was wrong with my father's heart that it gave out. I could hear this and I guess I began to realize that I didn't have to feel guilty about "killing" him. I started to cry; I began to feel different. I knew my mother was telling me the truth and not making it up to make me feel better.

Not all children of this age like to hear the whole truth, however. While they know on some level that the dead can't come back to life, many still harbor fantasies about a miraculous return. Even if they saw the person die, children can believe that this was all some terrible mistake. One eleven-year-old is still angry at his mother for telling him, when he was eight, that the scenarios he'd created to describe how his father could still be alive were impossible:

I've forgiven her as much as I'm able to, but I'll always be a little bit mad.

His mother replies:

I did what I thought best at the time. He was telling me these stories and asking me what I thought. At first I said I didn't know, but then he kept after me, asking how I knew he was really dead, and why didn't I think the same way he did. Finally, I thought maybe he was asking so often because he really knew the truth but needed me to say it. I also worried about how disappointed he'd be if he kept on thinking his dad would come back, and he never did. I thought that would have been like losing him over and over again. I feel terrible that what I told him hurt him, but also upset that it's made him mad at me. I feel like he's taking out some of his anger that his father died onto me.

Wishing doesn't make people die, nor will it bring them back. Yet there is always a piece, even in adults, that wants to believe that death is not final. There is no right answer to whether or not you challenge magical thinking; perhaps the best you can do is to try to be sensitive to how much reality your children can accept at a given moment. You might want to just listen to their ideas without judgment, but even that might not work, as in the case of that widow whose son kept coming back with more questions. If your child doesn't demand a response from you, patience may be a good solution; your children's thinking will change with time, as their ability to connect to the real world grows.

You can assist that growth by giving them a framework that will help them cope. School-age children don't like to be different, and they have very few points of reference for how others feel in this situation. Your children need to know that most people feel sad, scared, and alone when someone dies; that crying is appropriate, but they often won't cry; that they might be anxious and worried about the rest of the family, but they should not act on that anger in any way harmful to themselves or others; and that it is natural to be angry. They want to know that you will be there for them, as will other family members and friends, and that it's all right if they want to stay close, or go out and play, whichever works for them. You don't want to play armchair analyst, explaining where you think their ideas are coming from or what you think they mean.

Instead, you want to help them understand that what they're going through is completely natural and to be expected under these sad circumstances.

School-age children are in a period of rapid change; a first grader and a fifth grader are in very different places. First graders are just starting to see a world apart from their family, whereas by fifth grade, they are already operating in that outside world. Along the way, relationships with peers and teachers become more and more important. Children begin to be able to maintain inner pictures of objects and people, differentiating between what comes from their own imagination and what exists outside themselves. They can give you a pretty good description of who they are and what they like, and they are beginning to organize and classify things and people in their environment. Consider how this young girl describes herself:

> I'm eight, I live in a white house, I have a sister, my name is Barbara and I have a cat that's fat. I'm a girl and I like to ride my bike, to play house and I would like to try a car.

Since children at this age have an expanding vocabulary to go along with their expanding world, they may seem more grown up than they really are. They still see themselves as the center of their world, and it may still be difficult for them to hold on to more than one feeling at a time. They lack self-control. What they are starting to be able to do, though, is to see the connection between feelings and actions, like this eight-year-old does when describing his response to the news of his mother's death:

> I could not believe how it was possible to go on living without her. I trashed everything around me in my room. It was as if I didn't need them anymore.

Children this age still have concrete questions after a death: Who will play ball with me? Who will help me with my homework? Who will get me to school in the morning? They do not have a developed sense of the future; rather, they live in the near-present. They may not know how to ask for reassurance, yet it is clear that this is what they need. Letting your children know how you plan to fill some of those holes in their lives, and which things will go unchanged, will go a long way toward providing that reassurance.

No two children will respond in the same way to a death in the family—their reactions depend as much on their personality styles as on their ages. A good example can be seen in how six-year-old twins responded to their father's sudden death. One talks about how her father went to the hospital and her mother came home alone; she describes the shock and numbness she felt when her mother told them their father was dead. Her sister, on the other hand, can't talk about what happened. She talks instead about a bird her father gave her, the things the bird can do, how much pleasure the bird gives her, and the time she and her father spent feeding and playing with the bird. She focuses on what she can understand: the things she did with her father. Neither twin is dealing with the death better than the other; they're both coping in the best way they can. You can help your own children by respecting and appreciating their individual styles and working within them to help them fashion an approach that lets them cope.

It is often easier for children to reminisce about things they did with the person who died instead of talking about the death. After hearing that his father had had a heart attack and died, this eight-year-old-boy became very sad, and then rushed around from one activity to another—all related to things they had shared:

My father liked my piano playing. Listen.

Just like you, your children are overwhelmed by emotion and by all the changes that are taking place. There's too much to process. As this ten-year-old describes, children often can't, or don't want to, talk about what's happening:

I feel more comfortable when I don't talk about my father. I think about him a lot, but I am not sure what to say.

This reluctance to talk will last a long time. People of all ages have a hard time articulating and sharing how they really feel. Instead, much of the time, you'll have to extrapolate the feelings from the actions. It took years for this young widow to identify her child's fears:

My daughter was six when I had our third child. She seemed worried but I couldn't understand why. Our second child died shortly after she was born, when our oldest was four. I didn't realize what my oldest was worried about until she asked: "Will this baby come home from the hospital?" I was so grateful that I could reassure her that the baby was fine and I saw her relax, that yes, this baby would be coming home.

Bereaved children are full of fears. When someone they love dies, they lose their innocence about the permanence of relationships. As a result, one of their greatest fears is that another loved one, especially a second parent, might die.

They may only show their concern in behavior—by clinging, or sleeping in your bed—but some children at this age will talk about their fears. One girl remembers how she felt when she was ten years old:

> I was very scared. My father had just died. It was all so sudden. I remember asking my mother the very next morning, "So who will take care of us if something happens to you?" I remember I wouldn't let her out of my sight. Maybe it was because people weren't paying much attention to us kids, maybe it was because, as I saw it, this was a very frightening possibility.

Five-year-old children can ask this question, too, but it is more likely to come from an older child. Even if they don't ask, your children are likely wondering about it, and you can initiate the conversation by telling them what would happen to them if you died (although you all hope that won't happen for a long time). That kind of talk helped this nine-year-old:

> My dad asked me who I would like to live with. I was terrified to talk about this but I am glad he brought it up. I thought about it immediately after my mother died. It wasn't easy for him either. He mentioned his sister. I didn't know what to say. It didn't seem right to me. Then he mentioned his brother who had kids my age. That felt more comfortable. Dad explained about a will. I was glad when he said we don't have to talk about it anymore. That's decided.

In addition to worrying about other people dying, as they move toward adolescence bereaved children begin to be acutely aware of the inevitability of their own death. Coming on top of the death of a loved one, this fear can be paralyzing. One boy recalls:

> I think I was about nine years old when I woke up for several nights in a row. I was shaking and scared. I suddenly realized that I could die, too. My father came in and tried to comfort me. What could he say? It was all too real. My brother had died, and I began to understand that everyone dies.

Being open to painful conversations about your own death or theirs, consoling a fearful child, or accepting a clingy one into your bed, tells your children that their feelings have merit, their fears will be addressed, and their needs will be met. These are all essential comforts to children who are feeling lost, comforts that will be needed throughout their childhood, as they continue to revisit, and reprocess, the death.

Another big concern children have in the later elementary years is how other people will respond to their loss. By the time they are in fourth or fifth grade, as peer acceptance becomes more important, some children do not want to stand out for having lost a parent or a sibling, and they try to keep it to themselves. This girl says even though she wouldn't talk about her father, she was still thinking about him, and what his death meant:

> I was ten when my father died. I knew that it meant he wasn't coming back. I don't know how I knew, I just did. No one in the family ever talked about heaven so I didn't think about that. I didn't want anyone in school to ask me about him. I'm not sure why but that was important to me then—I didn't want to appear to be different in any way.

Your child's classmates probably don't know what to say, either. Most of them have little or no experience with death; they don't know how to act, and they're puzzled by what they see or don't see, and that can make it difficult for your grieving child. Just after her father died, girls at school kept asking ten-year-old Kathleen why she wasn't crying all the time. For Kathleen, their inability to understand her situation meant the loss of another connection to a world in which friends are a stable component. Kathleen was devastated. It took her mother a while to understand that it wasn't simply her father's death that was upsetting her but also the way her friends at school were reacting. You, too, will be surprised and dismayed by the reactions of some of your friends, but for youngsters, whose social interactions are still developing, those responses can be devastating. It may help if you explain to your children that their friends are not trying to hurt them; they just don't know what to expect when someone is grieving. They do not know how to react to the methods your children must employ to make it through the day as they begin to rebuild their lives.

You can anticipate some of these issues by talking to your children's teachers and guidance counselors, and encouraging them to talk to other students about how to approach a grieving child. Perhaps the best approach they could take is being friendly and open but not asking too many questions. This widow says even words of sympathy were too much for her child:

> My older son's class had sent him cards and a gift at home, and before he went back to school, the guidance counselor had advised them to be his friend, but not to ask him any questions. She even stayed near the classroom on his first day back. Everyone was very

nice, but he still found it difficult to have so many people coming up to him and saying they were sorry. He just wanted people to know, but not to say anything.

Some children do want the death acknowledged while others prefer that things go on as usual. It is often difficult to know in advance what the appropriate approach is, and your children may not know, except in hindsight. What is clear is that children don't want others telling them how they should feel or how they should behave.

Most adults don't know what to do or say to your children, either, and will sometimes fall back on old platitudes that may make it harder for your children—and you. This widow finds that particularly upsetting:

It drives me crazy when people (usually older than me) tell my boys that they have to take care of their mother now. I try to say something in a light tone, like "Oh, I'd rather take care of *them*." I wasn't so nice to this guy who said, "You're the man of the family now." I told him flat out, "No, he's not; he's only seven."

Your children want to know that you recognize them as mourners, as people in need, and, yet, still as children. Grade-school children are desperately trying to find their places in the world, trying on new personae, trying out new interests, trying to fit in. A death in the family immediately sets them apart—which is, for many children, something to be feared at all costs. As much as possible, you want to reassure your children that what they're feeling is normal and that they are not alone.

Your children need to know that you will be with them on this journey and that they will survive. For their sense of self to remain intact, children need to believe that the world can continue despite the death. This thirteen-year-old boy doesn't have that. He's watching his family fall apart after the sudden death of his fifteen-year-old brother, and it's very frightening.

Since my brother died, nothing is the same; my parents don't seem to talk to each other, we don't act as a family like we used to. I try to think about what I can do to bring people together. I have a good sense of humor and sometimes I can get everyone to laugh and that feels good, even if it is only for a few minutes.

No matter what else is going on in your house, your children need the reassurance that your family will make it through this tragedy, and that you'll do it together. This will be an ongoing process for everyone, but while your trajectory will be about making your way without this person in your life, your children will actually be experiencing their grief all over again as they reach new developmental stages. Be patient with them, even when it means repeating discussions you had months or years before—as they get older, your children will be ready to go to a deeper level of meaning, and they need you there to help them find it.

THE TEENAGE YEARS:
A FULLER COMPREHENSION

The greatest shift in the way teenagers see themselves and others comes with their emerging ability to look in on their own feelings, behaviors, wishes, and needs, and to take another person's point of view. They can now begin to share their inner thoughts and feelings with others and to construct a personal history, looking back and ahead in their lives. With this ability to hold several views at once, they begin to see that relationships are dynamic and reciprocal. They can appreciate differences and are learning to coordinate independent points of view: their own and their friends'; their own and their parents'. Maintaining peer relationships and obtaining peer approval are central to their sense of well-being. It is as if their sense of self exists in the in-between, that is, in the relationship between themselves and others. If those relationships end, they are likely to feel not only sad or wounded but also incomplete. While in some ways adolescents and teenagers can seem quite grown up, it is important to remember that they are still, after all, children. They are in the midst of changing their relationship with the family as they mature, while now, paradoxically, needing to be included in the family's seismic shift after a death.

Teenagers can end up in a no-man's-land of grief when a loved one dies. Old enough to understand that everyone dies and that bad things happen, they're too young to fully synthesize these thoughts or be certain how their life will go on. The older the child is, the more likely people are to think he or she does not need the same attention that parents do or the same accommodations a younger child does. This thirteen-year-old remembers the house getting full of people who were there to support her mother—and ignoring her:

> I didn't know what to do, so I went out for a walk. I don't know when anyone missed me that evening. I finally called a friend and she came over, so then I had company too. She was stunned when I told her my father died. Her mother didn't have any problem

bringing her over. As I thought about it that night, I realized that with my father dead, everything was changed.

This seventeen-year-old girl felt ignored for weeks after her mother's death from breast cancer:

> My father was out of it. No one seemed to be paying attention to my needs and so I decided to go to a friend's house after the funeral and I spent most of my free time there.

Your teenagers need to be included in the mourning rituals from the start, to the extent that they are willing. You can keep your children involved by giving them concrete things to do, like helping you pick the music for the funeral. Let them roam, if they'd like, but encourage friends, relatives, and clergy to check in with them—they also need to be treated as mourners.

Teenagers' actions and reactions in this period after a death in the family will likely be in keeping with their general approach to the world—from wide open, to closed, to hostile, somewhere along the repertoire of emotion and attitudes. Some break down, as their known universe unravels. A thirteen-year-old explains:

> After my brother's death I needed to be sure that the world was still there. I wondered how that was possible when something so awful happened.

On the other end of the spectrum are the teenagers who seem quite stoic after the death. Many hide their tears or don't cry at all. This doesn't mean they're not feeling anything—they are. They're just putting on a facade, not only to hide their feelings from others but, to an extent, from themselves as well. This boy ignores his own needs by almost taking on his father's role, in helping his mother and siblings:

> I was there if my mother wanted to talk. She was there to listen and she knew she could count on me to help with my kid brother to see that he did OK in school.

It's not uncommon for teenagers to close down emotionally, remaining numb for quite some time. It can be hard to recognize that they're doing this because they often seem to be functioning well otherwise. Most of the time, when they're ready to take more in, they will. You can't rush this, but you can try to keep connected and open by sharing some of your own thoughts and your own dazed feelings, and letting them know that they're not alone.

Adolescents move back and forth between a maturity that is surprising, and a naive impulsiveness that is usually associated with a much younger child. Not long after her husband died, one widow was standing on a city sidewalk with her teenage son:

> All of a sudden, he started to cross the street without even looking—cars were coming— and I had to grab his arm and pull him back. I shrieked, "What were you thinking? You could have been killed!" and he said, "Well, at least I'd get to be with Dad." I couldn't believe it. He's fourteen! He knows better!

It is not unusual for a parent to see a child's behavior and assume that there is some reason for doing it, while their child may be acting without any understanding of why he is doing what he is doing. Here's how one mother interprets her children's behavior:

> I think that after the initial shock my older boys tried to hold up not only for each other but for me. Neither of them likes to talk about it a lot. My oldest, who's sixteen, went into the bathroom and got all of his father's aftershave and T-shirts, sweat shirts, and took them to his room. I wasn't surprised. My fourteen-year-old seemed to be a bit more grownup, I think, trying to help me and being part of the family unit. I tried to teach my kids that they have some control over their lives, if they work in school, if you put forth an effort, then you will succeed in whatever you do. And then something happens that we hadn't planned on happening, which they have no control over. That's hard to swallow.

Talk to that woman's older son, however, and you find he has no idea why he took his father's things. It may have been a kind of reflex to have some of his clothes. His brother took his father's favorite hat, which he had always wanted. He needed something at that point that was his father's. Neither of them tried to explain their behavior to their mother, nor were they aware of what she saw or thought. In fact, neither boy was really able to talk much about the death or his reactions.

It's not unusual for teenage boys to have a hard time discussing their feelings. By adolescence, boys' behavior reflects a movement toward self-reliance, autonomy, and independence—a self-analytical focus. Boys often report that they try hard to contain their feelings—*be a man*—and not talk about the person who died. Teenage girls are more likely to take a more emotional stance, to talk about their feelings, and even to show them. In some families, regardless of who died, this leads to boys trying to take over a paternal role, and girls, a maternal one.

It's not clear if these differences stem from the inherent natures of girls and boys or are the consequences of the different ways children are socialized. For example, boys are far more likely to be told to be the man in the family, whereas girls are more often told to look after their siblings or help their parent.

In looking at the ways teenage boys and girls respond to a death in the family, consider the noticeable differences you see in this family. When asked how long his father had been ill before he died, fourteen-year-old Joseph said, "It was a long time, maybe a year and a half." His thirteen-year-old sister, Claire, had a lot more to say about it:

> It was twenty-two weeks. I knew he wasn't getting much better, but I didn't expect him to die. I didn't talk very much at the funeral. At the viewing, people were saying "You have to be strong for your mother, and you have to hold up for your mother." Like, support her. My mother talked to us about this. She said, if people say that, you should know that it is all right: if you want to, you can still be a kid. You don't have to be big and mature and all that stuff. It is all right to brush off that kind of advice. My brother and I knew our mother can take care of herself. But we were just there if she needed the support. I listened and if she needed to talk I was there to listen.

Joseph and Claire have other siblings, too. Their mother describes how their age at the time their father died affected their responses:

> You know, it is up and down, up and down. Each of my children was different, when my husband died. The youngest one broke down and cried right away. My oldest is eighteen and he didn't cry at first but he did later on but never in front of me. His eyes would be always red. It's a real tough age with so many emotional things going on.

The teenage years are a time when children shift some of their focus from home to friends and outside interests. After the death of a loved one, many adolescents and teens will move back toward the family. You may start seeing your teens sitting at the kitchen table to do their homework, or coming home after school again, after years of just showing up in time for dinner. Your children are going to the place they feel safe, even if that means being in their rooms, playing video games, or listening to music through headphones. If you are unwilling or unable to make the home a safe haven for them, your teenagers may well take the opposite approach: going out and staying out most of the time, away from the place that exacerbates their pain.

Your teenagers might also find some of their friendships tested right now, even if their friends are available and standing by. Some things their friends find important, like invitations to parties, or who's going out with whom, may seem insignificant to bereaved children, who are trying to find the meaning of life, and death. The teenage years are also a time when children take chances, thinking that nothing will happen to them. Those who have experienced a death in the family look at things differently: all-too-aware of mortality, they want to re-exert control over their universe. This high school senior elaborates:

> As I have gotten older, my thinking about death and what I might lose became more real. I have had that fear since I first realized I could die. Now I know that what I fear most is that I will die young. Maybe I was influenced by my father's early death. I didn't think of that until recently. I want to live a long time. There is a lot to do. I see kids my age being reckless, driving drunk, not taking care, not looking at the fact that they could die from the way they were behaving. It doesn't always do much good to talk about it; they don't want to hear.

While you don't want your children to become so cautious that they're afraid to live in the world, it's not bad for them to have an awareness of the dangers of reckless behavior. As for the larger issue of social interaction, you might approach the subject by talking to your teenagers about your own difficulties with friends you don't seem to connect with in the same way you did before the death. Your children will be relieved to know that issues with friendship are common among the bereaved and not some failure on their part. You don't want to ask them to resolve your problems, but teenagers like to be given the respect of an adult conversation, and sometimes that may even give them the impetus to talk their problems over with you.

Adolescence is a time when children begin to develop a personal philosophy, one that will bridge what they've learned with what they perceive and believe. That's why the death of a loved one can challenge belief in a God who rewards good behavior, and alter the notion that people can control their own universe. But adolescence is also a time when children start to recognize that they can monitor and regulate their own behavior as well as step back and look at what's motivating them. The death might interrupt this process, but in time, your teenagers will start to apply their developing logical abilities to the loss. A seventeen-year-old boy reflects:

After a while I realized my mother wasn't coming back. Somehow life did go on. I thought of what she would want me to do, and I let that guide what I did.

A death in the family creates a vacuum in the lives of these young people. They may have just begun to appreciate their parent as a person in his or her own right, as a role model who helped in developing new perspectives and new identities. They have lost someone to talk with, someone whom they enjoyed being with. They can also now recognize that the deceased lost, too, by dying so young. A seventeen-year-old reports:

My mother would be so proud of me. I wish she had lived to see me graduate. It gave her great pleasure to see me do well.

It is important to keep in mind that as children grow, their sense of what they lost will change. They will continue to connect and reconnect to the person who died in different ways, and through those connections, that person remains a part of their lives. With their growing sense of empathy and awareness, adolescents can also begin to appreciate the work their surviving parents do to keep the house and family going. A sixteen-year-old high school junior reflects on his life since his mother died:

The most important thing for me was that I always knew my father was there and that nothing changed on a day-to-day basis. It was the natural thing for my father to take care of us and he did. I was sad, but I can't remember more than that. Everything continued as before. What I liked was that he was always helping us remember my mother. We have pictures in the house and we talk a lot about her. Now I realize what I lost. I think I am like her in some ways. For sure, I look like her. I don't know what my life would have been like if she had lived.

Bereaved children will struggle with that unanswerable question forever. Even if there were some way you could maintain everything else as it was before the death, things just wouldn't be the same. The only thing you can do is make sure your own growth doesn't end here and that your lives aren't diminished by the absence of this person you loved. They won't be the same lives you had thought they would be, but they will be your lives, and they will, and must, go on.

3

Someone I Love Is Dying

Before he got sick, we had a good life. He worked, he made a good living. I was home with the children and was beginning to think about doing something now that they were all in school. It is hard to believe that everything looked so comfortable. We played, we laughed. We couldn't have anticipated the changes that were just around the corner for us.

A thirty-five-year-old mother of two

It's impossible to describe the shock of hearing that your loved one has a serious illness that will lead to his or her death. And as if it's not enough to digest this terrible news yourself, you have to figure out a way to integrate it into the heart of your family, and to keep that family going at the same time. Everything changes, from your daily routines to your vocabulary for talking to each other and with your children about this shadow that now hangs over the family. While dealing with your own great impending loss, you also need to be tuned into the changing needs of every family member, including the one who is ill.

Each family does this work in its own way. There is a gradual decline that takes you from the time you must deal with the news of a potentially fatal illness to the time you must surrender any hope of control. Each day is different. Every time your loved one's condition changes, the family is affected differently. You will all know denial, anger, withdrawal, and fear, your emotions circling around and back again. There will be all too many moments of torture as you watch what's happening to someone you love, and all too few moments of pure and profound beauty as you steal moments to appreciate the love you have for each other. While each of you will go through this process at your own pace, you will all be changed by it in ways you would never have anticipated or wanted.

GETTING BAD NEWS

Josh was diagnosed with a brain tumor when he was four and a half. When they finally got the results there was this terrible silence. I basically had to scream at them, "Tell me what is going on!" It was very strange, being told that my child had a tumor and then having strangers trying to comfort me.

People often use the word "denial" to describe the feeling you have after receiving bad news. That doesn't mean simply that you're not accepting what is happening. It's also that you can only take in so much at a time. Everything you've assumed about your world and your family's future has just been disrupted. A sense of numbness and unreality results, and while it may look like it's keeping you from seeing the truth, it may also make it easier for you to modulate the full impact of the news. Nicole was ten years old when she was diagnosed with cancer. Her father recalls:

My first thought was that I will never walk her down the aisle. It was ludicrous. The doctor is talking life and death and all I could think about was a wedding I would never arrange.

At diagnosis, you may feel like you have been knocked down and don't know how you will ever stand up again. Josh's mother describes how, in the clear face of a life-threatening situation, both physicians and parents may look for whatever hope they can, like an alternate interpretation that would change the prognosis:

When the neurosurgeon said that maybe it could be a cyst, for a brief period we were foolishly optimistic. It was a fool's paradise. They weren't telling us everything. But we didn't question; we were too busy just surviving. After the biopsy, they said directly that it was inoperable but they would try radiation to shrink the tumor. In retrospect we see that our hope that with treatment it would get better made no sense. But we couldn't see it any other way at that time.

You may try to bargain with God; you may argue. You might refuse to accept what is happening, or give it a name. It might be some time before you can repeat diagnoses like "cancer," or "muscular dystrophy," or speak the words "inoperable," "progressive," or "fatal." But at the same time, you will begin the process of figuring out what to do and how to fight for every last day. In one sense, your denial allows you to keep going, even when that seems impossible.

What does it mean to accept the reality of the diagnosis? It means asking thousands of questions, being sure that what is being proposed for treatment is most appropriate. It means becoming an instant expert in a subject that you would not choose to study. It means finding a place in your family's world for the reality that this can and does happen. It means knowing when to fight for a life with every tool of modern medicine. And if all hope is extinguished and the illness prevails, it means preparing for the death.

This is a full-family ordeal. No one, not even the youngest children, will come through this experience unscathed.

Telling the Children

On top of the shock of the news that you are absorbing yourself, you have to figure out how to tell your children that someone important in their lives is gravely ill. You might be reluctant to do that, thinking you're sparing them. But while you don't have to give all the details right away, your children will likely be aware that something is going on—something that's causing anxiety in the family; something that's being kept from them. This woman describes the effect that the silent method had on her family:

> My husband wouldn't let us talk about what was wrong with him, and how sick he was. We had no way of talking to the children about what was happening. It was confusing. They were only four and six and didn't know what to make of Daddy's diminishing ability to function. And of course because he couldn't acknowledge what was happening, we couldn't have help from hospice.

Even if you don't tell your children what's wrong, they can see and hear what is going on. They'll draw their own conclusions. As this nine-year-old boy reveals, children often know the truth without being told:

> I knew my father had cancer. I am not blind. He was so thin and tired all the time. He kept getting sicker. Just like someone I saw on TV.

As painful as it may be to talk about it, it is harder still for children to make sense of such an unimaginable outcome without your help. You can give your children some time to adjust to news of an illness before talking to them about death, but at some point you have to start preparing them. Otherwise they're forced to go through this terrible experience blindly, and alone. Three years after his father died, twelve-year-old Andrew remembers:

No one told me he was dying but I could see, he was wicked skinny, and the day before,
he couldn't get up, couldn't talk or do anything he used to do.

One father was afraid that the news of his wife's impending death would
seriously upset his daughter. Since he couldn't imagine how to handle the information, he chose not to tell her what was really going on. Now, the daughter
follows his example of keeping silent:

To this day my father doesn't know I knew my mother had cancer. I saw it on her chart
at the hospital and I read all about the disease in the newspaper. She tried talking to
me, but I wouldn't listen and my father kept telling us that my mother was having an
operation for this or that that could make her better.

Children want you to acknowledge what is happening, to help them understand it. In this way, they learn to trust their own ability to make sense out of
what they see. Ben's mother describes how communication began in their house:

Ben was five when his father had what we learned was a seizure due to a brain tumor.
Ben saw him when he fell; he saw the blood from the wound on his face. There was no
way we could tell him that this was simply an accident.

Ben's parents chose to be honest and to involve him in what was happening to his father. He learned that while the coming times would not
be easy, his mother would make sure that the family life continued. Even
though his world was in many ways falling apart, he felt that there were
still pockets of safety. Several years after the death, Ben, now age nine,
recalls:

When my mother told me, I knew it was bad. I just knew when he fell it wasn't an
accident. He was sick but I didn't know what a brain tumor was or what it meant exactly
to die. She told me she would tell me whatever she knew and I wasn't as scared.

Your children need information, and you don't know what to tell them.
You probably don't even know how to begin. The truth is, nobody knows the
magic words—even some doctors who face death regularly don't know what
to say. One mother was furious when the doctor told her by phone that there
was nothing more they could do for her husband. When she asked him how
to tell their eight-year-old daughter, he did not answer. She talked to a nurse at

the hospital who suggested she call the local hospice, where workers have more experience in these matters:

> I knew I had to tell her but I didn't know how. This is what the lady at hospice told me to say. She said, "You have to tell her exactly what's happening," and she gave me the words. I told my daughter that Daddy had something growing inside of him that's called cancer and that sometimes people can get better from cancer, but most times they don't. And we really didn't expect Daddy to get better.

That mother found that accurate information about what was happening, in words she could understand, helped her daughter become more calm and better able to withstand the difficult days of dealing with the disease.

Depending on the illness, you may not have to talk about death for some time; you may be able to focus primarily on the course of treatment ahead. Even that can be hard to do. A mother of three recalls how painful it was to tell her teenagers that their father was ill.

> My husband was most upset that he will be leaving me with the children, that he will not see them grow up. We told them that he was very sick, we used the word cancer, but we never told them that he was going to die. Maybe it was too hard for us to say it?

Some children, particularly older ones, will ask point-blank if the person is going to die when they hear that a loved one is sick. In that case, you might have to go into greater detail than you were prepared for. If the death is not imminent, you have some time; you don't want to give false hope, but by providing some sense of the progression of the illness, you may help cushion the inevitable blow. This mother describes the day she talked to her daughter about death:

> She was four years old. I had to explain that when someone dies their body stops working, and you won't see them again. I said it was not like going to sleep. At this point I can't remember if I told her that her Daddy could die. I don't think I could say it. She became very quiet. She became more clingy than usual.

That mother understood the importance of not equating death with sleep or going on a trip—explanations that can end up scaring or confusing children even more. She's laying the groundwork for the terrible news to come—even without hearing that her father might die, the daughter understood that this danger now existed. She held on more tightly to her mother, her source of comfort in this newly threatening world.

You might think your children don't comprehend what they are being told. You might misinterpret their silence, or the fact that they continue with familiar activities, as a lack of understanding. One mother spoke very hesitantly with her children about how sick her husband was; she thought that they were not always hearing what was being said. The children tell a different story. Eight-year-old Patrick cried as he recalled the conversation when he was told that his father was very sick and might not live:

I understood. When my father was home from the hospital, I didn't know what to do. I just tried to stay close by him as much as I could.

Patrick's sister Jayne was fifteen at the time. She remembers that their father was involved in the conversation as well:

My father talked to me about the possibility of his not getting better when he first got sick. After the second operation I figured it out for myself that he could die. I understood very well what they were saying. Neither my brother nor I knew what to say so we didn't talk much about it.

As time goes on, you'll have to revisit these conversations, especially as the patient's condition worsens. These are delicate, difficult discussions to have with your children, and they may come up at unexpected, even inappropriate times. Sometimes your children will initiate the conversation; other times they may shy away from it.

News of any illness often leaves children unsure of what to do and how to behave. Words for talking about death are not part of a vocabulary that comes easily to children, or to any of us for that matter. Think about the times when you don't feel like talking to anyone about what is happening, when all you want to do is be by yourself or try to act as normal as possible, without talking about what is going on. Your silence does not mean you are not concerned; neither does your children's silence or discomfort mean that they are not worried, not caring, or not "getting it." They may simply be overwhelmed, and forcing them to talk could make it worse. Of course, there are times when you may have to bring the topic up, especially if your loved one is approaching the end and your children aren't prepared. But if it's not essential to talk right now, and your children seem to want some space, you're better off respecting their silence and giving them support to find their own way.

Some children keep all their feelings inside while others shout them out. Some curse the fates while others pray. Some stay as close to a parent as they can, in hopes of some reassurance, while others want to run away from their pain. This sixteen-year-old girl says:

> I needed time to take in what was happening. My mother only made me more nervous. She looked so worried and frightened. I needed to be by myself for a while. I don't think my mother understood what I was feeling. I couldn't explain it to her.

Children need to find someplace comfortable or familiar. This little boy needs a safe haven to go to when the reality of disease gets to be too much for him:

> I didn't know what to do. I went to my room and played on my Game Boy, trying to act as if nothing was happening.

While you need to understand and respect your children's reactions and responses to the devastating reality they're discovering, keep in mind that there may be a lot they don't understand about what's happening. Even if you speak to them directly about the prognosis, your children might not grasp the total concept. Part of this is developmental—the younger the child, the more unreal the thought of death. Part of it is a willful avoidance of imagining the worst. Whatever the reasons, your children may not be hearing what you're saying. This mother of teenagers thinks the lines of communication in her family are wide open:

> From the time he was sick, what we knew, they knew. It was completely open and honest. There was no denial. Once we told them he had cancer, they all came to the hospital. Everyone was in shock. As soon as we found out it was terminal, we told them he was going to die.

Her thirteen-year-old daughter may have been in the same room when these things were being said, but the possibility of death was clearly not a message she received:

> I knew he was not getting better but I didn't expect him to die. My mother did say he was very sick, but still. My father was very quiet about it after he found out. I didn't really want to talk about it with him either.

Living with Long-term Illness

Being diagnosed with a terminal illness doesn't necessarily mean the end is nigh; many people live for a long time with disease. In those situations, the family has to adapt twice—first to an altered daily routine and then to the uncertainty of the future. You can know that the person will not survive, but years can pass between that discovery and death. In these cases, you can give more thought to planning for the time you have, as well as how and when to reveal things to your children. While you might be tempted to wait until death is imminent, this is usually not the best choice. Your children need time to adjust to what's ahead. Like you, they need to spend what time they have with the ailing parent or sibling, to share stories and lessons and love, and to not feel, in the end, that they've been blindsided, ending up with too many things left unsaid.

As time passes after the diagnosis, you'll all need to keep talking about what's happening. As your children grow, so will their understanding of death. The way you talk to them during the course of the illness will need to change accordingly, over time, as they become increasingly able to comprehend what's happening and what's in store for your family. Billy lived from the age of two with a father who was gradually becoming more and more debilitated from cancer. When their father first became ill, Billy and his older sister, Jan, were told that he had cancer and would eventually die from it. Yet their father continued to work for several years. When he could no longer work, he stayed home and cared for the children while his wife worked. Five years after his original diagnosis, the cancer impaired his ability to function physically and cognitively. While the children had become accustomed to seeing him in an increasingly debilitated condition, the original news that he would die had long since been pushed aside. In the last few weeks of his life, the children were told again. For Billy, it was as if it were the first time he'd heard it—he says he only knew his father was going to die about three weeks before it happened. On the other hand, Jan, now fifteen, says she never forgot:

I followed what was happening and after each operation I knew that he wasn't getting any better and I knew where it was going to end. I wanted to know what the various medicines he was taking were for and I always asked what the doctor said. My mother was pretty honest with me.

Over time, your children will need to be updated periodically about their loved one's condition, even if they seem reluctant to hear the news. While it's important to respect their desire to process information on their own terms, you do sometimes have to override that. You can present it as "I just want you to know where things stand right now," or "Let me give you a quick update about what the doctor is saying," and then take their cue about following up with a discussion. Often your children will say little when you first bring up the subject but come back with more questions or want to talk at greater length in the days following.

Telling children the truth from the beginning sets the stage for an openness that needs to be there throughout the illness, and afterward. They need to know that there are no family secrets that isolate them from each other and that do not honor what they see, what they know, and what they feel. Claudia's father lived with AIDS for more than five years. As the disease progressed to end-stage dementia, her mother's openness made it easier for her:

> We decided she should know what her father was sick with. As she got older and went to school, even her teachers, knew. They were very supportive. I don't know how much she understood about the disease when she was so young, but we always answered all her questions. When he was in an inpatient hospice, she really liked going to visit him there.

Claudia was seven at the time and comfortable being around her father. She was not frightened by his illness but rather took it for granted as the ways things were. The support and care she received sustained her. She never felt alone or left out. She describes her visits to him at hospice:

> I liked going there. I knew what was going on. I liked going up to his room and knowing they were doing the right thing. They were very friendly.

Children, like adults, often find it easier to deal with a crisis when there's something they can actively do to help. You can facilitate this by giving your children some age-appropriate responsibilities for the person who's sick. These can be chores, care-taking, or sitting by the bedside, but whatever the tasks, they have the added advantage of giving your children some more shared time to remember the person by. One mother reflects on the stability it gave her eighteen-year-old son to take on a helping role:

As my husband got sicker, I think my son lost his role model. It was a very hard time in his life for this to happen. After school he helped his father bathe and shave and I think that was good for him. I think his helping to care for his father got him through.

One of your many responsibilities at this horrendous time is to prepare your family for what lies ahead. Fragile as your own state is now, you have to find some way to impart the reassurance your children need that even though someone they love is going to die too soon, the rest of the family will survive, and their world will not end. You are a family, and you are all in this together.

HOW TO GET HELP

In the midst of this utter upheaval in your family, you also have to, at some point, let your extended family and close friends know about the illness. You're barely keeping it together yourself, and then you have to bear the bad news to other people who will be devastated by it. It can be scary and embarrassing to anticipate, and then see, other people's reactions. Each retelling is a compounding of your pain, a cementing of the reality.

Friends and family can become a primary source of support during most of the illness, and there are many things to be done. You need help with the details of daily living: shopping, being there when children come home from school, doing laundry, and the like. Claudia's mother reflects on how much her family helped while her husband was dying:

My family was always there, his parents, my parents, our siblings and their children. They accepted that he had AIDS, they stayed by him and they did whatever I needed. I see other families where people are rejected by their family or they have no family. I don't know how they get through this. I think their kids suffer. No matter how bad it got, Claudia always felt cared for.

As doctor's visits and hospital stays become a normal part of the family's routine, it can seem impossible to juggle everyone's needs on your own. Maureen was diagnosed with a rare malignant tumor when she was three-and-a-half. Her mother describes how their family managed:

I went to the hospital with Maureen. My husband went to work, and either my mother or my mother-in-law came to take care of our other children. We were lucky they were nearby.

You may be surprised and touched by how many people want to help in some way, whether it be cooking meals, running errands, babysitting, or spending time with the person who's sick. You may also be surprised, though, by some people who don't really step up to the plate. Sometimes their emotions get the better of them; sometimes it's their fear; and some people are just too caught up in their own lives to help you with a crisis. It would be nice to say that there's something you can do when this happens, but as this widow explains, that probably isn't possible:

> I found when my husband was sick that there were some friends who kind of dropped off the face of the earth, and some who would only help if I asked for something. I just couldn't ask twice, with all that I had going on. I also found that a few women I hadn't considered really close friends were the ones who would just show up to drop off a meal or to take the dog for a walk. After he died, some of those bad friends came back, but I had moved on. I can't say all of the helpers are now my closest friends but some are. I still see all of them and I'll never forget their kindness.

Dealing with Unhelpful Ideas and Attitudes

Friends and family may bring their own notions to your house, along with their assistance. They might ask too many questions about the course of the disease and the treatment options, challenge the way you're talking to your children, or critique how you're handling this momentous event.

Gone are the days when people thought cancer was contagious, but some of today's attitudes about that disease can still hurt. Patients with late-stage diagnoses are asked why they ignored warning signs. Those with lung cancer have to defend themselves against the suggestion that they somehow deserved the outcome; if they never smoked, they often take pains to make that point when telling people their diagnosis. People may ask if the patient ate meat, or didn't take vitamins, or failed to wear sunscreen before developing cancer . . . and if they now do yoga, visualizations, or pray, to combat the disease. Well-meaning friends often tell a cancer patient to "have a positive attitude." All of these notions can carry the implication that the person who's sick was somehow responsible for getting cancer or for not being able to make himself better. In the words of one widow:

It drove my husband crazy when people would act like all he had to do was wish his way out of cancer. It was as if they thought he got cancer because he wasn't thinking good enough thoughts.

Community reactions can be even trickier when the diagnosis is AIDS. Claudia's father had experimented with drugs as an adolescent but didn't discover he had contracted AIDS until she was two years old. Neither Claudia nor her mother was infected. Her mother was concerned not only with her husband's diagnosis, but also with the stigma associated with the disease:

I didn't care for me. I had to be sure our neighbors were OK with Claudia. My husband was very protective of us. We were very careful who we told. He said, tell them I have cancer. Our families were wonderful; they knew the truth. But there were neighbors who might not understand. One neighbor did find out and wouldn't let her daughter play with Claudia. She was sure she could transmit the disease. I also had to protect my husband's reputation. People who didn't know him, I was afraid to consider what they thought. Even now, four years later, it is still an issue if I tell people what he died of.

It's not your responsibility to tell people all the details—sometimes less is really more. As for all of the advice, if it's coming from those close to you and you have the emotional strength to address it, you might tell them that their comments are only making things harder for you. Otherwise, with those who wouldn't respond well to that or with those who aren't as close, you can simply answer with something mild, like "Thanks, we'll look into it," or "We're following the advice of the doctors right now," or "We're a little overwhelmed at the moment; thanks for thinking about us."

It might help you to remember that your friends and family aren't trying to hurt you; they're feeling lost and scared, just like you are, and trying to find a way to make sense of this tragedy. Many of them will feel better if they have something to do, a way to show you how much they care. They want to hear from you about what would be most helpful.

Zach was ten when he was diagnosed with cancer. His mother realized how important it was for him, as he got sicker, to not feel cut off from his peers. Near the end of his life, at age fifteen, his mother talked to neighborhood parents and encouraged their children to come visit, play computer games, and just be there. She felt that everyone learned something from this experience.

Unfortunately, things were quite different for Josh when he was very sick. Neighbors would not allow their children to play with him. They thought it would frighten the youngsters to see Josh bloated from the steroids he was taking to treat his brain tumor, and they didn't want to explain to their children that he could die. These sorts of situations are tricky to deal with. You might ask a friend to intervene, to talk to the other parents about how their children would benefit in the long run from spending time with their sick friend. But ultimately there's not a lot you can do to change other people's minds, and you may have to focus instead on protecting your own child from feeling hurt.

Working with Your Children's Schools

Schools can go a long way toward making things easier for sick children and for children living in a house with someone who is seriously ill. Teachers can help an ailing child stay in school as long as possible, and provide support to healthy siblings and classmates during this period. Children are grateful when a teacher is understanding if their school work suffers from time to time. You can also check to see whether your school has any counseling services available. Some children take advantage of the opportunity to talk while others prefer to keep quiet, but both types appreciate knowing that their school is supporting them in this difficult time.

You will likely have to help direct your children's care at school, first by informing the staff of what's going on in your family, and then helping them understand what your children need and what can be done specifically to help them. Some hospitals have programs to help keep a sick child in school and will send medical staff to visit the school along with you, to help other students understand the needs of a child returning to class after chemotherapy, in a wheelchair, or otherwise ailing. Most teachers and school administrators have little preparation for dealing with these sorts of traumatic situations themselves and will appreciate the input.

Hospitals Provide Support and Care

Hospital services can have a significant impact on how your family manages this crisis. When a member of the family is seriously ill, you will become intimately involved in the health-care system, spending a good deal of time going back and forth to the hospital. Hospital policies that allow healthy children to visit, let family members stay in a loved one's room, or encourage the family to decorate the hospital room, can help children feel more connected to what is happening around them. If your hospital doesn't have flexible family policies like these, you can ask if there's a social worker or administrator on staff who might help your family design a program that benefits you all—the sick and the healthy— without getting in the way of medical care.

While hospital staff can never respond to all of your needs at this time, they can play an important role in supporting your family in meeting its own needs. Hospital staff can point you toward appropriate resources and prepare you for what lies ahead. Remember, though, that just because they work around serious illness doesn't mean that all medical personnel will be helpful or accessible. You may have to seek out those who are able to talk frankly and sensitively to you and your children. For this family, the doctor's involvement made a big difference:

> I've heard parents talk about doctors who walk away once they cannot cure the patient. We were very lucky. Our doctor continued to visit and then to call. He knew we were being cared for by the hospice doctor but he was always ready to answer our questions and to show concern for how we were doing. We were people to him, and that meant a lot in helping us carry on.

You may be fortunate enough to have a doctor like that one, who can give both medical and emotional support. But, as you've no doubt experienced at some point in your life, being a good doctor doesn't necessarily mean having a great bedside manner. Physicians are there primarily to deal with the physical issues at hand. As long as your doctors are good at medical care, instead of demanding more from them, you might be better off looking elsewhere for the emotional support and attention you also need.

Finding Someone to Talk To

Therapists can be a great source of support: having someone to talk to about what's happening can be very helpful for everyone in your family. Therapists can give valuable advice and feedback and make you feel less alone. Maureen's father recalls the guidance he got when she was being treated for cancer:

> I talked to a child psychiatrist. We wanted to do the right thing in how we involved our younger children. He said, "Don't push." We knew that naturally as parents. He just

reinforced what we knew. He pointed out that having my sisters and their cousins there also gave the children's life a little continuity and made them more secure.

Don't take it personally if one therapist doesn't feel right to you, because not all of them are trained in the kinds of issues you need to discuss at this time. Dale's parents felt that the psychologist they consulted was not very helpful. He wanted to know about their own childhoods, a line of questioning they found to be irrelevant to their current situation. They had more success finding a therapist for Dale, who felt he needed someone other than his parents and friends to talk to. He found the staff psychologist at the hospital very helpful and talked with this therapist on and off until he died. You should feel free to shop around for the kind of help that suits you and your family. You don't need to worry about hurting the feelings of a therapist who isn't working for you; finding the right person to talk to is what really matters.

Children who are living with an ailing sibling or parent often find it useful to talk to other children in the same situation. That helped this father and his children:

The hospice nurse told me about this program, "Kids Can Cope Too!" that the Cancer Society in our community was sponsoring. Children came together to talk about what was happening in the family when someone was dying. My kids were delighted to be able to share. I guess the little ones did a lot of art work. I also had a chance to talk with other parents about how to keep the children posted about all the changes in my wife's condition. I realized there were people who understood and we learned from each other. It helped me think through, as painful as the thought was, how I would manage after she was gone.

When Hospice Is There

When hospice is recommended and available, it can become another important aid for your family. Hospice staff members help in many ways, providing nursing care in the home and physical and emotional support to the family. They may encourage you to make plans for the funeral and other realities in advance, to make things a little easier to manage when the death occurs. Social work or psychology staff may also offer assistance with other family issues. Hospice helped this woman communicate with her own extended family when their idea of how to help didn't jibe with what she and her husband wanted:

The hospice social worker said we should have a family meeting. She met with us and our extended family, who were all living nearby and were here all the time. She helped us explain our need for a bit more privacy. We talked about our children's need to know what was going on, that trying to cheer them up was making us uncomfortable. We didn't want them to be out of the house so that they wouldn't be there when their father died. The children were young teenagers and they didn't know how to deal with these different messages. Our family needed to hear all this. She helped them to listen and helped us to talk. Some of them felt hurt but then they began to listen to each other and to us. They were able to change and were so good through it all.

These kinds of interventions help everyone feel less frightened as you learn what to expect as your loved one gets closer to death and hear what you can do to prepare yourself and your children. Adults are often more anxious than children about the children's seeing someone in the end stage of a disease. If children are supported and do not feel alone, they seem to be reasonably comfortable being present. Ben, who was seven at the time, visited his father the day he died. He remembers his last visit:

I said all those things to him and the doctor said it was no use, he wasn't going to hear and I wanted him to hear. I think in some ways he did hear. I wanted him to know that I love him. I think he already knew, but—I remember my uncle was with me. We went outside. We cried, he bought me some candy and we walked around for a while. My mother stayed upstairs for a while.

Hospice is, in one sense, an organization that helps you deal with the impossible and imagine the unimaginable. Someone you love is going to die, and along with the horror of that knowledge, you have even more decisions to make, about how and where that will happen. This requires taking everyone's needs and wishes into account, from youngest to oldest, from the person who's dying to those who will survive. Some people choose to die in the familiarity of their home, while others prefer the security of a hospital setting. Some survivors want to be at the bedside at the final moment, while others want to remember their loved one in life.

Josh's parents resisted a hospice referral because they thought hospice was only concerned with helping people die in their home. They felt like they couldn't go back into their house if Josh died there. In the end, they did accept hospice help, but with the understanding that he would go to the hospital as he approached death. Josh's mother describes the last hours:

> I felt something changed in him, because he sensed it was all right for him to die. If it is OK, then let me go, I'll be able to run and jump. He couldn't speak, sit up, or walk. It was time to take him to the hospital. I remember throwing things into a suitcase and I started filing my nails. I realized I didn't know what I was doing. We had the baby with us and when we got to the hospital, he wanted to be fed. I couldn't breast feed at that point. A hospice volunteer appeared and took him home where I had breast milk in the freezer. We had to tell the doctors not to give Josh antibiotics. It just wasn't fair, his body really wasn't working. We watched him stop breathing. That was very tough.

Zach's parents also felt uncomfortable about the idea of his dying in the house. They took him to the hospital when he was close to death:

> We didn't have hospice. That might have helped. My husband and I agreed that with all the other children in the house it was better that he not die at home. We didn't want the responsibility at this time. Zach was used to going to the hospital.

Children's Presence at the Death

Whether your loved one dies in the hospital or at home, at some point you'll also have to decide whether your children should be present at the death. Here, again, there's often pressure from outsiders who usually counsel that it's important to say good-bye. But those are adults talking about other adults. You might worry about whether your children will be traumatized by watching someone die.

There's no hard and fast answer to this question. You can ask doctors, nurses, or hospice workers what the end might look like, and you can ask your children for their input. You can consider your children's ages and ability to understand and cope with what they'll see. One girl who was in the room as her father died remembers with horror the agonizing pain and seizures he suffered at the end. Thirteen-year-old Betsy, on the other hand, was present when her father died peacefully, and she's glad she was:

> Most of the day, he slipped into a coma-like thing. He was alert in the morning and then until he died, about 2:30, he was asleep like in a coma. We had a hospice nurse and she said he had taken his last breath. I just went into my room and stayed there. I was sort

of angry in a way that that could happen to my father but I felt relieved that he wasn't suffering anymore. Then I started to cry. I was glad that I was there when it happened.

Luke was seventeen when his father died from a very short debilitating illness. Despite the difficulty of seeing his father in this condition, Luke is glad he was there when his father died:

My father was very religious. He thought he was seeing God. It was important to him that we be there and pray with him. We think it made the end easier for him. It was easier for us not to have to imagine what was happening. That would have been worse.

Elinor thought it would have been worse to be there when her mother died; the reality of the final moment was too much to bear. Her father describes how Elinor spent her mother's last hours:

She had gotten so used to her mother being in her room, sick but still there. Then, when it got near the end, and there were so many people coming and going, hospice and nurses and friends and relatives crying, my daughter just wanted to be in her own room, playing with dolls and toys and hanging out with her friends and cousins. She said she didn't want to see her mom that way.

You can't expect to know how you or your children will feel in hindsight; you can only know what you feel now. One widow wanted to protect her young son from seeing his father die. Four years later, he admonished her for sending him to a neighbor in the last hours of his father's life:

I explained to him that he was only seven and, at the time, what I did felt right. If he was eleven as he is now, I would have done it differently. I tried to explain to him that his understanding today was very different from where he was when he was seven. I think he could see that.

There's no right age or personality type or relationship that determines what will work for your family at death. Keeping your children aware and involved in what's going on throughout the illness is more important than the decision you make at the end. There's nothing wrong with keeping your children away at the last moments, just as there's nothing wrong with allowing those who can handle it to be there. Maureen died from her cancer, at home. Her younger siblings were five and three at the time:

We had promised her she would be at home with us. By this point, she was so sedated that she didn't know us. We tried to make things as natural as we could under the circumstances. Her younger sister and brother would come into her room and visit. They took it for granted that the nurses were coming in and out. My sister, who came to be with my little ones, brought her four-year-old with her and they played, sometimes including Maureen. Sometimes they played music for her. Sometimes we read to her. In the end there were no big good-byes.

There isn't any adequate way to say goodbye to someone you love, someone who is so important to you all. Their suffering is ending, but yours is just beginning. The life you have been leading is about to change radically, and on the other side lies a wasteland of sorrow and pain. To slog through it will take more strength and energy than you think you have, but you will find it, and you will lead your children through.

MY SPOUSE IS DYING: ANTICIPATING LIVING AS A SINGLE PARENT

It is terrible to imagine your children growing up without one of their parents—so many life events ahead with a key person missing, so much wisdom and guidance lost. One father of very young children wrote out his life story so his children would know who he was. He knew they were too young to remember much about him otherwise. A mother wrote letters to her children to be given to them at every major life event: graduation, marriage, the birth of her grandchildren. Another father came up with a different way to help his children stay connected to him:

My husband worried that the children would not remember him. We had just gotten a video camera. He had this great idea, while he still looked OK, to tape himself talking to the children. He told them about himself and his growing up. They were old enough to ask questions and I put my two cents in. There we were a family.

Even if your spouse is unable or unwilling to participate, you can record some of your children's memories while they're still fresh, or ask friends and family members to share some of their recollections. One mother gathered some of her dying husband's things—his watch, a pair of ski gloves, a necktie, a silly note he'd written, a picture from his childhood—and put them in a box in his sickroom for their children to rummage through while spending time with him.

Anything you do now to create and preserve memory will be greatly appreciated in years to come.

The period before the death is also a time for you to prepare for your own new reality. For some women, this means learning to manage the family finances for the first time. Claudia's mother went back to school while her husband was still well enough to take care of Claudia. She knew this would help her support them after his death. Another widow remembers how insistent her husband was that she be prepared for his death:

> When he first found out, he said, "You know, you're going to have to go to work, I'm sorry I'm not leaving you with more." And I would just say, "Stop! What are you talking about?" He finally said: "There are things you have to know." I didn't want to talk about that. He made sure I knew about insurance, whatever resources we had. He made me write it all down in a notebook so all this information was in one place. We signed a will in the hospital. Now I appreciate what a gift he gave me.

When it is the wife who is dying, the conversation often has a different focus, one less about money and other specifics and more about the children and their needs. One mother talked to her husband before she died about what kind of care their children would need. He reveals she even encouraged him to find a new wife to help him care for their youngest child:

> She knew she was going to die. Our older children were already on their own, and we had one still at home. She told me that she wanted me to remarry. I already knew a lot about taking care of things in the house.

Fathers may need to begin the transition to becoming the children's primary caretaker. This father of three, the oldest of whom was sixteen when her mother died, recalls:

> We talked to the children. They all knew. When it was clear that there was no hope anymore, I told the children that now their mother was dying and that they should be on extra special behavior around her and not to try to pin her and me into an argument—not to ask me and I say no, ask her and she says yes, or vice versa. I asked them to be more cooperative around the house with chores.

Notice the difference between these last messages. These parents are aware of the major issues their surviving spouses will have to face—each will have to assume responsibility for an aspect of family life largely the domain of the other partner, and they will have to do it alone.

It is not easy to talk about these issues. There are those dying parents who refuse to discuss death, perhaps out of fear, or because they are concentrating so hard on staying alive. Others choose to be more actively involved to the end, passing on important information and giving last-minute guidance. In the long run, facing the meaning of this change can be very helpful to your surviving family. It is not so much about exploring feelings as it is dealing with aspects of the new reality that is so imminent.

Your Children's Fears

It's important to pay attention to just how much reality your children can accept at a given time, and to be aware of their feelings. Your attention is often, by necessity, focused more on your dying spouse than on your children. As much as possible, you need to take notice of your children's suffering, too. One father describes the assumptions he made when his wife was diagnosed with stage four cancer:

> My son, fifteen at the time, didn't want to know until two weeks before his mother died. I thought he should understand. And just a few months ago, he told me, "Dad when you told me Mom was going to die, I went numb." He has gone through a long period of difficulty and until recently I had no idea. We can't assume that because our children understand what death is, that they can cope. We need to be there for them. Five years later I begin to understand that.

Your children will be full of fear when the end is near: fear of abandonment; fear that their healthy parent might die, as well, and leave them orphaned; fear that their lives will never be the same; and fear that changes in family finances will force them to move or otherwise alter their way of life. They might not share those fears with you, but you can start the conversation on your own— acknowledging and addressing their concerns is a gift you can give your children, who may feel ashamed or selfish to be thinking of themselves in the midst of the family crisis. Eleven-year-old Christian says it helped to talk about what was worrying him:

My mother talked about stuff like not to worry about the financial situation and that's about it. That did help because I worried about how we would manage. I didn't know as much what cancer was. I was going to ask my father what it was. But he got too sick I guess. But I asked my mother.

Your children's fears won't go away with one discussion; they will have to be addressed again and again, and yet again after the death. Even with preparation, things will change then. Knowing that a parent will die is not the same as the fact that a parent has died. No matter how much is said or done before the death, until the door is closed, none of this is really real. Even when you know it's coming, death is still a shock.

MY CHILD IS DYING: ANTICIPATING AN ALTERED FAMILY

Children are our link between the past and the future. They are combinations of their parents, yet uniquely themselves. They are part of the rhythm of the life cycle, bringing you the pure joy of watching the next generation emerge. For you to be denied that journey is nothing less than a traumatic violation of the sense of order. This parent describes the agony:

Something is very wrong here! Children are not supposed to die before their parents. How could I take it in that this was happening to our child and to us?

Even though a diagnosis is news to you, you'll have some understanding of what it means. Not so for your children, who might not be scared by the news, perhaps because they don't comprehend its meaning. They will, however, likely be terrified by all the tests and doctors' visits and general anxiety that surrounds you all now. Helping them understand what is going on and what it means is tremendously challenging and tremendously important, so that they can cope as you all adjust to these new circumstances. Ellen was born with severe brain damage when her older brother Nick was four. Their mother recalls:

We decided to take her off the respirator and she lived, to everyone's surprise. We didn't know what to tell Nick. Nick would talk about when Ellen grows up and has her own children. I then decided to tell him the truth, that Ellen will not grow up. She is sick. I now think that I cut off his imagination. He then gave his sister a hug and said oh. He

> just took the news in stride. I talked with people at the bereavement center and they said
> that he needs the truth and to let his imagination grow into the truth.

"Growing into the truth" requires an open communication channel, where your children know what's happening and what to expect. Their daily existence will be tied to the vicissitudes of illness. Dale battled leukemia for three years. His mother describes its effect on the family:

> Whenever we felt he was a little better, or the visit had not revealed any new problem,
> we found ourselves getting our hopes up. These were false hopes that would soon be
> smashed. It was very difficult.

Everyone in your family will be riding the waves of false hope and reality, with you and your spouse trying to keep it together as your worst nightmare comes true, the sick child grappling with a concept too big to contemplate and your other children dealing with their own fears and their impending loss. Many children don't even know it's possible for young people to die. Discovering that a sibling could die is terrifying and includes the realization that *they* could die, too. Worse still, they figure out that you can't save them, just like you can't save their sister or brother. This is a time that tests your awareness of your children's feelings and behaviors. Sometimes, for example, withdrawal may look like indifference; fear resembles anxiety; confusion may make children uncooperative.

Of course, this is a dreadful time for you, too, and you won't be able to maintain a warm, even manner. You'll experience rage and despair and sometimes self-loathing for your feelings, frustrations, and reactions. You might feel anger toward your loved one for causing so much pain, impatience with all the care that can be required, all the family space your sick child is taking up. Hospital staff report seeing situations where the tension, anxiety, and even resentment has built up so much that families are ready to give up before either the child or the staff feels it is time. For Josh's mother, the frustration led to an uncomfortable moment of blaming the victim:

> My little prince was lying there sleeping and suddenly I felt betrayed by him. I couldn't
> put my finger on it until later. How could this perfect little boy have this thing inside his
> head? This perfect God-like exterior, how could he have this?

Parents who are genetic carriers of a disease sometimes suffer from a particularly insidious emotion: guilt. Even though it's not their fault, the guilt can take over and only make things harder on the rest of the family. Colin's mother described her reaction to his diagnosis, at the age of five, with Spinal Muscular Atrophy, a form of muscular dystrophy:

I got mail from the Muscular Dystrophy Society and threw it away for a whole year. I was a basket case. Although my family couldn't have been more supportive, I kept thinking, you don't know what I am going through. In our very large families no one had ever had anything like this happen. It was a fluke that my husband and I both had these genes. Finally I went to a parents' meeting. I met a mother who spent thirteen years being a mess, taking drugs, and feeling very sorry for herself. That did it for me. I'm not going to be like that. That's not what I want for my child. I am going to be positive, to give him the best I can. I began to realize with this disease you can't really forget. I am learning that I have to constantly adapt to different changes in his body. As I became more honest with myself, I was more honest with him. The disease just progresses and I have to make a new adjustment, and so does he. But we are living and that is what is important.

It helps if you try not to assign your child the role of a dying person when the death is still relatively far off. To the extent that you can, look for moments of respite from the onslaught of illness. Living in the present and for the moment is something families learn to value. It seems like human nature to adapt to even the worst circumstances; even while taking your crash course in bedside care, you will likely learn to compartmentalize the part of your life that is full of the pain and mess of illness and keep it separate from some of the rest of your family interaction.

Balancing the Sick and the Healthy

It is exceedingly difficult to balance the needs of the sick child with those of the rest of the family. The attention a sick child requires is often an added problem for the healthy siblings; they may feel neglected and unloved, and then be angry at themselves for having those feelings. On top of that, you can become so obsessed with your own despair that you fail to see the impact of the disease on your children. In the ideal situation, you'll recognize the need to be child-centered, attending to both the sick and healthy children. One way to do this is by having both parents take turns, as in Zach's family:

My husband went to work and I was left home to take care of Zach and my other children. He knew when I was reaching my limit and would try to come home early so I could have some time off. I liked to just go out by myself—to a movie, to the mall, shopping. We had trained a special baby sitter so sometimes we could just take off and try to find something special we both enjoyed, even like going dancing. We sort of learned that we needed to replenish ourselves to have what to give.

Janice was diagnosed with cystic fibrosis when she was a toddler. Her mother focused on the affirming aspects of what the family was living through:

Each day was a gift that we enjoyed as much as we could. We always had to remind ourselves that we had today, for which we should be grateful. We dwelt on what she could do, not on what she couldn't do. We gave the illness a name, and everyone in the family was involved in understanding what treatment was necessary and how things had to change in our daily routine. We tried to make it as easy for her as for her healthy siblings, who had so much more energy and could do so many more things.

You will find it a bit easier to keep up this positive outlook if friends and family support you. You may have to ask for their presence and encouragement, and give them some guidance about what you need. Maureen's cousins came to play with her as they always did; in this sense, little in her world had changed and she continued to live as before. Friends can also play an important role, especially for older children. Jessica was sixteen when she was diagnosed with cancer. Her mother remembers:

Her friends were wonderful. She told them she had cancer from the very beginning. They all seemed to grow up as they tried to understand what was going on and what could happen. No one talked about death, but at the end they all knew. I was so grateful their parents never tried to stop them from visiting, even at the very end. They helped my nine-year-old son with his homework and talked to him when we were all involved in Jessica's care. It meant so much to her that one of them would come and hang out at our house every afternoon after school.

Faith Challenged, Faith Strengthened

Beyond friends and family, beyond the pain of your daily reality, many of you may turn to a higher power for support. While some may find their religious beliefs challenged by this catastrophe, those beliefs can also bring comfort in the final hours, both for the dying and for those who love them. One woman describes sitting around the bed of a dying child, reciting prayers with her healthy children and some close friends, and feeling God's presence in the room. Josh's father says faith helped bring him strength and direction at a time when nothing made sense:

> The experience in some ways actually strengthened my faith. After I married I slowly drifted away from church. I wasn't even feeling guilty. We were actually looking for alternatives at about the time Josh got sick. It was around Christmas and somewhere around there I started to go to church again, and to go every week. I asked for forgiveness and then I started to bargain. I said I would be a good Catholic if my son could be saved. Then I prayed for enough strength to just get me through this. I got that. Then I prayed that I would be there when Josh passed away . . . and for that to have happened was a great blessing. We do not know what God's plan is. Sometimes I think that things are pretty much preordained. What I can ask is to make this, as painful as it is going to be, as palatable as possible. And that did take place.

Josh's mother describes those last few minutes as a time of transition into the unknown, but also a time of love:

> I had read all the books about seeing the light. I had been packing my bag preparing for this birth or death, treating it like I was going into labor for the first time. For me it was an unknown quantity, whatever it was. I had decided that at the point when he died, if I remembered I would look up and say I loved him. I wanted him to see my face, and not the back of my head.

When the fight is over, you may feel relief that your child is no longer suffering and that the rest of your family can now move on. But while you may be exhausted from all you've done until now, there's still more pain and adjustment to come. Death brings with it an even more terrible reality. There are phrases you hear all the time, like "go on living" and "live for the moment." These are true and good intentions, but it can be really difficult to put them into action. Try not to be too hard on yourself. Watching a child in pain is horrendous. Watching your child die is worse. Knowing you are losing a child, and that your other children are losing a sibling, is earth shattering. Saying good-bye is unimaginable. There is no magic potion that can change that. Sometimes, all you can do is just keep going.

4

Someone I Love Has Died

The last time we saw our mother alive, my sister and I went to visit her in the hospital at night. That was the time she said, "I don't know why I think this, but you're both so beautiful!" We all laughed. So when the call came at around 4 or 5 A.M. and I picked up the phone and heard the news, I couldn't believe it. My sister heard my voice (we were in our mother and father's bed), and we just held each other. We both began to cry. We were worried, if you can imagine, that we'd wake everyone. I quickly realized that that was crazy and immediately said, "Why are we worrying about anyone else, it was our mommy who died." Whew—this is really hard to talk about. So, the thing is, while we knew all year that this was inevitable, when she did die, we were inconsolable, as if it was unexpected. It had an unreal quality to it.

A young woman, remembering her mother's death from cancer

There is perhaps no greater blow than the death of someone you love. Sometimes it's news that comes in a phone call; sometimes it happens before your eyes. An accident, a sudden heart attack, an overdose, a long illness, a violent death, a bee sting, a suicide: no matter what the cause, it rips out the core of who you are.

Parents are supposed to die before their children, but not while their children are young and still at home, leaving them to grow up in a single-parent family. Children are not supposed to die young either, especially in today's world. How can these things happen? How do you accept the fact that life will go on, but without this person? If you have a hard time making sense of it, you can imagine how much more difficult it is for your children, who are just learning about the way the world works, and who might not even know what death is.

A sudden death is like having the wind knocked out of your existence; it's a kind of assault on the family that cannot be underestimated. Your whole life changes in the space of a sentence. This widow describes hearing the news:

> The phone rang. It was the hospital. They said there'd been an accident. My husband was dead. It was like a buzzing noise in my ears and it kept getting louder and louder until I couldn't hear anything else.

Even when it follows an illness, death is a shock; knowing that it is coming does not mean that you are prepared for it. There always seems to be an element of disbelief, a sense that it won't happen today, not now! These parents admit they couldn't absorb the news that their son had died, even though they'd known it was coming since he was a small child, diagnosed with Duchenne muscular dystrophy:

> We realized that what we heard from other parents was true: at first when you hear, you say it can't be true, not to our son, our child. It was as if it was a sudden, unexpected death.

Although you might have hoped for your family member to be released from pain, you still don't feel ready. Your relief that your loved one isn't suffering any more is little consolation when the person is no longer there to see, to talk to, and to hold. When the door is finally closed, a new reality sets in. One minute there is life and then there is none. There is a shocking silence from the grave.

Whatever the circumstances surrounding the death, you will want to deny the reality that is right in front of you. The initial period after a death brings disbelief, numbness, shock, a sensation of moving reflexively, and a clouding or veiling of the mind. A young widow feels utterly disconnected from her accustomed place in the world:

> Some of my friends are still dating, looking for the right man and here I am burying my husband. If anyone had suggested this was possible I would have said they were crazy. How am I supposed to make this real—but it is!

You feel like you're not really in charge at the time, but in reality, this daze you're in helps you to put one foot in front of another. It will seem like you're on automatic pilot, allowing you to do what needs to be done to share the sad news with your children, other family members, and friends, and to get through the rituals of the funeral and burial. It is almost as if your body is protecting you from the full impact of the death, which might otherwise overwhelm you and keep you from your responsibilities. As this woman relates, many of your actions will become a blur down the road:

> My husband had a heart attack. I'm not exactly clear what happened afterward. I know I went with the children in the morning, when no one else was there, to see the body. That was the funeral director's advice and it was good advice. They could look and ask questions and we didn't have to worry about how they reacted. We could pay attention to them. They were in the building during the wake, but it is all a fog to me beyond that.

You may wonder how you're even functioning. You'll question all your reactions, from the moments when you can't stop the tears to those when you or your children are casually chatting with friends. This is all a part of mourning. Sadness, rage, despair, and feeling forlorn all come in bits and pieces. Those around you are often not aware of what may be going on underneath, nor might you be. As a result of the numbness and the almost reflexive behavior, you are able to maintain control and manage the early grieving period. This man has little recollection of the first week after his wife's death, even though he got his family through it:

> I can't remember how I involved the children in my wife's funeral. I wasn't sure if they made an offering at the funeral Mass. They later told me that I told them that when a person died the body is buried and the spirit goes to heaven. I had no memory of this.

You have probably heard of the stages of mourning the bereaved supposedly go through. You might be wondering what stage you're in; sometimes friends or family might ask you if you've gotten through one stage and started another. Trying to identify stages of mourning can give a feeling of making progress, and a sense of order to an otherwise chaotic experience. But mourning doesn't really happen that clearly—there are no hard and fast rules, no invariable process that every mourner experiences. The "stages" overlap and circle around each other, from disbelief to anger to acceptance to disbelief again. Things will change over time, the pain will lessen, and you will create a new life for yourself and family, but there's no one path. You will find your way to a different place, but it will happen in your own time.

THE FINALITY OF DEATH: THE DOOR IS CLOSED

Right when you're in the first throes of shock, it only gets worse: you have to tell your children that their parent or sibling has died. Even if they actually witness the death, whether it's from an accident or a medical event, they still need some sort of explanation. A mother of an eight-year-old boy and a sixteen-year-old girl describes how the scene unfolded at their home:

> It was all so sudden. The children found him after he collapsed in the front hall. They saw the EMTs work on him and take him to the hospital. It was almost as if they knew before I got home from the hospital to tell them. What could I say? I just blurted out—Dad is dead. Who could believe it? He was out running the evening before. I did worry about whether there was a right way of doing this. At the funeral home they gave me a book to read and what I did was what they recommended. But in the end, maybe there is no right way, except what feels right to you.

She's correct: there *is* no right way to do it, and there is no way to make this easy, not for you or for your children. You can't really separate how you feel from what you have to say. Even if you think they've figured it out already, you can't take that for granted. You have to say the words, perhaps for the first time. Often, in their own shock and disbelief, children make you repeat the words again and again. One widow remembers:

> I was advised to tell my children that I had some terrible news, that daddy had been in an accident, and died. Before I could even finish, my seven-year-old said, "Is he dead?" and I said yes. My four-year-old said, "What? He's dead? He's not coming back?" He must have asked those same questions fifty times.

No one can be comfortable giving children bad news, and you might even be tempted to try to keep them in the dark as long as possible. Even though you're trying to spare them some pain, this is not a good idea because it sets the stage for secrets at a time when openness is needed. Your children may also be more aware that something is terribly wrong than you think they are. One father waited two days before telling his children their mother died. Though she had been seriously ill in the hospital for several weeks, the doctors had held out some hope for recovery, if she could get a transplant in time. The father was sure his children were not aware of how ill their mother was, but his eleven-year-old son, Judd, says:

> I guessed that there was a danger my mother could die. She looked so sick and everyone was walking around looking very sad. Maybe I even guessed when she died but I didn't say anything.

In keeping the sad news secret, the father had to make sure that other family members didn't inadvertently tell the children, which created even more tensions in the family. That, in turn, meant isolating the children from those who could have offered them some comfort.

Much as you'd like to spare your children's pain, there's no getting around it. Much as you'd like to ease the blow, there aren't words that will make the news any easier to digest. Not so many years ago, it was common for people to use euphemisms equating death with sleep, like "Daddy's sleeping with the angels," but children ended up being afraid to go to bed at night, in fear that they, like Daddy, would never wake up. Some people try to ease the blow by using such phrases as "passed on," "passed away," or "gone to Jesus," but that only works if your children know what those words mean; otherwise you still end up having to translate. In the end, the stark words have to be said: Daddy or Mommy, or your brother or sister, has died. No matter what the words, the message is the same: someone you love is gone.

HOW CHILDREN REACT

Children's response to the loss of a loved one will depend on their ages, their stages of development, and their individual behavior styles; your conversation after the death will reflect, to some extent, your children's personalities, your ability to understand and respond to their behavior, and the kind of communication that already exists in your family. Children who do not like to talk things out or discuss their feelings under normal circumstances will not likely change their communication style now. Children who wear their emotions for the world to see may be more vocal with their grief, while others may become very quiet, and pull away. Either way, your children are managing the pain and terror of this new reality the only way they know how. As one mother discovered, this is not a time when you can tell your children how to respond:

> My son was at camp. He knew his father was very sick. I went to get him and told him. I thought he would want to talk but he just listened. He was fourteen. I thought he would cry, but he didn't. I thought he might want to help plan the funeral. He said no. I knew he was devastated. I had to learn to respect his way of coping.

When death follows an illness, children may initially say they're grateful the suffering is over, but they seem to be almost as dazed and confused as those who were taken by surprise. Sixteen-year-old Rachel, whose mother had been sick for a long time, says:

> I certainly didn't want my mother to die, but I am so relieved she is not in pain anymore. All I remember after they told me was that I just sat down in the living room. I couldn't cry any more and I just watched people taking care of things around me. I just sat.

When the death is sudden, most children say they can't believe the news. Later, they'll use words like "shocked" or "stunned" to describe their reactions. One teenage boy, when told by his cousin that his father had died, thought it was a cruel joke. When he realized it was true, he says he became confused and not sure what to do. This is probably the way most children—and adults—feel at this point.

Despite your desire to protect and shelter your children from the worst, their minds can be very concrete and literal, and they may want to hear all the details, to know the why and the how. This woman's husband died while out running at night. Her children had gone to bed before he went out; when they woke up, he was dead. The younger daughter couldn't make sense of it:

> She was five when he died and she wanted to know EXACTLY how he died. How did his heart just stop? Did he fall? Was he on the grass or the street? Did it hurt when he fell? *How* did he fall? Did he fall flat on his face or backward? A friend and I tried our best to explain that sometimes the heart stops working, in a way that wouldn't make her think this was an everyday occurrence. Then my friend demonstrated how he must have fallen. She "fell" in the most gentle way imaginable in our living room, kind of ending up in the fetal position so she looked like she was simply napping. I have never seen *anyone* fall like that but my daughter was satisfied—for a few weeks, and then the questions began again: Can we dig up Daddy's body? I would like to see it one more time. Do you think his skin has fallen off his bones yet?

Finding Comfort in the Familiar

Children may cry when they are given the news, or express their sadness in some other way. But they often seem to recover quickly, so much so that an observer might not be able to tell just how upsetting the news of a death has been. Just sitting with their feelings is not something most children can do well (nor can adults, for that matter). It's very common for children to physically remove themselves from the shocking news, even acting as if nothing has happened. Some children will go for a walk, a bike ride, or retreat to their room. Being with a friend can be very reassuring. Finding that their regular activities are still available helps them feel secure in a world that has turned upside down. One widow describes how her five-year-old reacted:

> When I told him his dad had died, he asked a few questions and then we sat there quietly together for a few minutes. We sort of didn't have anything to say. Then he said, sort of abruptly, "Can I go watch TV?" And I thought, well, I don't know what else he can do right now.

Escapes come in all forms, and in the short term, they can help your children by removing them from a situation that's just too hard to deal with. That little boy ended up watching TV on and off all day, while people came in and out of the house to express their sympathy. Other children leave their home, and all the commotion, and go to a friend's house. Anna remembers what happened when she found out her father had died:

> When I was nine, my uncle sat my siblings and me down and told us our father was "gone." My mother, too hysterical to tell us herself, had to be sedated. It was very hard for me to process; my father was the person I loved more than anyone in the world. Still, almost as soon as he told us, I remember leaving and going across the yard to my friend's house where there was a tether ball strung on a pole. I played by myself for a while, until my friend came out of her house and played with me. I told her, "My father just died." She didn't know what to say, so we said nothing, playing tether ball together for the rest of the afternoon while my house filled with adults seeking to console my mother.

Spending time with friends immediately after the death, or otherwise removing themselves, can give children the crucial sense that parts of their lives are unchanged, and life will go on—a notion you're too busy, and too upset, to give them yourself. You don't need to intervene or insist that your children be with you and other mourners. There's time ahead for that. But as the days stretch on, you do need to check in with them to make sure that the escape doesn't become destructive, or self-destructive. Anna sees a direct link between her mother's inability to recognize her children's grief or try to help them, and her response:

> Within a few days, that friend and I started stealing cigarettes and smoking them behind her house, another form of escape.

In Anna's family, the person she was closest to was the one who died, leaving her with a mother who was so caught up in her own grief that she was blind to her children's. Even before the death, Anna's mother had had a problematic relationship with her children. In some other situations, the person who died was the main source of conflict in the house. Children struggle with their mixed feelings when death brings an end to an emotionally painful situation, whether in the form of an abusive parent, an absent parent, an addicted parent, or a troubled parent. One thirteen-year-old boy, whose father died suddenly in an alcoholic stupor, reveals:

> Now we don't have to worry about Daddy coming home drunk anymore.

It's not like the only spouses who die are those in happy marriages. Almost every couple struggles with their relationship at some point, and if one of them dies during a period of turmoil, it eliminates the possibility of some sort of resolution. That can be frustrating, whether you thought you could work things out or whether you wanted the marriage to end. This widow describes a feeling of relief that her difficult marriage was ending and understands that her children's emotions will be different than hers:

> We were talking divorce. He was very depressed. I was so grateful when they told me he simply had a heart attack—it looked as if it might have been suicide. I was relieved. I started to feel guilty but as I thought about it, it was true I wouldn't have to face a divorce and it was also true that now he was at peace. It somehow made it easier for me to talk to the children about all his good points.

That mother was able to see what her children needed—to remember the good in their father—and to help them find this. Her approach is a good one to take if you were divorced or separated from the person who died, to concentrate on the good qualities your children will miss. There will be ample time in the future to talk about whatever problems there were. For now, your children are just beginning the process common to all mourners, of creating a mental picture of the person who died that they can carry within themselves.

When the cause of death is suicide, it can be especially difficult to tell your children what has happened. Children can be tormented by the thought that their loved one chose to leave them, by taking his or her own life, and they need to be reminded often that this was not the case. It is tremendously challenging to broach a subject that is so full of pain. This woman was fortunate that the coroner suggested she call the hotline of a children's bereavement program in her city for advice on how to tell her twelve-year-old son what had happened to his father:

> I was surprised. They told me to just be honest. They said to say his mind wasn't clear. He was having problems that had nothing to do with anything we did. To even say directly, "Daddy hung himself," and use the word suicide. It worked, and it was much easier at the funeral, because I didn't have to worry that someone would let it out.

In contrast, after twelve-year-old Bruce committed suicide, his mother discovered that community response made it more difficult for her younger son to understand and accept what had happened. She and her husband had to deal with family members, including their own parents, who would not believe that Bruce had really killed himself. This made their younger child question what his parents were telling him. In the long run, the parents learned to share their horror, their sadness, and their own difficulty in understanding what had happened, so that their other child was able to trust them with his own feelings and sadness.

Words are important; talking is essential. But whatever the cause of death, and whatever the family circumstances, many young children need more than words to help them deal with their emotions. They need to express their confusion and fury more actively. This woman recalls her son's response to hearing the bad news:

> He was only five years old. When I first told him that Daddy was dead, he beat on me. All I could do was hug him. Later, every time someone mentioned what happened he ran into his room and hid under his bed. I felt like hiding myself. It was so hard to take in that my husband was dead. Murdered. These were not words I wanted to use with a five-year-old.

Younger boys in particular seem to show their distress through their behavior. They can lash out physically or use angry words to express what they feel, but they are often unable to describe their emotions directly. This eight-year-old boy admits sheepishly:

> I showed my feelings by swearing, saying the "F" word and words like "crap." I wanted to break something, but I didn't. My mom didn't care at the time.

Outbursts of anger are not reserved for children whose parent died suddenly. This nine-year-old was in bed when his mother died at home after a long struggle with cancer:

> My brother came in and he said, "Ma died" and he just started crying. Then I started punching walls and stuff. I was punching stuff all over the place. I broke one of the pictures in my room. I smashed it all over the place. I was mad. I just went around the house punching everything. Getting mad and freaking out, punching everything and just crying and stuff. I cried the whole night. I didn't even sleep. I guess my father would have liked me not to be mad and stuff and punch things, but I couldn't stop.

When considering your children's reactions, keep in mind where they are developmentally. While everyone has a difficult time grasping what has happened, adults at least know at some level what death means. You know that death is final, that there is no returning from the grave, that you cannot go up to heaven to visit, and that all of us will die someday. You may not believe it's really happened; you might feel as if your world has come crumbling down on you; but you know that there will be a tomorrow and, in spite of your wishes to the contrary, that your loved one will not be there. Children's views of death, on the other hand, will vary with their age. The younger they are, the less they understand. Notice the confusion in this child's perceptions:

> I was seven when my father died. I knew he was going to die. But I had no idea that I wouldn't see him again. I didn't really know what was going on. I didn't understand, and when he died, I wondered why people were so upset. I was watching people because I didn't understand what was bothering them that night when he died. Then I gradually realized he was gone. I can't remember everything. I asked my mother, a doctor, medical questions. She explained it medically but even then I didn't understand.

Children tend to fare better when they're allowed to ask questions and share their pain and their fears. You can help them most by being honest and truthful, even if they are too young to fully understand what you are saying, and by recognizing that they are mourners too, grappling with the pain, just like you are. One of the most important things you can do is to reassure them, tell them that they are not alone, and that you will do your best to be there for them.

STAGGERING THROUGH

At this very moment when you and your children are completely dazed and unclear about what's happening, there's often a dizzying frenzy of activity all around you. The phone rings constantly. People come over, bringing words of sympathy, along with food or coffee. This widow describes it:

> I don't know how everybody found out he died but it seemed like all of a sudden people just showed up. I looked into the kitchen at some point and there must have been ten people in there, just standing there. They didn't know what to do, but they wanted to be there. I wasn't thinking very clearly but every time I looked over at them it felt good. I was so touched that they came.

Another widow remembers the scene at her house very differently:

> I'm usually really sociable but I was so bothered when people I wasn't close to just dropped in. I felt like they were vultures. I just wanted to be with my close friends and family.

Your children might also have differing perspectives on the activity in your house. Some find it comforting while others feel lost in the crowd. A sixteen-year-old girl describes her perception:

> So many people around. For a time I felt that no one realized that I lost my father too. One of our neighbors came over and took me out for a walk. That felt better. I told him I understood what my mother was going through, but I guess I needed something too.

Children, especially younger ones, may not always be able to verbalize what they need for comfort. You can help by finding them diversions, something to distract them and occupy their minds and hands. This widow explains how she turned to her family to help, when her own responsibilities kept her too busy to be with her daughter:

My five-year-old kept talking about the Easter eggs we were making when my husband collapsed. One of the smartest things I did was ask my niece to come over. They spent the day making Easter eggs, and my daughter was excited. She could not wait to show me what she had done. She couldn't connect to what I was doing—arranging for her father's funeral.

Almost no one can do this alone. There are so many decisions to make and so many people needing you at the same time. If you're lucky, people will come to you, asking what they can do to help, and there are many things they can do—answer the phones, coordinate with clergy and your house of worship, watch your children, keep food and drink in the house for you and your visitors, or stay by your side, taking notes, as you face all the questions that need to be answered and all the decisions that demand your attention. In the best of cases, you'll have friends and relatives who will also be able to help by offering some comfort to you and your children, despite their own shock, as happened in this family:

My brother kept saying we will get through it. He was shattered by my husband's death, but he was still my big brother. I didn't have to say a word but he understood what I needed. His family came over, and somehow we got through the funeral and there was food on the table.

In that kind of family, children receive the nurturing and support, love and care that helps them thrive. Families are the place that children learn how to deal with others, develop relationships, discover a sense of who they are. When everyone shares their grief, it may help children feel more safe and less alone.

In some families, this system of help is not available after a death. Sometimes family members will express opinions that can confuse and upset your children. These opinions might be about death and dying, or, too often, about how you should be grieving. Many adults grew up at a time when children weren't involved in the mourning process, and they still think of grief as something to get over. They don't keep these sentiments to themselves, either. One woman whose soldier son was killed in Afghanistan was told by a friend a few days later, "You can leave the pictures of him up for a month but after that, you have to pick only one and put the rest away." The mother took the advice and moved away the pictures. The fact that it didn't make her feel any better didn't really register with her, in her grief, but it did send a message to her other children that their loss and their sorrow should be put away after a short while, too, and it left them anxious and confused when they found it hadn't lessened their hurt.

If people give you advice about what you should do to feel better or to get on with your life, you can say something like "thank you, I'll think about that," and then evaluate it on your own terms. You don't have to act on something just because somebody suggested it. Try taking a step back and asking yourself whether the advice sounds right for you and your family. Sometimes you'll find the recommendation helpful, especially if it involves ways to stay connected to the person who died. If the message involves trying to bury your memories or push them aside, that's probably not the way to go.

Be wary of people who tell you how you "should" behave or feel. Be wary of those who try to minimize your pain or control the way you express it. Be wary of people who turn their supportive shoulder away from you, recommending instead that you take medication to help you control your feelings. While medication can be invaluable in some cases, it is not a panacea and shouldn't be treated as such.

What you do need to do is to let yourself and your family grieve. Don't ask or expect too much of yourself or of anyone else. Find some way to convey your attention and your support to your children; they need to know that you can and will take care of them. Even in this moment when you can barely function, they need to know that you are there, and that you won't abandon them. They've lost enough already.

MAKING DECISIONS

In the midst of all the pain and shock and turmoil, you find yourself thrown into a monumental, almost incomprehensible, task: arranging the funeral. You still haven't quite grasped that your loved one has died, and you have to figure out what to do next. One mother remembers the feeling of two worlds colliding:

> I had a lot of people in the house so there was someone to take care of and play with my children—the youngest was two and David was nine. It all happened so suddenly. I had to take care of all the details for the funeral. Every time I went by where the children were, they asked again what happened. We must have gone over it at least one hundred times that day.

Arranging what to do with the body of someone you love is not easy, but it must be done. The services and ceremonies that follow a death provide a way of honoring your loved one and a way for the community to console your family and share your grief. If the death was anticipated, you may have had the chance to discuss some of the options for rituals and burial with your loved one:

> Once we knew how sick he was, we did talk about where he wanted to be laid out, but that was as far as we got. I had to figure out the rest on my own.

Chances are that this was a discussion that most of you did not have, and what you choose will rely on family beliefs, traditions, and experience. When the death was unanticipated, there is a very active learning curve. You need to connect with a funeral director, clergy, a cemetery, and a whole world you may be exploring for the first time. You need to find out how your children can be involved and whether there is a role for them in the rituals of your tradition. You may be asked to consider an open or closed casket, where the body will be buried, the cremation alternative, and what kind of service you want. This is one of the times when the numbness you're feeling will serve you well, by allowing you to push on through these issues that speak to your terrible loss. One new widow describes the strangeness of navigating through this time:

> I was really surprised that I could make choices and decisions, and for the most part I was fine, but I found it was completely impossible for me to say words like "body" or "casket" or "bury." I just couldn't use those words in reference to my husband.

As you approach these decisions, keep in mind that finding some way to involve your children in rituals is one of the most reassuring things that you can do for them. It reinforces their place in the innermost circle and identifies them as mourners—active members of this family that has taken a blow but is not broken.

Cremation or Burial

Most likely, your first decision will be between burial and cremation. For Richard's family, the idea of cremation was comforting:

> We all three of us saw cremation as very symbolic—freeing him from the body that had imprisoned him. It gave him the freedom to be where he is now. We had gone

to a spiritual fair not long before Richard died. This reader said he will walk, he will be free. Then I realized she is right—it will happen with his death. This is another reason why it was important to have him cremated. It was about this time that I had what I call a vision, for lack of a better word, of two teachers we knew who had died. I saw the three of them playing basketball. We believe Richard will come back in a different body some place, somewhere in this world. There has to be something else.

When cremation is chosen, you may opt to wait before deciding where to place the ashes, or you may choose to bury or scatter them now. Some cemeteries have areas where you can have a plaque next to the cremains, or you might prefer to keep the ashes in your house or scatter them in a favorite location. One woman divided her husband's remains and had friends scatter them during trips to locations around the world; she and her son like knowing that his ashes are strewn from America to the Great Wall of China and back again.

When burial is the choice, you need to find a cemetery. For this woman, that was the moment when the reality and finality of death truly hit:

This decision was in all ways much harder for me than making choices about the funeral. It was terrible because I was deciding not only where my husband would be buried, but where I would be. I didn't know anything about different burial options. I didn't know what he wanted, beyond knowing that he did not want to be cremated. The first cemetery I went to was incredibly depressing—all those indistinguishable shiny granite stones in a row, right by the railroad tracks. How does anybody tell one grave from another in those kinds of places? How would we get any comfort there, standing around our little plot while the trains whizzed by? I really lost it when I went there. Then I heard about another cemetery, where you can sit and reflect, wander around, and the kids can play. As soon as I went to see it, I knew it was right. It cost more than I could afford, but I felt like it was important for the kids and for me. We like to go to the cemetery; it is beautiful and calm and peaceful. I sometimes wonder what would have happened if I had taken the first place, and my husband was buried somewhere that I knew he would have hated.

Unlike that woman, you might not be ready to make a decision about a double grave; many widows and widowers find it too hard to even contemplate what their own disposition will be in death, many years hence. This widow exclaims:

> I know it's too soon to think about the rest of my life, but I'm still young. What if I remarry? What if I move? How do I know where I'll want to be buried? How can I decide all this right now?

This is something you can talk about with the cemetery management; in some places, there's a way to hold a spot and then sell it back, if you later opt not to use it. You might also consult your extended family about a group plot, where others could be buried, even if you choose not to be.

Planning a Funeral or Memorial Service

Once you've made the burial or cremation decision, you have to think about the funeral or memorial service. You probably have some sort of religious or cultural tradition in your families that you'll want to consider in making your plans. This may be your first experience with the details of a service, and you might not know exactly how they work. Don't be embarrassed to ask a relative, your clergy, or the funeral director to describe what will happen and what you are expected to do. Then, you need to tell your children what to expect, what to do and where to sit, and what role they'll have, if any. In their own numb state, your children may not remember what they were told. But, like this thirteen-year-old boy, they'll know that someone took the time to explain it to them:

> I remembered that my neighbor talked to us. She told me her father was a funeral director. I remembered that she talked to us about the funeral but it was going in one ear and out the other. All I could think about was if it really was my father who died.

Funeral directors are used to the confusion and uncertainty that may define your interaction, and they'll know how to get the answers they need while providing the information and support you want. There is probably no situation funeral directors haven't seen, no question they haven't been asked. One told us he considers his job a calling and feels blessed to be able to be there for people in their darkest hour. This woman reflects on how helpful that was after her daughter was killed in a drunk driving crash:

> Before, I was always very independent and liked to find my own solutions. Now I was so pleased that the funeral director and our minister were very specific that I needed to do this first and then that. It seemed to me that I needed their help simply so that I could walk. I couldn't even do that by myself.

Members of the clergy can also be a big help to you and your family. Children are especially appreciative when clergy consult with them and include them in the process. This teenager remembers the rabbi who came to talk to her:

> He said it was important that we be at the funeral and he wanted us to tell him about our father—what we thought he should say. I appreciated that.

What's most important is for clergy to create an accepting atmosphere for your children that respects them as mourners. This woman describes her family's experience:

> My religion is very important to me. I immediately called my minister and he came over. He was as shocked as we were to learn that my husband collapsed in a hotel while away on a business trip. He spent time with my two girls who had a lot of questions about what happens to people after they die. They wanted to know what happens at a funeral. They were very curious at ages twelve and fourteen about how their father could die this way. The minister wisely said we should talk with our doctor, but he then described a funeral and asked if the children wanted to be involved. They wanted the minister to conduct the service, but they decided they wanted to pick out the casket. Their father was a woodworker and they wanted to have him buried in a coffin made out of his favorite wood. We all went to the funeral home and they chose the casket. All this activity quieted them for a bit and I guess I began to feel that maybe we could survive.

Involving Your Children

During this time, your children need as much support as you do. They may not always be able to say what will comfort them, but children need some sort of reassurance that even though one aspect of their world has crumbled, the walls of their own existence will hold. Involving them in the funeral and giving them some voice in the planning gives them this reassurance, as well as a sense of power when they're feeling particularly weak. One widow explains:

> My son was seventeen. He helped me plan everything. We decided that when my husband was in the casket, if it didn't look like him, we'd not open it. We agreed he looked like himself and kept the casket open.

You don't have to include your children to that extent if it doesn't feel right for you or them; the important thing is letting them feel like they're playing some part in what's happening. This widow did not want to give her children that much of a voice. She involved them in the service, but she made the decisions:

> I felt that one person is in charge. I decided what the funeral would be like and I didn't really involve the children in that. I then gave them each a job to do and told them how they should act in the receiving line. We all felt comfortable with this.

Children feel better when they are participating somehow—if not in the planning, then in having some task to perform. Your children might not know what to do, or what they can do, so concrete guidance is helpful to let them know what is expected of them in this unusual situation. You can involve your children in different ways, according to their interests. Some will want to help pick out clothes for their loved one to be buried in, or choose flowers or music to be played at the service. Some will find comfort in putting letters, mementos, poems, or pictures they drew in the coffin. This widow describes her daughter's choice:

> I made arrangements myself, but Jane (who was eight) put a teddy bear in the coffin. She had brought it to him when he was in the hospital, and she wanted to put it in the coffin.

The specific choices you make to involve your children in the rituals of a funeral or other memorial service are not as important as the overall idea: to let them participate in a way that brings them some comfort. Your goal is to provide them with some sense of finality to this part of their mourning and at the same time to implant the notion that your family will continue on, together.

RITES AND RITUALS

If your family has a religious background and you're comfortable with it, you can let those traditions guide you through the funeral service and whatever comes after. When Zach died, his family found solace in the rituals of their synagogue. His mother explains:

> We didn't have to think about anything. He was buried the next day according to our tradition and we sat shiva [period of mourning] for seven days. Tradition guided how we

should behave and what to expect from the community. All the children were home from school for the week. They were mourning, too. My husband and Aaron, who was now over thirteen, helped form the minyan [prayer group] we needed every morning and evening, and men came from the community to participate.

For this widower, the ritual of the Catholic service was equally soothing:

I was an altar boy at our church and our kids have been active members there their whole lives. Hearing our own priest recite the familiar Mass somehow kept the bedrock under our feet.

Even if you aren't involved in organized religion, rituals can still provide a guide at a time when you are feeling unmoored. Some people like to adopt customs and rituals of various traditions and create their own service, with a willing clergy member or another kind of spiritual leader officiating, or simply run it themselves. Dale's parents were very clear that they did not find formal religion very helpful. They did not think that they would meet again after death, or that Dale's spirit lived on in any form. However, when he died, they followed Jewish burial rituals on their own, and found comfort in having their family around them for a period after the death, albeit not for the traditional seven days. In retrospect, they were grateful for the order and direction this tradition gave them in the face of the vacuum Dale's death created.

Death itself can inspire a crisis of faith. You might view death as a reality of life, with no spiritual overtones. But it's more likely that the role of God and faith is inexorably tied up in your ideas about death and dying. You may become angry at God for taking your loved ones away, feel He's taken them to His embrace, or alternate wildly between the poles of belief. Some lose faith, some find it. In the words of a new widow with young children:

We do believe in God. I am Christian. God is in control and there is a better place. I think that's why we can deal with this, even though it is enough to make you not want to be here. I have days where I don't want to even bother.

It's not uncommon in funerals and other services to hear statements like "It is God's will" or "God has taken her home." This mother thinks that language helped her daughter:

My fifteen-year-old felt comforted when the priest said her father was in a better place.

But such words can also be frightening or upsetting, especially to younger children, who are quite literal in their understanding. One mother with young children asked the priest to modify his language:

> I didn't want the priest saying that to my children because I didn't want them to think their father would find any place better than being with them.

The funeral or memorial service may be your first exposure to phrases or advice that are well-meaning but in conflict with your own beliefs or attitudes. It probably won't be your last. This mother wants her son to understand that his place is as a mourner, and not something else:

> I told my son that if anyone tells him that he has to be the man in the house, to listen and be polite, but that is not his job. People seem to forget that he lost his father. He's mourning too. He can cry if he wants to and be sad and he doesn't have to worry about taking care of me.

Another young widow mixed the same message with guidance for making it through the funeral:

> Be polite, greet people, and if anyone tells you that now you are the man of the family, just ignore that advice. You can't take your father's place nor should you be told to.

Juggling Your In-laws' Needs

Parents who leave behind young children when they die are usually relatively young, and their own parents may still be alive. When it's a child who has died, their grandparents may have outlived them. As a result, you could have mourners at the funeral who have very different needs and expectations from yours. They, too, are burying a child they loved; they, too, are in mourning. This is not a time for learning new ways of getting along, although necessity may bring some of that about, as this widow discovered:

> My mother-in-law was upset that we brought the children. I wanted a small funeral and I wanted the children to be involved in the planning. I am not Catholic and I knew that my husband would have preferred something that would be comfortable for the children. I couldn't fight with my mother-in-law and his siblings and we ended up with a big funeral Mass. They came to the funeral home and overrode all my decisions. It was awful for all

of us. Somehow all the attention went to her. That's not how it should have been. I wasn't comfortable in that church that she arranged for. It was where my husband had his first communion, but we didn't feel any connection to him in that setting. It is not where we went with the children. I know she lost her son, but my children lost their father. They seemed to just take it in their stride, watching everything. I guess they took their clue from me. I was stoic and strong. I think we were all simply numb. Nothing seemed real, as far as I could tell.

The conflict is exacerbated by the fact that other family members are not at their best or their most flexible at this time; they're numb, just like you are. You may feel unable to muster the kind of energy necessary to withstand this kind of upstaging. In a situation like this, you might try to find a compromise, such as holding the funeral service at one location and a separate memorial service at another one. One widow came up with another way to merge traditions:

We had both the priest who married us, from the church I grew up in, and the minister from my husband's church, involved in his funeral service. That was very important to us.

Some family members, especially older ones, may balk at the way you're involving your children. Previous generations were raised with the idea that children don't really mourn the way adults do; they thought children just needed somebody to take care of them, and they'd be fine. It was not at all uncommon for children to be raised without ever really hearing about a parent or a sibling who died. This woman lost her mother twenty years ago, when she was seven:

My father married within the year. I called her mom. Nobody ever mentioned my real mother again.

Her father wasn't being intentionally cruel; that was the way things were done then, and many of those notions persist today. If you run up against this sort of criticism, you might need to explain that being open with children and having them participate in these rituals has proved to be important in helping them deal with the loss of a loved one. Most relatives will be understanding and embrace your idea, especially if this sparks a memory from their own childhood, when they were left out of such a ritual and were angry or upset about it. Of course, you may also meet continued resistance from some people and be left just to calmly reiterate that this is the course you consider best.

Asking Your Children What They Want

Your children will have ideas, too, about what's best for them. Judd's father had not been planning to take him to his mother's wake and funeral. Eleven-year-old Judd was so sure of what he needed to do that he prevailed. Judd reflects:

> She was my mother. I would have felt weird not to have gone. I had to see her for the last time.

Children usually make it clear that they don't want to be excluded from the funeral of someone they love. You may be concerned about your children's reactions to seeing a coffin, or going to the graveside for the actual burial. As it turns out, children don't always understand all the details of what they saw. But when they look back on these early days, what they say is that what mattered most was just being there. In the words of one boy:

> I'm his son. It would have been disrespectful to not be there. It did help me. I got used to being near a dead body and now it doesn't scare me any more.

Some of you may worry about including younger children, under the age of four or five, feeling that a wake or graveside service might be too frightening. Looking back three years later, an eight-year-old disagrees:

> He was my father and no matter how young I was, I had to be there.

Your children might not be sure if they want to participate, or even to attend the wake, funeral, or burial. In that case, you might sit down with them and describe what is going to happen, and let them decide whether to stay home, attend, or come for a short time, and then leave if it gets to be too much for them. That's what this mother did:

> I really thought that they should be there. Sandy hadn't gone to her aunt's funeral. Now she kept saying that she was too young to come to the wake. I didn't agree. I told them that this was their father and they should go. I was pretty clear about that and that made me feel good about myself. I said, if they couldn't stay, that would be OK. Sandy lasted twenty minutes and my brother took her home. Alice stayed another ten minutes and she said she had to leave. The next day they were fine.

Your children don't have to come if they don't want to, and they don't have to stay if they do come. The key is being flexible and taking your cues from your child. This widow's eight-year-old son changed his mind:

> We were all set to go to the wake and he just said no, he wants to stay at his friend's house. I didn't think it was time to pressure him. He did want to go to the church service and he did.

It was the other way around for this family; the daughter wanted to be in attendance but her father didn't want her there. He listened to her, and changed his mind:

> I told my twelve-year-old that I didn't want her to go to the funeral Mass or to the cemetery. She was adamant and made quite a fuss. She kept yelling it was her mother. I finally had to let her go. I don't know why I was worried. She cried, but really she was fine.

As emotionally fraught as this time is, be careful of the words you choose when talking to your children, so that you're not talking them into, or out of, something. This father thinks he left the decisions up to his son, but his words tell another story:

> I gave him a choice. I told him it was an open casket so I preferred that he did not go to the wake, and as far as the funeral Mass, I gave him a choice. He chose not to go.

If you take young children to the funeral home, to the service, or to the cemetery, it's a good idea to ask someone to stay by them, to support and comfort them, and to be able to leave with them, if that seems appropriate. One father explains how he worked it out:

> I asked my cousin, whom she knew very well, to sit by my five-year-old daughter. The service was at the chapel in the funeral home. I didn't know what to expect. Several times my cousin offered to take her out, especially while the rabbi was giving the eulogy, but Jenny wouldn't go. She clung to my cousin and sat there wailing into her lap through the whole service. Some people were bothered by this but I said, if she wants to be there, this is where she belongs. It's her mother lying there. Maybe she was wailing for all of us; that's how we felt but we were too self-conscious to express it.

It helps if you can find out in advance if there's any place your children can go, just to get away from it all. This fourteen-year-old boy, whose father died suddenly, recalls:

> The funeral director had what he called a children's room, where we could be with our friends. It was good to be away from the wake and from the grownups for a while. No one got mad that we were being disrespectful when we made a joke about something or got a little noisy.

That same kind of room was also a welcome respite for this seven-year-old:

> This nice man let us sit in this room with all our friends so we didn't have to be with all the adults all the time.

Don't be surprised if, after the funeral, your children have difficulty talking about the experience. They may not be very clear about what had taken place or only focus on a few specific things, like what the room looked like or who they saw. For this little girl, it's more impressionistic than memory:

> There were lots of people around; all my cousins were there. I remember all the flowers.

Children will forget details, or talk about a "box," unable to remember the word "coffin." Like you, like this child, they walked through the service in a daze:

> I remember I was just sort of blank and wanted it to be over. Everyone was crying. All I remember was snow and tears.

More important and lasting than any specific memory is the general feeling most children think back on, of a time and a place where other people honored their loved one. It's important for them to see who was there, mourning with them. One boy says:

> I remember my uncle doing a reading. So many people came. My dad had a lot of friends. He was kind of good.

Children perceive things differently than adults do, partly because they don't have the same frames of reference. So much of what's happening will be new for them; they can't understand it all. Even with your explanations, your children might not really get what's going on. They can be confused and disturbed that friends and family are there for the burial. This girl was six when her mother died in a house fire:

> After the funeral, I couldn't understand why everybody had come back to the house. It seemed like a party. I was mad at them for years.

She was so disturbed by the party scene, she says, she couldn't stand the smell of flowers for years afterward. You can help your children with these sorts of feelings by explaining that while it may have looked and even sounded like a party, the gathering was about remembering the person who died and honoring him or her and your family. Even after hearing that, it can take children a long time to be able to reflect on the experience and modify their understanding of what went on. There's not much you can do to speed that up; it's something that happens naturally over time, as they process all this monumental change in their lives.

Another notion that takes years to come to terms with is the feeling children commonly have that the death is not real; it's all a terrible mistake. This belief can persist for a long time, and some adults who lost a family member in their childhood say it never really goes away completely. Many children, like this sixteen-year-old girl, say it's hard to believe that their loved one is in the coffin:

> I kept expecting the cover to be pushed open and my father would come out alive. At that point, I could not believe he was really dead.

You don't want to push too much reality on your children before they're ready, but being present for the service and the burial helps impose a little logic on this magical thinking. It's painful, but necessary, as this teenager describes:

> I was glad that I was there; people needed me, but I also went for myself. I needed to know what happened. OK. This is it. Here's this hole. He is not alive anymore. I saw it.

Being part of the ritual recognizes your children's roles as mourners and gives them a piece of their loved one to hold on to. Rachel, now eighteen, thinks that going to her mother's funeral let her begin finding her way to a new understanding:

> It helped me realize that she was not coming back and I appreciated seeing all the people there who knew her and liked her. I realized how special she was.

On the other hand, if your children don't attend any mourning ceremonies, it doesn't mean they are going to be forever scarred. If they don't want to go, or you don't think it's a good idea for them, there are other things you can do to help make clear the separation between the death and the new family reality that lies ahead. Reminiscing, writing down memories, and looking through pictures are all ways of saying good-bye. The goal is the same as it is at any ceremony— the deeper meaning that this teenage boy found in going to the funeral:

> The purpose is to get everyone feeling OK about the death. Anybody who wanted to could come. It is for children too, a way for little kids to understand that people have a life on earth but they die. Maybe bring religion into it, but not bring in hell because it might scare the children.

The funeral is the last public ritual in which the person who died has the central role. After the funeral, raw as you are, you have to begin to deal with the real impact of the death. The numbness and disbelief will stay with you for a while to cushion the hours, but reality will break through repeatedly and randomly. Your children are also coming in contact with their new reality and their new needs and demands, and they'll be looking to you for guidance. Whether you are ready or not, you have to begin new roles for yourself and your family. The ways in which you develop these roles will have direct consequences for all of you in the years to come.

5

After a Parent's Death:
A World Upside Down

*Inside of me, I feel as though everything has just died, but you still go along with
life's routines. You have to get to another place where you can sort it out. Some day
maybe you'll feel good. I don't know.*

A mother of three teenagers, two months after her husband died

There's no time line for pain. The funeral and the first worst days are over, but
there will be countless difficult and harrowing days ahead. It is tremendously
disorienting to return to the life you once had, minus your partner, because in
many ways, that life does not exist any longer. You are now living between a
tomorrow that will not happen and one that you never could have anticipated.
Calm, happy days when your family moves smoothly through its routines are a
thing of the past, and it may be a long time before they return.

You may feel as if you are on a merry-go-round; there is now a void that
you could never have imagined before. One day, a sense of the new reality is
there in full bloom; other times, all you want to do is crawl in bed and avoid
the pain. But there's no escaping it: reality does not go away. Your cloudy mind
and sense of disbelief will remain, and the feeling that you're just going through
the motions might continue on and off for many months. A mother of two
describes a family totally disrupted by death:

> When my husband died, I just went along with whatever they wanted to do. I would look
> at their faces and see their sadness. I couldn't refuse them anything. My heart broke for
> them. "You want a chocolate bar before supper? Eat a chocolate bar!" I was helpless. I
> keep worrying about how I can keep the children in line. My son needs his father. He was
> a great role model and he did keep things in order. I don't know if I can do it. Sometimes
> I think we have to learn a whole new way of living together as a family.

You might not be aware of how numb you are until you look back on what you have gotten through. It is almost as if your body has a way of protecting you from the full impact of the death, which might otherwise overwhelm you. Sadness, crying, and despair may come in bits and pieces. A widow whose husband died of a brain tumor tells us about her overwhelming feeling of lethargy:

> After he died, I was like numb, in a crazy funk. I felt like I was chronically jet lagged. Fortunately, my son didn't feel much better most of the time, but he still needed my attention. I'm not sure what he got. It was school vacation. He watched TV while I stayed in bed. Sometimes a friend came to visit and got us out. School pushed us into a working routine.

For you and your family, there has been a total disruption of the life you were living. Family routines are altered, and the orderly progression you count on in your lives is essentially gone. Sophie was seven when her father died of a heart attack. She has a literal measure of the loss of continuity:

> I was reading a book with my father and he said we were going to continue tomorrow, but he didn't, because he died.

Your children may cling; they may disappear with friends; they may want to share your bed; they may want to be alone in their room; they may want one thing at one minute and the opposite thing the next. At the center of all of your worlds is a new and profound emptiness you are only beginning to understand, as this widow describes:

> After he died, the house was full of people. Everyone went home to their lives after the funeral. I needed the quiet, but then it became too real. He was gone. I could not have imagined what it was going to be like. In the end when I held his warm hand, even if he was in a coma, he was there, and now, nothing.

LOSING YOUR PAST, PRESENT, AND FUTURE

It helps to realize that what you've lost is more than a person. You have lost your spouse and the relationship you had; you have lost a way of life; you have lost the person you were in the relationship. As one widow asks, what's left for you now?

> I am John's mother, but I feel like I don't know who I am any more, now that Jim is dead. If I am not his wife, then who am I?

Susan is a Unitarian Universalist minister who writes and sometimes gives sermons about the aftermath of her husband's sudden death. She writes:

> I used to hate it when someone referred to a dead person as lost. It was worse than passed away. "We lost Jeffrey during the war." "She lost her daughter last year." People who are lost often find their way home. Or find their way to another home. People who are dead are not lost. They are dead.

> But then my husband died on a Wednesday night in June. Along with my husband, the "I" I had known was instantly lost and so was the life I had been leading. The loss that struck that spring night keeps multiplying and multiplying like loss to the zillionth power. Bob is dead but I keep losing him too. I have lost him as a husband, as my girls' father, as a companion, as a confidante, as a lover, as the one who shared the chores (loose definition of sharing here). I have lost a built-in child-care provider, a hand-holder, a movie-going buddy, and someone to yell at when I am in a bad mood and no one else is over. I lost the only person who loved my children anywhere close to the way I love them.

Even if you were separated or divorced from the person who died, your lives will be thrown into chaos. You have to come up with a way to reconcile the difficulties and disappointments of your marriage with your children's need to mourn the parent they've now lost for good. That doesn't mean mythologizing or rewriting history, but your children will be hungry for positive memories that they can hold on to.

WHAT YOUR CHILDREN HAVE LOST

Whatever the status of your marriage, with death, your children also lose a part of themselves. They lose a parent; they lose the relationship they had with that parent; and, most importantly, they lose a very real presence that helped give their lives shape and form. Most children take this sense of security and certainty in the world for granted. Sophie's older brother, Alex, misses that feeling:

> It hurts the most in the beginning. It's two years now. You get used to it so it doesn't hurt as much. You have to get used to the idea that he is not there anymore. That was hard because I could always count on his being there. It is hard when you go over to your friend's house and their father comes home and asks how you're doing and then you go

home and your father isn't there. It's only your mother. And then you hear kids, like, say
they hate their parents and stuff. It's like you don't know how much you like them until
you lose them.

Death leaves a gap not only from the lack of the physical presence but also
from the part the parent played in defining and directing the family life. Parents
are role models, teachers, nurturers, and framers of family traditions. Each child
loses someone different, depending on their parent's role in the family and also
on the child's relationship to that parent. A nine-year-old boy wonders:

Who will help me with my homework? Who will play baseball with me? Who will be there
when I get home from school?

It's incomprehensible that one minute there is life and then there is none,
and it's excruciatingly difficult to accept the notion that life will go on without
this person you love. But even though it's not easy to accept, adults understand
that life does go on, albeit in a different direction from the one you'd anticipated.
This may not be so apparent to children and teenagers, who have neither the
sense of history nor enough experience to be certain that the world will not
come to an end. In the words of a ten-year-old:

When my mom died, I couldn't imagine how anything would continue.

Sally was ten years old when her father died very suddenly. She recalls
knowing that:

. . . all of sudden everything was going to be changed.

But Sally didn't know what that meant. The need to deal with change is a
very real part of what we call grief, but understanding how to do it doesn't come
from one action or one activity; it develops a bit at a time, as you also deal with
the myriad other issues facing you, with all that is now changed in your life and
in your children's lives as well.

It may have been years, even decades, since you lived without your spouse,
and for many of you there were no children involved then. Now, like this widow,
you are making decisions for an entire family:

I didn't like it; I didn't want to be here, but I was determined to do whatever I needed
to be sure we would make it. I never lived alone. I went from my parents' home to
my marriage.

Your own grief means that you may not be able to think clearly, to even consider the future; you may be moving one foot in front of the other without being sure where you are going to put that foot down. The whole world around you may seem unreal, and yet you need to be there for your children. Having dependent children who still need care and attention keeps you grounded and forces you to start formulating a new life, at least on some level. After his wife's sudden death from what had been seen as a chronic but not terminal condition, Russell's father says:

> If I didn't have children, sure it would have been easier. But really knowing that they were there and needed me kept me going, sort of pulled me through.

While caring for your children might feel like more than you're up for right now, they also do give you a reason to go on. Without them, it might be even harder to get up in the morning, even harder to deal with a world where everyone else is moving right along while you are stopped short. Your children are sharing your agony, and cobbling something together now is your joint purpose. Be patient with yourself. And with your children. They're staggering along blindly, right behind you, and at a time when nothing is right, they need to know that what they feel, and how they show it, is not wrong. In the words of an eleven-year-old boy:

> I was in shock. I wasn't sure what to do. My mother said it was OK to cry, and I sure did a lot of that.

DIFFERENT WAYS OF SHOWING GRIEF

If you or your children don't cry, it doesn't mean you are not mourning or that something is wrong with you. There's no single way to cope, because everyone responds differently to grief. Some children can let it all out; others try to hide their tears or fight them back. When nine parents in a bereavement group were asked if their children cried a lot after the death, seven of them replied that they had seen tears only a handful of times. All of them agreed that their children had a hard time seeing adults cry. This widow watches her daughter:

> I know that she goes through these times when she doesn't want to tell me she is sad because if she sees my eyes fill up, she wants to protect me. I told her that there's nothing wrong with feeling sad. I would feel that way even if she didn't say anything.

Feelings after a death are dynamic, changing all the time, and they don't always fit the stereotypes of what a bereaved person should look like or act like. Those around you are often not aware of what may be going on underneath, nor might you be. Ten-year-old Sally thinks back:

> In hindsight, I think I was numb. I simply couldn't take in all that was happening, and just followed my mother around.

Thanks to an almost reflexive behavior, the autopilot of human interaction, you'll often be able to maintain control and get through what needs doing. The numbness disguises much of what's going on inside, and others may think that you are really doing pretty well. This teenager says even those closest to you won't necessarily know what you're feeling:

> I was fifteen when my mother died. I became numb and that really made it possible for me to go on with school. I didn't realize until three years after how numb I really was. As things started to unravel, my father said he had no idea. I was going to school and so he thought I was okay.

But it's just a facade: in hindsight, most people report that they were not really in charge at this point. They didn't always realize how numb they were. This can last, with you floating in and out for months, sometimes for a year or more. The automatic pilot that is steering the family makes it possible for you to carry on and get through what needs doing.

LIVES REEXAMINED

One major undercurrent that runs behind the facade will likely take you by surprise because almost nobody talks about it: after the death of a spouse, or a former spouse, you enter a period of deep self-evaluation. When you lose such a big part of your life, all the rest of it becomes open to scrutiny. Widows and widowers spend months, if not years, running their minds over their marriages, for better and for worse, trying to see who they were before, who they are now, and how they got from there to here. Susan found that out in the months after her husband died of a heart attack. She writes:

> I am starting to doubt the many myths I have told myself about myself growing up. My love of this person or that thing. It's all come under harsh review, microscopic analysis.

> I shouldn't wonder why I am tired all of the time. All this thinking. I have lost my past as well as my future. When Bob died it took a while to realize that the future I had planned on and relied on having, the one I leaned on in times of stress and happiness—that future was gone. It took even longer to realize that my past was going to get an overhaul as well. So much of what has happened to me has been told to Bob. . . . Without him here, the past is opened for reinterpretation.

You will mythologize your spouse; you'll rehash old arguments. You'll find yourself awash in regret over words spoken or actions taken that now can never be undone. It can be confusing to be angry at people who are not there to defend themselves, and it can be easy to remember only what you did wrong and not the part the other person played. In the end, you're left to reconcile it on your own, whether your marriage was happy or sad, peaceful or contentious, and to come to an understanding about the relationship that you can hold on to, as part of who you were, and who you are.

REDESIGNING THE ROLE OF PARENT

After the death of a spouse, the structure of your family life cracks in some ways and crumbles in others. You won't even know where to begin to reestablish some order. A mother of two small children remembers begging other widows for something to look forward to:

> Tell me it will get better. I remember going up to anyone, almost, and saying—just tell me it is going to get better. I wanted that HOPE. It was very powerful to meet people who say you can get through this.

In the early days, your daily existence might feel unfamiliar, upsetting, and empty. There you are in the home you shared; all of the rituals are over and the guests have left. Now it's just you and your children, making the transition to a different life, while your previous life is still visible, just out of reach. Mandi remembers the juxtaposition of worlds, just after her father died:

> We had just moved into the house. The new washing machine arrived the afternoon he died. He had decided he would install it himself. It was sitting in the back hall, looking out of place, just like we all felt. It was chaos. I guess Mom took care of getting it installed, eventually; I can't remember, except I kept worrying about how we were going to manage.

The whole family is worrying about what's to come, and the depth of the change ahead becomes clear only gradually with each new task you must face. This widow explains:

> Probably the worse thing I had to do was clean out his office. It made me realize how real this all was.

There are tasks all around you that make the loss more real, that still have to get done. You need to get your papers in order, find out about insurance and pensions, arrange for social security, look at your financial planning, and make plans for child care that is sensitive to the cataclysm in your children's lives. In the words of one woman:

> I knew it was coming. I sort of practiced while he was dying. But when it really happened and I had to check the box "widow," I said it can't be me. But it was.

An Empty Space

You and your family must find new routines to build around the space left by the death. Virtually every activity can feel altered. For example, one newly bereaved parent admits to not knowing what to do at dinnertime:

> We ate a lot of pizza and were regulars at McDonald's.

Mealtimes are often family times, an opportunity to talk about the day and catch up on events in each other's lives. Now, there's a giant crack in that routine and an empty chair that symbolizes what is missing. A seven-year-old, after her father's sudden death, says:

> I didn't really feel like eating because my Dad's not there. Mom said I know how you feel. I feel that way too. Sometimes I can't stand the empty spaces.

It may sound odd to outsiders, but this empty space really can loom so large that it makes mealtime an awkward, painful experience. Some families rotate seating, so that every night a different person sits in the empty chair. Other families eat at a different table for a while. Many families, like this one, end up fleeing to restaurants, where old memories aren't as present:

> My husband was a good cook. I just managed. Now it seems there is less food on the table and we eat out more.

If the death was expected, you may have already made the mealtime adjustment. Even so, there's still something missing when the person dies, as this child describes:

> Sometimes I notice it's more empty at the table, but I don't feel uneasy about it. We got used to it when Daddy couldn't come to the table when he was sick.

In these early days when everything seems like a blur, just getting the family to sit down together—whether at the kitchen table or at a restaurant—is a small triumph. One of your biggest challenges and most important tasks right now is to begin instilling the idea in your children's minds that you are still a family and that your lives will go on. Some of you will find it easier to do that by minimizing the change in your family routines. That's the approach this widower takes:

> I worked very hard to make sure nothing changed in my son's life.

This mother took a similar approach after her husband died:

> I tried to keep his life just as absolutely normal as possible. I went to work as I had done before, and Philip was involved with school and his friends. I am a private person and I didn't show my grief visibly. I have no doubt that he is grieving in his own way. Christmas we went skiing with a friend of his. He is an adolescent and I thought he would enjoy the holiday if this is what we did. He liked the idea and we had a good time.

Reestablishing a sense of order in the house, with someone who cares for your children, is crucial. Russell describes how it helps:

> My grandmother was always there after school. I'd help her with the baby. Playing with him made me feel better and helped me not think so much about my mom not being there.

No matter how hard you try to make the routine the same, though, it can feel very different, and that can make your children anxious and disoriented. Leslie's father was sick before he died. Now, the teenager says, there's an emptiness in the house:

> I got used to my father's being there when I got home. Even if he was in bed, we talked, and I could tell him about my day. When I come home now, I miss his voice. The house is so quiet.

After his father died suddenly, thirteen-year-old Alex also noticed how empty the house felt:

> It was strange coming home from school. Mom was usually not there. We stayed with a neighbor until she came home from work, or I had to babysit my kid sister.

For better or for worse, out of choice or necessity, babysitting is often one of the new responsibilities that older siblings are given in the revised family order, if you return to work, start working, or change your hours. Suzie finds this frustrating:

> I'm twelve; my little brother is only eight. He really doesn't see things as I do. I can't talk to him—he is really too young.

Other children, like this boy, appreciate having a new family role that gives him something to be proud of:

> I'm the big brother. Sometimes I try to help with my younger brother, help him in his baseball like my father used to do. We both get a kick out of that.

You can help your children adjust by being very clear and fair about their new roles and responsibilities. Explain some of the tasks the family has to absorb, now that one member isn't there any more, and point out that while you are picking up many of those jobs, the children will need to help. Then apportion your children some tasks they can do, with the acknowledgment that these responsibilities will likely change as they grow older and more capable. This fourteen-year-old boy appreciates the chores his father has given each child, bringing the family more structure:

> I felt better when he said I was in charge of taking out the garbage every day. My sister would help with the laundry, he would do the shopping, and we could all help with the cooking and help with the dishes. I began to feel that we could survive. It was important that I could help.

You might not want to give your grieving children new responsibilities to manage on top of your grief. But even if you don't dispense new chores and you do get meals on the table and make very few tangible changes, everything is still different because there's a big hole in the family. No matter how hard you try to make things "normal," or not burden your children with the day-to-day problems that will inevitably come up, the absence is there, and it is felt. It will be a long time before that sense that something is missing diminishes. This widow explains:

> Our daytime life has not changed. For me the big problem comes in the evening when he doesn't come home. I was comfortable in the knowledge that I was the parent, but now we weren't going to be as happy as we were.

Taking On Your Spouse's Role

Perhaps your biggest challenge as a bereaved parent is recreating an identity for yourself in the absence of your spouse, while taking on some of his or her responsibilities. This mother describes how that's working for her:

> I suck as a father.

It's a brave new world out there for single parents. Or, as one widow asks:

> Why do they call us single parents, when we're really double parents?

An only parent, doing double duty. This is not a job that comes easily. You are suddenly required to take on this double role at a time when not only are you at a low point in your life, but your children are scared, angry, and in need of comfort. Vickie's father died after a long illness. While her mother reassured her that in the long run, everything would work out, Vickie still finds her new reality challenging:

> Mom yells a little more now but she was always stricter about our doing well. She says we will be OK and I know her—we'll be OK. She says I have to get used to the fact that it is different now. I'm trying. It sure isn't easy.

Things are not any easier in the home of this widower, who is losing control and pushing his children away. His children feel the strain:

> My father set up rules for us but they don't always work when we have things to do after school. Then he gets angry and yells when we don't do what he wants. He finally gave up! That's not a solution either. He scared me when he threatened that if we didn't obey we could leave. I don't think he really meant it.

Your identity as part of a couple gave meaning to your daily life, providing a framework and focus for how you related to yourself and to each member of the family. By yourself now, you have to learn the role your spouse played in the family, and take on some of those responsibilities on top of your own.

For men, that often means becoming the family's primary caretaker. This father of young children says his wife was the glue that held the family together; now, he has to take over for her:

> I left child care to my wife. Now I have to learn how to do it.

Another widower only sees the need to have someone take over with the carpools, the after-school activities, and the other care-taking tasks that a babysitter can perform. He doesn't see the other responsibilities that go along with raising children:

> My only concern is to find someone to care for the children after school while I work, that's all I need. Otherwise I am sure they will be fine.

It's true that your children might be fine in the sense that they are safe and getting where they need to go, but grieving children need more than that. This father explains how wrong he was when he thought it would be simple to meet his children's needs:

> I had teenage children. I assumed they would get to school and come home and be okay. I was wrong. They shouldn't have come home to an empty house. They were alone too much and they filled that emptiness in ways that were not so good for them.

A common problem for many widowers is dealing with the needs of daughters, especially as they enter puberty. This man rose to the occasion:

> My neighbor said she would take the girls bra shopping when the time came. Of course she was nowhere to be seen and I didn't know how to ask her. We got through it. We went to a local store and the saleswoman sensed the situation and took charge. My daughter was very pleased as she got her first bra.

While that father managed on his own, don't be uncomfortable asking for help. Your neighbor might not be watching your daughter's development closely, but she'd most likely be happy to pitch in, if asked. People understand that you're in uncharted waters, and they want to help steer you.

Since it is more common in our society for women to be the primary care-givers, widows usually have fewer adjustments to make in the daily child-care arena than men do. In the words of one widow:

I just went on doing what I always did—that was the easy part.

They might be things you did before, but now there's no help with home-work and bedtime, no one to take the kids on an outing, no easy way for you to get a break. And, there are a lot of other roles left unfilled with the death of a spouse, from household responsibilities to family decisions that become a lot more difficult when you make them alone, without your partner to talk to and to have by your side. This widow misses the support:

My husband knew how to take care of all the little things in the house. He was always there to back me up. I don't know how I can be alone. I think there is always the worry.

It's overwhelming. Widows often talk about wanting someone to mow the lawn, or shovel the driveway, or know what to do when the roof starts to leak. It gets tiresome and even embarrassing to ask for help. As this widow describes, it takes a lot to keep a household going:

I quickly learned that when something went wrong with my car, I wasn't sure what to do. There were things to fix in the house. My brother lived nearby and he came over at the beginning to advise me. I didn't know I could do some of those things.

There will be some tasks you'll find easy to incorporate into your life, chores you can manage. But this is not a case of finding strength to do things you never had to do before; it's about managing the impossible. You are raw and vulnerable and guiding your family through a cataclysm. No matter how strong you are, you can't do everything, but what you can do is identify people who can help. Make a list of friends or relatives whose counsel you trust, and ask them for advice and backup when you're uncertain about your decisions. Find a responsible teenager who can change lightbulbs, hang pictures, or pick up the toys in the playroom for a reasonable price. In a perfect world, you wouldn't have to ask for help and you wouldn't have to pay, but you have surely learned the hard way that this world is far from perfect. This mother thinks the most important thing is to do whatever you can to minimize the disruption in your house:

My kids are still the same. My youngest is still a little boy. I want my oldest to be a teenager. I am careful about not making them feel they have to be different. I want them to feel that they are children and now because Daddy died it doesn't mean you have to help me with barrels, you know, I am capable, I am very careful.

Beyond running the household, there are other, more subtle dynamics you now need to parse. Every couple balances roles in one way or another: one more strict, one more lenient; one funny, one serious; one energetic, one slower moving; and so forth. Figuring out how those qualities were divided helps give direction to the changes you have to make now. Losing your spouse means taking on both characteristics—it's like you have to play good cop and bad cop, often at the same time, in the same scene. Ben's mother sees how difficult this can be:

Some of the life went out of our family. I was always more earnest about things. He was the one with the humor and was always finding fun things to do. They also had a father-son thing going, doing fun things, that I can't replace. I enjoyed a lot of what we did, so I have to take some initiative now. I didn't know this for a long time.

Everyone who loses a spouse has to change the way they are involved in parenting. Russell's father already knew what he would do:

I changed my job immediately to be closer to home and to be available during the day if I was needed. I was lucky; my mother was able to take care of the baby and be there when Russell came home from school. I was able to do the housework because I had always helped my wife, who never had a lot of energy.

You might not be able to respond so quickly, and you might not want to. Many fathers are used to seeing their main role as the family breadwinner. Some men, like this one, try to go on as before, maintaining their previous routines at work:

I lost a lot of time when my wife was sick. I needed to get back. I found a babysitter and I was out of there. It felt good to be back.

These men are not used to attending to the small details that make up a large part of daily family living, and they aren't planning to change; they keep themselves busy outside the home and leave the child care to others. This may work in some cases, but one widower who tried that approach found that it didn't work in his family:

> I'm a cook. I threw myself into my work so I didn't have to think about my wife. I rationalized that I needed the money to make up for the time I didn't work when she was sick. Work helped keep me going, as long as things were quiet at home. I realized one day that I had a young son to raise and it was my responsibility, not that of his older sister. It was bad enough he lost his mother. He needed his father now. That's my job.

Work, Family, and Finances

Managing the twin pulls of work and family can be extremely challenging. You have new financial realities, whether because your two-income family is now down to one, a stay-home parent has to go to work, or you need to pay for a caregiver to help fill in the gaps. These widows and widowers speak for all those who say that financial concerns keep them up at night:

> My husband's employer paid for our health insurance. I wasn't sure how long that would continue. I knew I had to find a job where I would get coverage. I don't know how easy that is going to be.

> Can I hang on to the house, am I going to raise my kids well enough? Can I get a job with mother's hours and health insurance, to carry us through, so I can be with the children as much as possible?.

> I wasn't sure where I was at. I decided whatever energy I had, I had to be home for the children, so I found a job in the local school as a substitute teacher. I was scared. I wasn't sure I could handle everything by myself.

Your needs and concerns at this time are serious—and real. You might not have the strength to deal with them in the earliest days, but pretty soon, you're going to have to come up with a plan. If you already work, you might start by talking to your employer about how best to manage your time while staying on the job. If you haven't been working and now need to start, or if your current job won't give you the flexibility you now need, try taking advantage of those people who've offered help by asking for recommendations of companies or jobs that might be better for you. Once again, people will be understanding and want to help—they can appreciate how much your life is changing.

Financial worries are also on the minds of your children, often expressed as "What's going to happen to me?" One sixteen-year-old boy asked how they would manage; he offered to quit school and go to work. His mother responded by treating his concerns with respect, but reassuring him at the same time:

> Daddy didn't leave us with a lot. I think we have enough to get by. We can pay the rent. I'll need to work, you may have to get a job after school and we all have to work together, but we will be OK.

Your work defines a part of you, but even that "you" is altered when you go back after the death of a spouse. This is true as well for parents who do not work, when they return to their daily activities. Your sense of what's important has changed. It may be hard to focus. This widow feels that her work has become just a job:

> I took a week off from work. I should have probably taken more time. I went to work when he got sick partly to get out of the house and partly because we needed the money. Work used to be an escape; I'd go there for fun. Now it is more of a responsibility. Now it feels like I have to be there. We get health insurance through my job as well.

You may have less time and patience for colleagues, office intrigues, or paperwork. On the contrary, you may also find it comforting to throw yourself into those very things—burying your troubles in projects or distracting yourself with the tasks at hand. More likely, you will alternate between the two feelings.

These same contradictions exist for your children as they make their return to the central part of their daily life: school. Going back to class, like your return to work or to the workforce, is fraught with conflicting feelings: escape, relief, worry, sadness. Difficulty focusing. Anxiety about what to say, and what other people will say. Your children are carrying these weights, just like you are.

GOING BACK TO SCHOOL

School makes up a huge part of your children's lives. It's much more than a place of intellectual growth and academic knowledge; school is where children learn to organize their minds and their lives, exist alongside other personality types and interpersonal styles, relate to authority figures, and make and break friendships. For children who have lost a parent, all of these parts come together in a new way. Nine-year-old Russell remembers:

> I went back to school the day after the funeral—that seemed like what I should do. Most kids in the class didn't say anything, although I think the teacher told them. They looked uncomfortable but no one knew exactly what to say.

Mike feels a new sense of purpose at school:

> We always did well in school. But now my mother would tell us that we are working hard to please Daddy's soul. It was important to keep that in mind.

Mandi finds school to be a relief:

> Going back to school made it easier—at least for part of the day my mind was occupied with things I could understand.

Sally explains why school was important for her:

> It was the place where I felt I had some control. Everything else had changed, but here I managed my work, my activities, my friends. I was in charge and I sure needed that.

Both because of their own discomfort and their fear of others' reactions, children are often reluctant to talk to their classmates about how they feel after the death. They may be concerned that their raw emotions will get the better of them, that they'll lose control, and the sympathy will only make them feel worse. Some children say they have one or two friends who they think will understand; others don't talk to anyone about their emotions.

Working Together with Your School

It helps if you or another adult who is close to your child can talk to the school in advance, to prepare administrators, teachers, and students as well as your children. You'll want to learn how the school plans to deal with your children's grief and to find out what other students might already know. In elementary school, classmates may have been told what has happened before your children return to class. In middle and high schools, where people switch from classroom to classroom, there may be teachers and students who are not aware of the death. This widow describes the steps she took to help:

I tried to keep my son's school routines as they always were. As far as I could see, nothing changed. He was in high school. I did tell the principal, who knew how sick my husband had been. I don't know if he told the teachers. But James was very clear that he would tell those friends he wanted to know.

Even when they do know what happened, teachers and students are often unsure or uncomfortable about what to say or do. Thirteen-year-old Leslie says she doesn't know what she wants them to do, either:

Going to school is good. I go to school to get away from things. I don't want to talk about it. I don't want to be reminded every single day about the fact that my father is dead. But they still come up and ask me how I am doing. In a way I think my friends treat it like my parents are divorced. A lot of friends have divorced parents and they don't see their father at all. I don't honestly know what they—that's how it looks to me—like they're just treating it like, "OK, her father's dead. She doesn't want to talk about it. That's fine."

You might think that teachers are prepared to deal with all aspects of a child's life, but this is not true. Teachers can spend a career without having a student in their class who's lost a family member, so they'll need your help to guide them. You might forewarn the teacher, for example, before events when your child might be especially stressed, like school plays, first and last days of school, graduation ceremonies, and other events when their parent will not be present. There are certain days that can be particularly painful: Bring-a-Parent-to-School Day; Career Day; and, perhaps the most difficult, Mother's or Father's Day. This widow explains how an elementary teacher dealt with one of those days:

My first grader's teacher was really sensitive and asked me if I wanted her to not do a class Father's Day project at all. I told her to go ahead, and prepared my son, suggesting he do the project and put it in a memory box he keeps. My fourth-grade son's teacher wasn't that thoughtful. She just went ahead and had the class do a project without asking me, but I had prepared him for it, just in case.

It's important that you stay on top of things and anticipate potential problems like that one whenever possible. Ask your children periodically how their teachers and classmates are responding to them, whether they're bringing up the death and whether your children are comfortable. They may not be able to give you concrete answers, but you may learn something important in what they say (or don't say), nonetheless.

Schoolwork itself can become quite challenging for children who have lost a parent, and therefore, for their teachers. Bereaved children often have trouble focusing in class and concentrating on their work. Vickie finds herself thinking about her father when she's in school:

> Every day I think about him. He was sick and didn't work. I got used to his being at home when I came home from school. I just wish he was here. Sometimes it's an excuse. During a test, when all is quiet, I think about him and then I get a C. I can blame it on the stress, but I can't use that excuse to myself.

Your children might not be thinking specifically about their parent, but just spacing out—taking a break from the reality of their lives right now. They may also react to their stress with angry outbursts, and this kind of response may continue for some time. Both girls and boys can get angry, but school-age boys in particular seem to let their feelings out in their tone of voice, in restlessness, and by lashing out. This anger may come, in part, from the confusion and uncertainty they feel, without having the words to describe it. Duncan describes the trouble he had after his mother died:

> I didn't think that I would ever feel better. When I went back to school I couldn't concentrate or think about anything but my mother. I thought that the world was going to end without her. I was yelling at everyone. I wouldn't talk to anyone. I can't believe that one year later, I can study and I'm getting along with my friends. I'm lucky they stayed with me.

Ben also found himself in turmoil:

> I was always angry at school. Kids thought I was stuck up, but I figured I had better stay out of their way, to keep from fighting. I didn't connect this to my father's death.

Of course, fighting often brings children the opposite of what they want. People pull away, or fight back. Ben's mother says what he needed was someone to understand that he was in mourning:

> His teacher kept saying he was looking for a fight. When it finally happened, Ben kept saying it wasn't his fault, he didn't start it. The principal wouldn't listen and said Ben had to change. I finally started to listen to what Ben was saying and I understood that he was right. I was able to change schools. The new school said OK, he is grieving—what can we do to help? What a different attitude! Ben began to relax immediately.

Like Ben's mother, you might have to intervene to help your children get the understanding they need. You don't want the school to simply excuse violent behavior, but if there's anything you can do to show teachers how to ease your children's anxiety and pain, and move them out of that self-destructive mode, it can make a real difference.

Bullies

Intervention may also be needed to deal with the behavior of other students. Hard as it is to comprehend, it's not uncommon for bereaved children to be bullied or harassed by their classmates. Vickie is in the sixth grade:

> One girl tried to give me a hard time. She thought I was a snob. She'd say, "Oh, you've been so stuck up since your father died and everything." So I just stopped that. I gave it right back. I said "You've been stuck up since you were born, since your parents were divorced." So I gave it right back to her and she hasn't bothered me since.

Claudia's father died of AIDS; she has a friend whose parent committed suicide. While they shared the common bond of a father who had died, they were both taunted by other classmates:

> The kids said we didn't have a father. We thought about that and I said loudly, "Yes, we do, only he's dead." Kids don't tease me too much. I stare them down and they know I have friends who will get after them. That was last year, in fourth grade.

No one really understands why children tease or bully in any situation, but it's even harder to imagine someone wanting to further hurt a child who is grieving. Perhaps the teasing stems from ignorance: the bully does not know what kind of behavior is appropriate for someone whose parent has died. The death might also make bullies act out from the fear it inspires about their own parents' safety or their own mortality. Whatever is fueling the behavior, though, there's no excuse—the victim still suffers. Eight-year-old Sophie responds to taunts in the only way she knows how:

> Other children sometimes think if we don't talk about it and cry about it, we don't care. A girl on my block teases me. She laughs and calls out "You don't have a father," and "You don't care. If you cared you'd be crying." My mother is going to talk to her mother. I yell at her that she's fat and ugly.

Left to their own devices, these children are just reflecting back the bullying, fighting fire with fire. While that tactic actually does often work with bullies, your children can use your help to learn other ways to negotiate such situations. In some cases, that may mean talking to the bully's parents, like Sophie's mother plans to do, or getting teachers and school administrators involved. The first step is listening to your children, to gently ask questions about what happened to help you clarify what they are feeling and experiencing. They need to know that you can respect and understand their feelings, and you need to know what they're dealing with.

Eight-year-old Billy announced one day that he did not want to go to school any more. Neither his mother nor his teacher had any idea why. A month later, while on his first visit to his father's grave, Billy told his mother what a friend had said to him at school, in a mean tone of voice:

"Why aren't you crying all the time? If my father died, I'd cry every day, all the time."

Not knowing how to respond, Billy told his mother instead that he hated his friend, and that's why he didn't want to go to school. His mother explained that his friend was probably trying to make sense of what Billy was going through and that it isn't easy to do that. As painful as the experience was, Billy's mother admits she learned a lot from it:

It's all very strange, like each day brings a kind of unknown. You have to keep your antennae up. If I had not paid attention to what he said, and if we hadn't gone to the cemetery and not asked questions about his friend, we never would have gotten to the bottom of that one.

Keeping your antennae up is crucial. A good school will welcome the feedback and work with you to ease your children's way. If your school isn't like that, you'll have to pay even closer attention. You won't necessarily have to change schools; if there's no behavioral, academic, or social fallout, you're probably better off just monitoring the situation and staying on top of any problems.

This sort of monitoring is a good idea for all bereaved children, including the majority who are neither bullied nor teased in school. Many children who are mourning manage to attend school with little or no difficulty and find it both a respite from some of their strongest grief and a place where their life does, indeed, continue as before. But even when teachers are sensitive and classmates are considerate and caring, your children will still feel different, because they are.

They know a truth that their peers can't wholly imagine, that truly bad things can happen, sometimes in the space of a second. One of their great challenges is finding a way to incorporate that knowledge into their lives in order to go on.

FEELINGS AND WHAT TO DO WITH THEM

Virtually all bereaved children have a fear that lives side-by-side with their grief: fear that something will happen to their remaining parent. Even if they cannot find words to ask about it, they're wondering: what will happen to us if something happens to you? Sally describes it from the child's point of view:

> When I saw how my father could die so suddenly I was really scared about something happening to my mother. She forced herself to make out a will and talk with us about who would take care of us if something happened to her. It helped a little bit, but I still got scared if I didn't know where she was.

You are their link to the past and the future, and they need to be sure you are all right. Children whose parent has died are often nervous about being separated from their surviving parent for even a short while. This widow says that anxiety can be painful to see:

> When my children don't find me where they think I am supposed to be they can get panicked. They really worry about me and cling for a few minutes when they find me.

As frustrating and exasperating as this clinging can be for you, your children are experiencing real fear. They're not unlike the clinging newborns who don't yet know that you will still be there the next time they cry—and just like those newborns, you can't spoil grieving children by showing them that you will, in fact, be there. This is a time of intense emotional turmoil and upheaval for them, and it may be different from the sadness, emptiness, and yearning for the past that you're experiencing. One widow tries to grapple with the emotional divide:

> I don't know their pain and they do not know mine. I don't know how it feels to lose a father at this age.

Trying to Make Sense of It

Even when you try to find out how they feel, your children are even further from understanding this experience than you are. Bereaved children, at any age, have trouble putting together a picture of their family with only one parent. It takes time for them to learn that their parent really will not return. Nine-year-old Jason remembers how startled he was, about a month after his father's death, when he thought:

> Oh my God, he is not coming back.

When asked about his mother several months after her death, fourteen-year-old Dean says:

> I don't want to think about her, it hurts too much to think that she isn't here any more.

It also took Philip a long time before he realized that his father was truly gone:

> I woke up and I suddenly realized that it was the time of night when he died and it was a year later. I really started to cry and I knew then he wasn't coming back and all my sadness came out. Nothing was going to be the same. I think my mom came in, but I don't remember.

Thoughts of the dead parent seem to come in and out of consciousness—unbidden, and sometimes, unwanted. Fifteen-year-old Thea talks about going to a school concert, something she used to do with her father:

> I was just sitting there thinking that I am here without him. Then I realized that my mind is just floating in and out, I wasn't listening to the music. Ordinarily I wouldn't miss a note.

Bereaved children are faced with strong and strange feelings that they never experienced before. They are crying, they are sad, they are confused and angry. They may not know what to do with these feelings; they have no words for them and no experience in expressing them in any kind of orderly fashion. They are trying to figure out what dying means and to understand that death is final. Their parent will not return. There is an emptiness, a space in their lives that makes their world look and feel very different. This child is heartbroken:

At first I was shocked; that was the only feeling I can remember at the beginning. Now it is just sad and angry. Angry because she had to go and sad because I loved my mom more than anything.

Sadness and anger often go hand-in-hand, perhaps because anger is a way to take on the emptiness. Vickie's mother says she never thought her children were angry, but Vickie reveals that she is:

I don't cry too often. There's no real reason for crying about my father; it won't bring him back. He was such a good guy. I am still angry because I don't understand why he had to die.

Some people have suggested that bereaved children feel guilt after a parent dies, but this does not commonly show up in research or in talking to children. There are exceptions, though, as when the parent who died was not taking care of their health. The father of this sixteen-year-old had a serious drinking problem that contributed to his death:

Sometimes I feel guilty. Maybe I should have said something to him about watching his health, but part of me knows there was nothing I could have done.

Children may worry that they caused the death by thinking bad thoughts about the person who died or by behaving badly. They might remember an argument or a parental request they had ignored, and blame their actions for the death. Children may suffer from survivor's guilt, if they survived an accident in which their parent died. You can hear that in the words of this seventeen-year-old:

My mother fell asleep at the wheel. I think I was asleep. It was at night. When I woke up, the police were there. She was dead. At first I thought, if I had stayed awake . . . and I felt guilty. It took me a while to sort it out. I got some help. I understand now that sometimes things happen and we can't control everything. It is not OK that she died, but I know it wasn't my fault.

Nobody understands why bad things happen, and that can make children frustrated and angry at the deceased, the surviving parent, or, if applicable, a drunk driver, or a doctor, or a boss who caused the parent stress. It is a frustration with a world in which this kind of thing can happen, and it seems to develop as children grow, often turning into the question this child asks:

> If God is good, how could He take my father?

Faith and Beliefs

Children take in the religious beliefs they learn at home, and as they age, they refine these beliefs for their own use. Peter, at fifteen, is able to understand that not everyone has the same belief system, and he's made a conscious choice of his own:

> I know some people don't believe that there is anything after death. I was raised to believe that there is, and I prefer to think that my father is in heaven.

Not all families have constructs that include a place like heaven. Elizabeth's mother thinks of herself as too matter-of-fact to believe in an afterlife. Eleven-year-old Elizabeth wishes she felt otherwise:

> Most of my family don't believe in heaven. My mother thinks once you are dead, you are dead. I'd rather have something after that. He was really a great person and so he deserves more. He was only forty-five years old.

Children seem to want to believe that there is something after you die; they're looking for something that makes death seem less frightening. While many of you will be struggling with these concepts yourselves right now, this might not be the best time to try to change your children's minds. If you don't believe yourself, you don't have to lie to them, but you can tell them that some people believe in heaven, others in a different kind of spiritual afterlife, and still others in reincarnation, and leave it to your children to think what they'd like. Their ideas will mature as they do, as their worldview expands, but in the short term, at least, leaving the door open to belief is probably a good idea.

Struggling with the Pain

Your children have never experienced any feelings this intense before, and it can be difficult for them to hold such strong emotions for any length of time. Younger children have a hard time finding the words to articulate what they're feeling or even to tell a story in a straight line and stay with it for more than a minute. Eight–year-old Seth tells us about his father and what he has lost, in a way that reflects his anxiety and confusion:

> Let me play the piano for you. I know how to play Mozart. My father liked that I could do that. He won't hear me now. I like to read books. I'm learning to write on the computer. My friend's waiting, I can't talk to you anymore.

Sophie, in second grade, tries to find concrete ways to recognize that her father is not there any more. Her sadness is almost palpable, but she cannot talk about her father beyond describing the impact his death has had on her daily life:

> I'm sad. I miss him. He used to take me to 7-Eleven. My mother doesn't do that. My mother used to be home when I came home from school. Now my brother is there. When I think about him sometimes I cry. My mother taught me how to make pancakes so I can make something to eat. Sometimes I worry if things would be OK. That's what my mother says—"You'll get over it."

That is not the best way for her mother to respond. It is not very realistic to think that someone can "get over" this loss and all that has changed because of it. It's more helpful to talk about feelings and experiences, to ask your children to say more about what worries them, or to help them talk about their parent and what they miss most. It's also a good idea to give them ways to express what they're feeling by introducing some language of change: that your new life is different on many levels, in terms of daily routines and in terms of feelings you never experienced before. These words legitimate how difficult it is to accept the fact that this person is really gone.

Shortly after the death, children often describe an amorphous emptiness that seems almost bottomless. It takes a lot of support to learn to live with this pain, to feel it, and to accept it as part of dealing with what is lost. Eleven-year-old Claudia remembers how she felt just after her father's death:

> I don't know . . . I was kind of sad . . . kind of a lot of different things . . . sometimes I just sat in my room or lay on my bed. Some nights I just lay down with my mom.

You'll want to make your children's sadness disappear and alleviate their pain. But it's not possible. You are all grieving; you are all in mourning. Sometimes you have to share the sorrow, as the mother of eight-year-old Alice describes:

> After he died she started yelling and screaming for several months, and nothing I did seemed to help. Finally, she burst out and said I didn't love Daddy because I wasn't crying. I explained that I am a private person and cry when I am alone. It seemed to reassure her and she did calm down. I am always having to learn how to say things to her in a way she understands. I never put things together by myself like this before. It's hard work.

Alice was looking at things literally: what she saw was what she believed, and she was old enough to verbalize it. Most younger children usually can't explain what they think. Preschoolers don't have words to express what they have lost. They may be able to say "dead" or "all gone"; they may make a sad face. They can feel the emptiness and longing; they know something is missing. But they don't always know what it means. As children approach school age, they can describe their loss a little more clearly: a parent who bought them toys, who did things with them and for them. This six-year-old says he is sad

> . . . because I understand Daddy will not be there to throw me in the air when he comes home.

Young children describe their parent with simple words like "nice" or "funny," as a person who was important in their lives because he or she did things for them. They talk about what the person looked like, in concrete specific language, like "he had brown hair," or "she wore turtleneck sweaters." Sophie sees her loss through that sort of lens:

> I was lonely. There was no one to snuggle with watching TV. It was empty. So I had to watch TV by myself. He used to have a surprise for us when he came home, like candy or a special toy. I miss that.

Russell tells us:

> What I miss most is—she was always there when I got home from school. She wanted to know what I had done at school, and she always had a snack for me.

Younger children focus on the loss of someone who did things <u>for</u> them. As they get older, children begin to appreciate that their parent did things <u>with</u> them, as well. Andrew was twelve when his father died:

> He always wanted to help us so we could do better. Like if I wanted to build a magic trick he would always help me with that. He was sometimes strict, but that's how all parents are, I think. He wanted me to get involved in anything I could.

This connection to their parent has been broken, and it takes a while for your children to realize just how many moments have been lost. One year after his father's sudden death, Jason is giving up on an activity they used to share:

> My father kept a garden and I was trying to keep it up. He was teaching me and I try to remember what I learned. I have his tools and it is a lot of work. I did it after school and on the weekend. We had some nice vegetables last summer. I'm not doing it any more. It is too hard alone.

Children begin to realize the fullness of the absence in all aspects of their lives. A twelve-year-old misses his mother:

> She was a good cook. I could talk to her about anything.

David remembers the shared activities and the sheer pleasure of doing things with his father:

> I miss him too sometimes on regular days—not just Christmas—like when I'm playing softball or basketball. I'd like for him to see me play. He had taught me how to do most of it. He would be happy to see me play and see how good I was.

An eleven-year-old longs for the mother she could confide in, no matter what:

> I would have someone to talk to when things go wrong, like talk about personal things. If I ever got pregnant, she would understand more than anyone else.

Beyond the specifics, your children are mourning a more existential loss—the death of what was. This sixteen-year-old says things would be much different, and much better, if her mother were still alive:

> We'd be a family again and do family stuff.

In a sense, part of mourning is saying good-bye to the old ways of living as a family that cannot be retrieved. Your children, no matter how young, recognize on some level that their world is irrevocably changed. Each realization of gaps that can't be bridged and shoes that can't be filled brings them fresh pain. You will rebuild your family, and you can help your children find ways to keep the person who died in their memory and in their lives, but there's nothing you can do to take away that pain.

FALLING APART, AND COMING TOGETHER

It is hard to see your children in such pain, harder still to not know how to reach them. You'll no doubt try, as most widows and widowers do, to get your children to put their feelings into words, thinking that will make things better for them. But that kind of discussion is hard to have, as this teenage boy explains:

> I don't talk about it. It is too depressing and it makes me sad.

You'll wonder if your children are doing OK; you'll wonder what's going on behind the silence. Seth's mother worries that his reticence will get him into trouble down the road:

> They say it is important for children to talk about how they feel. Sometimes I worry as he gets older that he will break if he doesn't let it out.

The idea of talking about how you feel, letting it all out, getting it off your chest, or some similar phrase, is ubiquitous in today's world, but it's usually not realistic, especially for children. There's nothing wrong with your children keeping some of their thoughts to themselves; talking isn't some magic pill that will make everything all right. When the magnitude of loss is so great, it can seem impossible to articulate what you're feeling. This fourteen-year-old girl says it just hurts too much to discuss:

> I don't talk about it. I try to forget so I don't feel sad or anything. My brother and my friend know how much I miss mom.

You'll ask yourself a hundred times whether it's normal for your children to not talk about their parent, or, if they do talk, you'll ask whether what they feel is normal. But there is no normal, no one right way for children to deal with death. What they're struggling with is so huge and runs so deep that, for the most part, you have to let it unfold. You'll want to remain accessible for the times your children do want to talk, and you'll want to make sure they're not slipping into behaviors that get in the way of their progress, but you can't take these steps for them.

Most children find it easier to talk about the person who died than to talk about their feelings. These sorts of conversations give them the sense of closeness that they crave. One thirteen-year-old boy describes how it works for him:

> I like it when my mother talks about my father and how he liked helping other people. My friends and I like to share things they remember about him. My mother sometimes pushes on me because I don't talk about my feelings. What can I say about them?

Try to create opportunities for discussions that feel natural and not forced. This mother used an indirect approach with her boys:

> I told them that sometimes I feel like talking about Dad, sometimes I feel sad, or I want to remember something he did. If they ever feel this way, they can tell me and I will be glad to listen. They seemed most comfortable keeping things to themselves.

Her older son, Mike, might keep things to himself, but he enjoys hearing his mother talk to her friends about what a good man his father was. It's even given him a way to join the conversation:

> I like to talk about my father when we do things like he used to do things. He would have been pleased that we did the vegetables on Thanksgiving the way he did. We all laughed and said we hoped he was watching.

Sometimes children do want to talk about what they're going through, but they hold back out of concern for your own feelings. Children often see themselves as needing to protect their surviving parent. They don't want to burden you or make you more sad. This is related to their fear that you will die as well, leaving them all alone. Mandi explains:

> My mother was having a hard enough time. I would cry when I was alone so as not to upset her. I try to keep my fears to myself to make her feel better. She is all I have now. I need to take care of her, too.

Even though you might not want them to try to protect you, your children's actions make some sense. Try as you might to be strong for them, you are in your own period of upheaval, and they can tell. Dean describes how he watches his father:

> I just knew when it wasn't a good time to ask any questions. My father would have a short fuse on some days. I would then decide the best I could do was behave myself and be quiet. It wasn't as if he said, "be good," or anything.

Losing Track of Your Children's Needs

It can feel like a tremendous challenge to push through what you're feeling in order to tend to your children's emotional needs. This widow admits it was terribly hard for her:

> It was like someone put a knife in me every time they talked about their father. I tried to pay attention but I think they knew I couldn't listen. It did get easier with time.

These sorts of communication problems happen as you all adjust to your new circumstances. One area of potential conflict comes from new responsibilities. You might worry about what you're asking of your children in this time of turmoil or disagree with them about their roles. Jason wishes he could do more around the house:

> I watched my father, and I thought I could fix the sink. My mother wouldn't let me. I wanted to teach my little sister about the train set I used to play with my father. My mother said no. It was hard for me.

Jason's mother sees his actions as a need for control and worries that he's trying to take on too much of a parental role. It's easier for her to focus on structure and discipline than it is to relate to his wish to help, and to understand that he is trying to figure all of this out, too. Jason's mother struggles with how to interpret her children's behavior and figure out what that behavior says about what they're feeling. This is how she perceived her daughter's actions, after her husband's death:

> I was sure my little girl was mad at me. She wanted to be with anybody else, or anywhere else.

While the girl was pulling away during the day, she insisted on sleeping with her mother every night after her father's sudden death. The mother could not understand her child's need for comfort, the meaning of her anger, or her anxiety about being left. She understood that some of what her children were doing was related to their grieving, but her own grief interfered with her ability to understand their behavior. Luckily, a friend helped by explaining the daughter's confusion and telling her that it is very common for children to want to sleep in the same bed as their surviving parent for months, or even years, after the death. Jason's mother has a new perspective now:

> I talked with another mother and she said her son did the same thing. This was how they felt safe. So I tried to relax, to give her this comfort. Someone said I would spoil her, but I can't see that as an issue now. As I started to pay attention, I realized she was scared of losing me too. Jason was wanting to sleep with me, too. I was able to let both children take turns sleeping with me. In that way, I could get some sleep too, and they did relax.

The burden falls on you, the parent, as it did for that mother, to decipher your children's mixed messages. It's a steep learning curve for everybody involved, but you can help find the right direction by keeping in mind that your children are lost and searching for answers just like you are. By taking a child-centered approach and letting your children's loss take center stage, these conflicts usually pass, and you will all find new directions and new ways to talk to each other about what has happened to your lives.

It's when you choose not to interact this way and you ignore what your children are going through that you can develop serious problems. By the time this father began to look at what was going on with his children, they were in trouble in school and with the law. His oldest daughter describes the household:

> It's so lonely. My grandmother tries to help. She lives downstairs but that doesn't help. I stay at my boyfriend's—so I'm not reminded all the time that she is gone.

If you can't get past your own pain or loss on your children's behalf, you leave them even more at sea. Seventeen-year-old Tony feels disconnected from his father because they can't communicate:

> I always think no one understands. I can talk to my godfather; he understands more than most, but even he was grown up when he lost his mother.

Your children need to know that there's someone there for them if and when they want to talk, whether it's about feelings, or the changes in their lives, or about the person they miss. Two years after her father died, Suzie says:

> I become frustrated when my mom won't listen to me. She says we just have to get on with things, that we can't focus on what we lost. I think my stuffed animals understand me best. They can't say anything back; they listen, they don't move, they sit there and I talk. And I write stuff in my diary. Diaries help a lot. Whenever I feel down, or whenever I don't like what my mom's doing, or something, I write it down in my diary. It's kind of hard to talk to my father's family. They get all upset and start to cry. My mom does, too. Actually, my aunts don't. They can talk to me; they tell me stories about when he was little. On my mom's side, I talk to my grandmother all the time, 'cause she knows things about my dad. I ask my mom lots of questions about my dad and that seems to be OK. But I don't talk about my feelings.

The pain and sadness these children express come not only from what is lost but from the absolute silence of death. The temptation is great at any age to run from these feelings. There are constructive, positive, temporary escapes, like sports, school work, and after-school activities. But there are also far more dangerous escape routes available, especially for teenagers, who can easily find themselves in situations where others offer them a quick way out of their pain. This sixteen-year-old struggled after her father's death from an industrial accident. Six months after he died, she recalls:

> I was really hurting. I couldn't tell my mother. It was so easy to go off with my friends. It felt good to be away from the sadness and to forget he was dead. One night I had a few drinks and then someone offered me a smoke, and then I realized it wasn't going to work. I began to think about my father, how he wouldn't like my getting into this kind of trouble. He wanted me to go to college. I was out all night. I had to deal with my mother's anger. She was also so worried. Somehow she began to listen and we both had a good cry together. It still hurts so much, but not as much as when I felt so alone. I think that talking about it helps a little—it helps me see that running doesn't help.

In the absence of clear direction from their surviving parent, children are left to try to piece together a new way of life by themselves. This would be asking a lot of any child, but it's asking too much of children who have lost a parent.

In this family, the children tried to get their father to come back into the family after his wife's death, with some small success:

> It was my daughters—Lianne was seventeen and Janice about fourteen. They called me on it four months after their mother died. They reminded me that I was needed at home, that this was not a good time to be working overtime and on weekends. I had to explain that I wasn't sure what needed doing, that I was a man, I was the only parent they had, and they had to accept my limitations. My oldest finally got me to see that she would be going off to college and it really wasn't her job to "mother" her younger sister.

In Tony's family, the surviving parent couldn't respond and couldn't come back to his children, even when asked. Tony's mother had been sick for a long time; when she died, the children felt very alone with their grief. Tony's father admits that he failed to recognize that his children had needs, too:

> I was like a couch potato. I would go to work early and work overtime. It kept me very busy, and I made up for the time I lost when my wife was sick. I would come home late and just sit. It took me maybe six months, maybe more, before I realized that my children had lost their mother, too. It wasn't just that my wife died. They had to get to school, eat—I didn't have the vaguest idea how that got done, or was getting done, for that matter.

Ideally, Tony's father would learn to recognize and acknowledge his children's grief as well as his own and would develop a role for himself as the single parent in the family. He needed to see that his absorption in his own loss and pain was in part responsible for some of the antisocial behavior his children were displaying. This was not what happened, however. While Tony's father sought help, it was only for the children's behavior, not for his relationship with them. A year after his wife's death, he was dating a woman who was willing to pay some attention to the children; he saw this as a way of taking care of their needs. This only angered the children and distanced them further from their father. They needed to hear that this new woman was not a replacement for their mother, just as women in this position need to understand that while they can give the children some of the routines and support they need, their father should not really be assigning girlfriends the care-taking role to relieve himself of the responsibility.

Another father we talked to also minimized his children's reactions to their mother's death. But in this case, his own mother was there every day to be with the children after school. She and their other grandmother took turns to be sure there was a support system, with good meals on the table and someone the children could count on. As one of the grandmothers says:

> We can't take their mother's place, but we can be sure they get a lot of loving.

Putting Your Children First

Keeping your children's needs at the top of your agenda will help you avoid these extreme situations and let you make the accommodations you need to function. Part of your family's adjustment involves recognizing that even though there are some spaces that no one can fill, they can be maneuvered. The father of eleven-year-old Darin reflects on how his family dynamics are shifting, a year after his wife's death:

> My son was always very close to his mother. They could talk to each other in a way that I couldn't. It was nice to watch. He won't have that again. I was forced to retire because of my health. I was home, that was no problem. I had to learn to be more open and to listen better. I am impressed with what I have done. We seem to be managing, and even having some fun.

Don't just ask your children what they're thinking; watch what they're doing. In the period right after his mother died, Duncan did not try to talk about his feelings: he lashed out. Then his father started staying home more, paying more attention to Duncan, and giving him a good deal of support. He also encouraged the hospice volunteer who had helped out when his mother was sick to continue to visit, and he let Duncan go see a favorite nun in a nearby convent whenever he felt like it. His father helped Duncan learn to ride his bike, giving him more freedom to move about the neighborhood to visit friends. Pretty soon, Duncan stopped acting out in school and at home. Duncan's father says he needed to find his own way to help his son:

> I'm not good at talking about feelings. But I am good at just being there and helping out, doing what needs doing, when I know I'm needed.

This might be as good as it can get in the traumatic months after the death—doing what needs doing, knowing when you're needed, and just being there for your grieving children. The depth of your family's loss cannot be overestimated, and each of you will go through significant changes as a result. David's mother sums up what she has learned since her husband's murder:

> What parents need is to be there and to listen. But it usually is a time when we may not know which side is up. Children may be young, but their feelings may be more powerful than anything we will ever hear. We are all grieving. Learning to listen, however, may take longer than we like.

BE PATIENT WITH YOURSELF AND WITH YOUR CHILDREN

None of these changes takes place overnight. You are as dizzy with grief and change as your children are, and the shifting sands of your family life will take months, if not years, to settle out. Be patient with yourself. Jason's mother is only partway through this process:

> I got to the point where I wasn't sure who I was. I knew I was my children's mother, but I wasn't a wife any more. It made me think. I realized that the house wasn't falling apart. I found a part-time job I really liked. I began to think that my husband would see me as a good manager and have faith in my ability to take care of our children. I started to feel in charge. I began to believe that we would make it.

The responsibilities of being on your own are enormous—and exhausting. Claudia's mother had gotten used to being on her own in the last months of her husband's life. Then, and afterward, her family helped with babysitting and taking care of the house. But, as she now realizes, nobody can keep up all the time:

> Being a single parent—I am ashamed of myself sometimes. I'm tired after work. I might be shriller than I like. I try to lie down with her before she goes to sleep. During this quiet time, if I need to, I can say I overreacted, I'm sorry. Then we each look at what is happening and she finds it easy to see her part and we try to change. I'm sometimes so tired of making all these decisions by myself, but I do, and we are really doing OK.

Like you, your children will struggle to make accommodations to their loss. They need to construct a sense of the parent they've lost and to adjust to the feeling that their surviving parent does not seem quite the same, either. They can rebel against the new roles that have been forced on you as they miss the parent who used to fill those shoes. It's a particularly painful part of the process; idealizing the dead parent, and demonizing the living. Tony misses the person who made things feel right in his family:

> She was nice all around. She brought us up well. She was always there when we needed her. I miss most how nice she was. If she was here, everything would be going good for me, school and everything; I'd be a lot happier. My father always gets angry when we don't react like he wants. I don't want to make it sound like I'm never close to my father, but he never lost his mother.

Tony's younger sister, Melissa, misses her mother's ability to keep her in line:

> I don't listen to my father the same way I listened to my mother. I wish my mother was here to yell at me. I need discipline. When she yelled, I felt that she cared. My father can't do that in the same way.

These attitudes will even out over time as your children find ways to keep a connection to the person who died that they can carry within themselves, and as they begin to erase that sense of active loss. It may take a long time of traveling on a very bumpy road, but if you put their well-being at the forefront and make accommodations for your family in a changed reality, your children will settle into your reconstructed family and maybe even become more emotionally accessible. They still might not talk about their feelings, but they'll talk more easily about the person who died and live more comfortably in their new roles. For them, and for you, dealing with the death, the grief, and the many changes in your lives, is an ongoing, unfolding process.

6

After a Child's Death:
A Family Disrupted

It is never going to stop hurting. People have to understand that. Never. This is someone you brought into this life. You bathed him, you nourished him, and you loved him. This pain remains the same; it is constant. What do you do about it? It is like a throbbing headache. At the beginning it can drive you crazy. Then you find ways of living with it. At first we were paralyzed by his death. Just accepting that every day this pain is there was what we had to do. Then we found ways of functioning around it. We are still finding ways.

A father, one year after his son's death

When a child dies, he does not stop being your child or your other children's sibling. Even though this child no longer fills your living space or makes daily demands on you, there is still a place for him or her in your family. You must learn to live with this painful paradox at the center of your life: you are a parent and yet not able to parent that child; a vital member of your family is missing, never to return, yet at the same time is still very present. The death of a child is a cataclysmic blow to body and soul, and it presents unique challenges, from the simple fact of your own devastating loss, to the turmoil it can create in your relationship with your spouse, to the special needs of your surviving children. These are three enormous burdens to carry at what is already probably the lowest point of your life. You'll need strategies to deal with this new reality of irremediable loss.

If you've been living with a sick child, you may have expected that you would somehow be ready for the death. But even though you might feel relief that your child's suffering has ended and that the vigil is over, you won't be prepared for what lies ahead. These parents were relatively prepared for their son's death but not for what they'd feel like afterward:

> We never went to bed leaving things unsaid. I just think of parents whose children die in an accident who didn't say I love you. That would have been hard for us, but then, we weren't there when he died. Bringing his body back to our house was our way of saying good-bye. Whatever we had done before, it was different now.

Now, as all of this becomes real, you'll face a new set of circumstances—living without your child's physical presence. Josh was diagnosed with a brain tumor when he was four. He went through numerous painful treatments, but nothing worked. His mother says death ended his pain, but hers was only beginning:

> Bereavement is traumatic. It is really a crisis in your life; it is awful. It amplified all my foibles. The hospice worker had told us, "You will never be the same again." I'm so grateful she warned me. A whole different set of issues is at work. It is different than when he was sick. Then, he was here and that's what we thought about.

If your child died suddenly, you'll feel like the very core of your being is spiraling out of control. You'll find it hard to talk, or breathe. You'll finally understand the literal meaning of words like "heartache," and "staggering blow." Shelly was killed by a drunk driver. Her mother remembers:

> How did I react? All I can say is I think I was in shock. The first night I was on her bed and I said to myself, I know that I am in shock. She was wearing a hat and they gave it to me. I sat there with this hat in my hand, and I just sat there. I couldn't even close my eyes. How could it be that this happened?

This father describes the shock of the news that his fifteen-year-old son, Darrell, had been the accidental victim of a street crime:

> When you first hear, your first response is to block it out and to pretend that everyone is wrong, that there is a terrible mistake here. When you are finally faced with the facts and you see it really is your son, you find yourself trying to find ways to soften the impact on the rest of the family... but it's also finding a way to better absorb it for yourself.

When your child's death is unexpected, you may be tormented by regret that you didn't have the time to say good-bye, or to comfort your child. This mother has realized that's not worth thinking about:

I used to think it might have been easier if Peter had died of a long disease, or a bullet, or an accident. But people who had that say no; for Peter, it was a good death. Everything was fine. He was having a good time, an aneurysm, we couldn't have known it was there, it was no one's fault. But these other parents are right. No matter how he died, Peter is gone, and that stays with me, and that's what I have to deal with.

If your child committed suicide, the torment takes on an added dimension. You'll be tempted to blame yourself, wondering what could have driven your child to do such a thing and what you could have done to prevent the suicide. Whether you had no clue of what was on your child's mind or whether you were aware of your child's intentions but were unable to prevent the death, you will still feel in some way culpable. That blame is rarely valid, but no matter how unrealistic and unfair, those feelings hang heavy and are not easily set aside.

Bruce's family had no idea that suicide was on his mind. He was twelve and left no note, but the way he died left little doubt that he intended to kill himself. Bruce's mother feels partly responsible:

Only later did I realize that he showed signs of depression and when someone says, "The day I was born was the worst day of my life," that can be a real danger signal. This is the hardest thing in the world to face. It would have been easier to say it was an accident, but it wasn't. I have to live with that. I keep saying, if only I had known, if only I had forced him to see a counselor, if only I had gotten to his room sooner.

With time, her burden has lifted, but it will never fully go away:

For a while I hibernated. I couldn't face people. Even my own mother said, "If he did do this—which I don't believe—then what did you do to him?" This is a small town, and I'm sure people were pointing fingers, saying this was a family doing terrible things. For a while, I felt myself to be suicidal. Even now, I still feel some responsibility. His personality contributed, but I wasn't there. I didn't respond in the way he needed. I just live with this.

Regardless of how your child died, even when there was absolutely nothing you could have done to change the outcome, you will feel that you have somehow failed by not being able to prevent the death. That's because as a parent, you consider raising a child to be your responsibility and your mission. You believe you were supposed to protect your child from harm. And you thought you had the power to do so. Sadly, as you are now learning, some things are beyond our control.

THE PARENT'S VIEW: COPING WITH YOUR OWN LOSS

No matter what the cause of death, the end result is the same. Numbness and disbelief give way to emptiness, pain, stress, distress, and change in almost every aspect of your family life. This is a process that shifts over time, but time will not remove the pain.

One of the early things you'll learn is how unpredictably the waves of pain and remembrance come. As Shelly's mother relates, it's often the little things that remind you that your child is not coming back:

> Sometimes I would get scared about how I will live without her love. I expected to have my daughter's love forever, you know, you go through all that pain of having and raising that child, and now—she was only seventeen and all excited about finishing high school and getting her first job. My husband talks about how much he misses just her touch when they watched TV together.

While your entire frame of reference is crumbling, the rest of the world continues on, as if nothing happened. This father describes how it felt after his son, Carl, died in a household accident:

> As soon as people went back to their routines and you try to go back to your routine, that's when you realize that that routine doesn't exist any more. We now had to get used to this new reality. Nothing is the same. All of a sudden there was this silence. The expectations of waking up in the morning, of hearing your son stomping up and down stairs going to the bathroom. You never knew you woke up expecting to hear them—it is automatic. You never realize that they meant anything to you except to irritate you for a while. Suddenly it is too quiet, and that's when it starts sinking in.

It sinks in, in little pieces, over time. After Dale's death from cancer, his parents observe:

> Dale was supposed to be going to college. After the funeral, all his friends went off to college. For us, for a while, it was as if he had gone to college, too. Sure, we knew the difference. We kept thinking this is what it would have been like, if he had gone to college. But then on Thanksgiving, they all came back and he didn't come back. They came to our house for leftovers. We also let each of them choose something from his room that they wanted. A part of him went with them. It was very hard for us. We laughed and got through it, but it was very hard.

With all of this turmoil in your life, be prepared to find a way, and a place, to let out the tension and pain. Dale's mother describes what outlet worked for her:

> If I was driving, I sometimes would pull over and just scream. I didn't bother anyone, and I felt better. I had a friend whose daughter died and she had young children at home. She couldn't simply leave. So she had a pillow in her basement where she could bury her head, scream as she needed to, and go back to the children.

This relief is only temporary, but it's better than nothing. Carl's mother found a different venue for escaping reality:

> Work was very important after my son died. It was a place where he wasn't present all the time like at home. I was just existing. All I could hope to do was get through a day where I had five minutes of relief from thinking that my son was dead—without thinking about how can I survive without my son.

Some days you move forward, and start to believe you have things under control. Other times you realize you have not really accepted the truth. Shelly's mother recalls:

> This happened in the summer and I remember at Christmas thinking, "OK, you can come out now. I did a good job, it is enough." But it didn't happen. She was really gone.

It's normal for your emotions to be on a slalom course, careening from horror to pain to disbelief to anger. People tell you "this, too, will pass," but they're wrong. The pain will diminish, but it will not end, and your life will never be the same. Sam was thirteen when he died in a bicycle accident. His father talks about how hard it has been:

> It has been a year; I still can't believe it. Of course I know he is dead, but his birthday was coming and I found myself thinking automatically of what we could do to celebrate and then I remembered. I began to realize that you never quite get used to it.

After the death of a child, you might get mad at your spouse, at God, at anybody and everybody, at the fates that brought you to this place. Ellen was born with severe brain damage and did not live for long. Several years after she died, her mother reflects:

I have to get angry at something because I am so sad. Why me, why am I the one? Why can't I be normal, mainstream, like everyone else?

Josh's mother simply gets mad because of what she lost. Josh was only four when he got sick:

Sometimes I get angry when I see a child who is not very nice. Josh had so much more to offer and he is not here. Luckily I'm getting over this. I don't ask as much why was he taken when he had so much to offer. Also, for a long time, it was very hard for me to realize that friends' children are growing up. I don't know what it means to have a nine-year-old. Now I can listen to friends who talk about their nine-year-olds without getting angry.

The anger is different and more focused, when the death is the result of a criminal act. Stephanie was killed in a drive-by shooting. Her mother says:

You are angry at yourself for not being able to prevent this; you are angry at the system around you for not being able to prevent it. You are also confused, because what you thought you could do to prevent it didn't work.

In anger, you want to strike back, get revenge, seek retribution—but you can't change what happened. After Darrell was accidentally shot in gang cross-fire, his parents had the opportunity to consider whether punishing his killer would ease their anger:

For a year after he was killed, they didn't know who did it. We didn't let that consume us. There was never any vengefulness. The media tried to fan our sense of vengeance, but what good would that do? For myself, I needed to step back to ask what would I get out of it? So yes, I was very angry. We are looking for solace, for a way to appease the pain, even something to feed the pain. Some people think vengeance will do that for them, then, that's what they seek. At the trial, after it was over, we heard people saying, now you can have closure. We said no, it is closure for the detective, for the District Attorney, and it is closure for the media. But we continue to live, and there will never be closure. We still have to find ways of living with our son's death, but vengeance won't help.

All of you will feel at least a spark of anger at some point, given this assault on your very being. Even years after the death, the anger may come back, because your sense of outrage over the death will always be a part of you. This is all normal under the circumstances, but try not to take your anger out on your spouse or your other children, and try to be understanding if they take their anger out on you. If you start to feel like your anger or theirs is taking over too often or getting between you and your family, you might want to seek professional help. Otherwise, manage it the best you can and try to channel your emotions more toward getting through this loss, rather than getting back at it.

Time does temper the anger and the pain, such that there are days when you can think of your child without breaking down. You no longer think of things as "easier" or "harder," but as "different." Even then, there will always be reminders, things that will bring your pain to the surface again. Four years after Dale's death, his dog died. His parents describe their reactions:

> The dog was part of him; he trained him, he took care of him. He was a part of Dale that was still here. We didn't think about it until he died. It hit us very hard because in a sense another part of Dale was gone and we felt bereft again in a new way. We still miss that dog.

These reminders will surface throughout your life. More than a decade after Carl's death, his mother reflects:

> I lost a twelve-year-old who would have been twenty-four now, so I also lost a twenty- four year old. As I put her hood on Linda at her college graduation, I suddenly realized that I would never do this with Carl and I lost it. That's not unresolved grief. It will always be there. You can't lose someone who was so much a part of your life and expect to fill that up or ever be able to act as if it didn't happen.

If you have a significant event coming up, you can try to prepare yourself for the inevitable thoughts about the child who's not there. Sometimes a moment's quiet contemplation will be enough to steel yourself against your child's absence, or you might try welcoming memories as a way of inviting the person who died into the life of the event. There's nothing you can do to speed up this grieving process; there's no "getting over it"; the empty space can never be filled. But there are steps you can take to make it easier for you and your family on this journey through pain. Eventually, the grief will become less frightening and less intense, but it will never entirely go away.

TWO PARENTS, AND AT LEAST TWO WAYS OF GRIEVING

The death of a child can have a profound impact on a marriage, as you face the hurdle of learning to deal with each other's grief. There are many different ways in which your relationship can play itself out as each of you confronts your loss. Ronald died of cancer when he was eight years old. His mother explains:

> We have come to the realization that we can't fix it. We have to have tolerance. At times we all become intolerant. A death like this disrupts the whole family. We had to renegotiate our whole relationship.

All marriages will go through some sort of reorientation in the aftermath of such a monumental occurrence. It's often said that the death of a child increases a couple's chance of getting a divorce, but research doesn't consistently bear that out. It turns out that when divorce does happen, usually the marriage was already in trouble and the crisis highlighted the problems. Three years after his son's death in a swimming accident, one father describes what happened to his marriage:

> We had gotten to a place where we were never agreeing about anything. Our son's death was the last straw. My wife wanted out. I took care of our other children and I said: "Go." I guess we became a statistic. But I wouldn't blame it on the death.

Bruce's parents were struggling with their marriage when Bruce killed himself. In this case, his mother reveals, the crisis acted as a different sort of catalyst:

> I can't say we were emotionally supportive, but we agreed to be here for each other and for our younger son. Every time I tried to talk about suicide, my husband wouldn't go there with me. He wanted to believe it was an accident. After a while, he changed. It was like he got jolted into a different place. We went into counseling. He became more attentive. Now he can ask about blame and his part, and we are beginning to talk about this. It is hard work.

At this time when you need each other the most, you and your spouse may be too overwhelmed by your own grief to try to understand or respond to each other's. Hard as it may be, it's essential at least to be aware that your spouse is suffering, too, even if that pain takes a different form from yours. There are some common traps parents fall into at this time; being aware of them may help keep you from becoming mired in their quicksand.

Guilt and Blame

One pernicious quagmire starts with guilt and its evil twin blame. As you struggle with the question of how your child could die, your frustration and sense of futility almost always lead you to ask: where did I fail, what didn't I see, what did I overlook? Clinging to the concept that you could have done something to avert the tragedy is a way of avoiding the helplessness and powerlessness that everyone feels when a child dies, regardless of the cause. Over time, as you adapt to these new emotions and begin to see events more clearly, you will find the ability to understand what can and can't be controlled, and you can put your own involvement into perspective.

It is a short distance from asking where you failed to asking where your spouse failed. Blaming someone else for the death might be a way to help displace some of your guilt and pain, but it can also be extremely divisive. People play the "if only" game: If only my husband hadn't bought her the roller blades; if only my wife had backed me up about not giving him the car that night; if only we had moved to a safer community. Unless your spouse did something intentional that contributed to the death, holding on to this sort of blame won't get you anywhere. Your child is dead regardless of what might have been done differently. Your spouse will feel enough guilt without your adding to it. Instead, you might try working through these feelings together, sharing your thoughts about what could have been instead of attacking each other for what's not.

Communication Breakdown

Another common area of conflict between spouses develops out of efforts to cope with and communicate your stress and emotions. In the aftermath of Peter's sudden death, his mother describes how this plays out in her relationship with her husband:

> In bed, I cry, and if I cry too long, then he starts changing the subject. I see crying in bed as my time when the other children aren't around. I get angry at him. I want to talk about

> Peter and things he did and what reminds me of him, and my husband has no patience.
> We know we need to learn to do things differently, but we don't know how to begin.

Peter's father tends to concentrate on "getting the job done" and getting on with his life. He knows what his wife wants but not how to give it to her:

> For me, everything in the family has changed. Now I see how we deal with difference.
> She wants me to be like her. I can't grieve as she does. I prefer to do it by myself. I can't
> keep crying and go over how awful I feel. You need to respect each other's differences.
> My wife and I are just not in the same place.

A similar dichotomy developed between Kevin's parents after he died in an automobile accident. His mother recalls:

> My husband has always been black and white: good/bad, happy/sad. This is the way he
> always is in our marriage. When Kevin died, my husband said, "You have another child."
> He said, "You have to be there for him and that's it." He sounded almost cold and matter
> of fact. There are times when a woman just wants to be held. I didn't want to have sex,
> but that's what he wanted and then he was upset and hurt. Then we both pulled away
> from each other. We certainly weren't helping each other.

Your approach to sexuality and its meaning in your life is one of the most sensitive areas where differences can emerge in a relationship. For some couples, both partners find that intimacy gives them comfort after a death. For others, there's the fear that by opening up to desire and closeness, the other emotions will come pouring out. In the early months after a child's death, women often report that their sexual desire has died as well. Some say that they associate sex with conception, which only brings back the sense of loss, especially in families where the child died at childbirth or shortly thereafter. Sometimes the sexual conflict relates to whether to have another child. The mother may be reluctant while the father is eager, or the other way around. It's important to recognize that your partner isn't wrong to have a different point of view from yours, just as he or she is not wrong to have different feelings about sex right now. In the best cases, you can respect each other's needs and try to find some common ground. If that's not possible, just try to be honest and open with each other about what you're experiencing and reassure each other that as time passes, so will these clashing feelings.

Trying to Make It Work

The journey of grief is long and slow, and the issues in your marriage will shift along the way. It's not as if you'll work this out once and be done with it. Your relationship will change many times as you deal with the loss over the years. In Dale's family, the struggle over personal needs and styles began while Dale was still alive. His father explains:

> While Dale was getting one of his bone marrow transplants I started to feel very angry about what was happening to my child. If I believed in God, I would have gotten angry with Him, so I figured out the only person to get angry with was my wife. I figured out how to get her so angry with me that we could get a divorce. Don't ask me what that would have accomplished. I couldn't convince myself or my wife that she deserved my anger. She kept looking at me strangely. It lasted about a week. We finally laughed and we cried together as we reflected on what I was doing.

After Dale's death, his parents kept working to be there for each other through the pain and despair. They say it's hard but it can be done:

> I think that the reason that our marriage lasted and got better after his death was because we were pretty much in agreement, even though our styles are so different. We were basically able to talk about most things, and we were able to live with each other's differences.

Openness to these differences in each other's grieving style is essential. Ellen's mother reflects:

> How do you survive as a couple? How did we work out our difference? We talked; we love each other and we held each other and we began to appreciate that we were different and also had our own lives. I always tell people to do things separately. Each of us was grieving on different levels. I was very sad at the beginning, and he was very rational. He was the type who was always very concerned about everyone else, but now he had to face what was happening in his life. When we went to bed, at first I would talk about my feelings so I could go to sleep—and then he would have it all and he couldn't sleep. He got to the point where he said, "Don't talk," and then that would breed resentment in me. It was a while after Ellen died, but we got to a place where we could hear each other. Coming to the bereavement center where we knew our son was getting some attention helped us to break this barrier.

In these kinds of relationships, you can acknowledge your pain but not be so consumed by it that you can't see your spouse's pain as well; you can see each other's points of view and try to be accommodating when there are differences. This couple is trying hard to make things work:

> My husband was ready to have a night out, and I thought that was a good idea. We got as far as the driveway before I changed my mind. At the door and looking at the babysitter, I would say, "Let's go!" We tried three times. I finally pushed myself, because he needed to just go out to dinner with me. We had a five-year-old who needed a lot of attention, and I still wasn't sure what the time of day was. We needed a lot of patience with each other. We sort of took turns being out of it. We were always good at pacing ourselves so we could continue to talk and be there for each other.

It's been a hard lesson, but in the five years since Ronald's death, his parents have learned to accept each other's needs and to help each other whenever they can. Ronald's mother reflects:

> My husband always said it is like reading the same book but being on different pages. It takes a lot of patience. We could comfort each other, but we always knew we each had our own pain. I think everyone is different with their pain and experiences it differently.

OTHER PEOPLE DO NOT ALWAYS HELP

The most common response from people, when they hear of the death, is to tell you they're sorry. Or, as one mother points out:

> People don't say "I'm sorry." They say "I'm so, SO, sorry." It's funny, even though I noticed it when people said it to me, I find myself doing the double-sorry whenever I hear that somebody's passed away.

Another woman describes the gesture that goes with the "sorry" as "the head tilt," a movement encompassing a wince and a neck roll. These are natural responses when words can't do justice to the situation; most people are just trying to find some way to give comfort and show their support.

But there are others who, for whatever reason, show a marked change in their attitudes toward you after a death. Every mourner has stories about inappropriate reactions and comments from others, ranging from the (almost) humorous to the deeply painful. Sometimes it feels as if everyone is looking at you like rubberneckers at the scene of an accident, with their shocked and sympathetic stares. Others will avoid meeting you face to face. They may think they are giving you "space," but people who back away at a time when you need them the most just put additional stress on you. This is especially true if your child's death was potentially avoidable, like an accident, suicide, murder, or sudden infant death syndrome. In these situations, people can react or ask questions that make it seem as if they think you did something to hurt your child or put them in harm's way. Perhaps this is the adult way of separating themselves from tragedy, but whatever the reason, these actions can sting. If your friends or relatives challenge you, you could try to explain how hurtful their comments are. If you don't have the strength or energy to confront this now, just ignore it and either write them off as clueless, or wait for a time when you're better equipped to talk about it.

Darrell's parents remember how criticized they felt by hospital personnel and, later, by the police investigating his killing. He died when he got caught between the crossfire of two gangs, fighting on a well-traveled street in his neighborhood:

> The way they asked questions, it made us feel that he was just another African American kid in trouble. We found ourselves defending him, to be sure they knew he was a good kid, never involved in gangs, and from a very caring family.

It can be painful to observe reactions, especially when there's a perception of judgment. This happens all too often in families of a suicide, and they are the most likely to report that people avoid them. Bruce's mother sees the stigma and judgment aimed at the whole family, including Bruce's younger brother Liam, lasting for years:

> His teacher the first year after Bruce died was wonderful. Liam was also a good little boy. By the next year, he decided it was time to show how he felt. This new teacher kept telling me "We have big problems." I kept saying, let's figure out what is going on and try to help him. But she never called me. Once I overheard her tell another teacher, "This boy needs a lot of attention because his brother committed suicide. This is a really problematic family. What can you expect?" She was condemning us. It helped her to not take any responsibility for her classroom.

Months and years down the road, you will continue to find yourself in awkward situations. Any mention of a child's death can be a conversation stopper. This can be especially true when you meet someone new, who asks how many children you have. Peter's mother wonders how to avoid making other people feel uncomfortable:

> What should I say when someone asks how many children we have? Sometimes when I see how people react, I wonder if I am too blunt. I say two living and one died. Now I think maybe I shouldn't use the word dead, maybe I should say, one passed away. Would that make it easier for people to hear?

In fact, there is little you can do; it is not your responsibility to help others feel better. Changing the words doesn't make the truth more palatable. People are responding to the horror of your news, not to you for telling them. Some parents choose to avoid the pain of the story by only counting their living children; others include those who passed away so as to not let them be forgotten. It's your choice, and you should make it by considering what seems right to you.

People mean no harm when they respond inappropriately; they just don't know what else to say or do. Nevertheless, it takes a good deal of energy, at a time when you least have it, to see what people are doing or saying in the larger context and to deal with their inability to cope with an uncomfortable situation. With time, some parents develop a sort of dark humor about it that serves them well. Three years after Ronald died, his mother says:

> Sometimes my husband and I test people to see how fast they will back off from us when we tell them we have two children, one who died of cancer when he was eight. The other reaction we get is, "Isn't it time you were over it? You should be moving on." It makes people feel better if we tell them we are using our experience to help others. That's true, but we also know that this idea of a limited time by which you should be over it is nonsense. You can't always get people to understand that.

For the most part, when people urge you to move on or act like you should not still be grieving, they are mirroring the kinds of messages they hear in the popular culture. Depending on the relationship and how comfortable you are with frank talk, you might say "Thanks, but, I'm finding that grief has its own timetable," or simply, "I'm not ready for that."

PARENTING YOUR OTHER CHILDREN

Beyond the difficulty of trying to hang on to the reins of your own relationship in the aftermath of a child's death, you also have to deal with changes in the way you parent your other children. Peter's mother was aware of the altered dynamic almost immediately after his sudden death:

> I went back to work. That's fine, but it is coming home that's the problem. I am used to saying, "Where are my three children?" Now I have to remember not to ask for Peter. We have to create a new normal. Priscilla is our oldest child now. Greg used to say, "I wish I had my own room." Now he does. I have a hard time at night when one of the kids asks for help with their homework, I find myself studying the same chapter I did with Peter— who would dream that it was the last time I would study with him? And then I start to cry. I think that upsets the children, but sometimes I can't help it.

Children may be upset by your tears because they fear losing you to your grief; they may also be uncomfortable about seeing you lose control. Peter's mother does not know what to do about her children's reactions:

> The kids come in. They say don't cry. I guess it upsets them, but if I didn't cry, it might be worse. I am not sure what I should say. It is all so turned around. I am the one who is used to comforting them. For the moment, nothing is in place.

Everything is mixed up for your children, too. They're used to you comforting and taking care of them, not the other way around. Carl's mother sees how her behavior after his death made life harder for her daughter:

> I was a fairly decisive person before Carl died. But afterward, I couldn't decide whether my sixteen-year-old should do certain things. I found myself phoning her best friend's mother, asking, are sixteen-year-olds doing this? I remember one of her teachers talked to me when I was at school: "You have no idea how much Linda is trying to protect you." I looked at him and said, "How can a sixteen-year-old protect me?" He said Linda told him, "I can't be late even five minutes; my mother gets upset." I remembered the first time she was late and I went through the ceiling.

You might not have any experience or models to draw on as you cope with the loss, so you might not have any idea what to expect. This mother describes her experience after her son was killed in a car accident:

This was my first brush with death. Both my parents are still alive. My husband was in Vietnam, so he had a lot of experience. As I think about Kevin's death, I realize now that I had to grow up fast. I watched our son. All of a sudden, he is an only child. He seems so alone and I am not sure we can help him.

Giving Your Children the Help They Need

It may not be easy for you, initially, to comprehend your children's pain and to see how to comfort them; it can be too overwhelming on top of your own grief. But you can start the conversation by letting them know how you're feeling. Knowing what is going on, even if it is only that you are overwhelmed, will make your children feel more secure.

It's important to remember that while each of you has suffered a loss, each of you will experience it differently and grieve differently. You have to learn to coordinate your own needs with your children's need for support and guidance. Five-year-old Denise talks about what helped, after her sister died:

My mother told me after my sister died that even when she was very sad, I should come and hug her. She was always hugging me, too, when I was sad or sometimes scared. They explained how much it hurt them, too, that my sister was dead, and it was going to be hard for everyone. It was OK to cry. My father said I should try to help: not nag, put my dish in the sink, pick up my room. I could do that. We helped each other.

Darrell's parents describe the ongoing process of being there for their other children after Darrell was killed in the crossfire of a gang fight he had nothing to do with:

It is difficult for us because there are times when you want to let it all out, but it wouldn't help the kids. You need to be there for them. When they are down, you have to be there. When our daughter is feeling that way, we are there and, as painful as it is, we continue to talk, and we cry. We don't try to put up a wall. We acknowledge her pain. She is learning that there are two kinds of pain. Pain when you get hurt that you can see, and pain that you feel that is in your heart; and she says it hurts so much, it hurts so bad. And we agree with her—it does hurt. We had to help her get to the stage where she could talk about Darrell and think about him. We were doing it for her, never realizing that we had to do it for ourselves. But we realized she needed us. In a way it was she who helped us.

Bruce's mother has learned from his suicide, and it's changing the way she interacts with her younger son, Liam:

Parents carry this horror with them all the time, but I think it has a positive effect. I'm more conscious now of what I'm doing. I ask, what are my issues that are getting in the way? At the beginning, my six-year-old could be loving and caring, and just like that, he would get angry. I tried to understand what a six-year-old can understand and what he can't. I wouldn't do that before. I realized I couldn't give him enough attention. I got him into counseling. If I can't be there with him, someone else can be. I try to follow his lead more. We talk a lot about Bruce. Sometimes he will approach how Bruce died with a little openness, and ask for details. But then he says "I don't want to talk about it," so we don't go there. I've learned we talk as much as he wants.

It will be difficult in the early days after the death for you to give yourselves fully to your surviving children—out of grief, out of guilt, out of fear that you will lose someone else you love. This is an understandable place for you to be, but your children won't like it. Some time after Janice died of cystic fibrosis, her siblings had to go to their parents to demand their attention. Their mother relates:

The children were very blunt, they said: "We want our mother and father back." It wasn't easy, but we listened. They were really surprised when we told them, "Those people are gone forever; you have to live with the mother and father you have now. Everything is changed. Your sister's death has turned everything around, and we *all* need to learn new ways. We are all hurting and we are in this together." It made a big difference in the way the children, even the six-year-old, reacted. They seemed to relax. We think it was because they felt included and began to understand what was happening.

Learning to cope isn't just about respecting each other's pain and being there for each other. Your children also have to navigate the outside world, and they'll need your help. Darrell's mother went to her four-year-old daughter's school, to make sure they knew how to help her:

I went to school. I told her teacher and the principal what had happened. I knew they knew, but I wanted them to hear it from me. I said, if she cries, just allow her to cry—don't tell her to stop crying. You have my permission to hold her. She is sad, and no one has an answer for what happened. If you can't deal with this, send her to the principal. I have done this every year because she still is dealing with his death. All the teachers so far have been most understanding. It is three years later and she is just beginning to understand that he is really not coming back. She talks a lot about him, and the teachers have to understand that this is OK.

Some children will act out at home or at school. It can be hard to interpret how much of that behavior is a reaction to the death of their sibling, their new circumstances at home, or a regular part of growing up. When her eight-year-old son started acting out after his sister's death, this mother struggled to understand what was happening:

> I soon learned what didn't work, dealing with Kyle. It didn't work trying to be angry when he did something that he knew wasn't right. What worked was understanding and hugging and letting him be a kid. Sometimes I had to put my foot down. It can get very confusing. It was very difficult to sort out what is part of death and what was related to other things. I didn't want him to use Leslie's death as an excuse to get away with things. It could also be his age or maybe because he is just bored. I realized it was everything.

You can never really know how much of your children's behavior is a direct result of the turmoil in their lives. Some of it would have been there anyway, but they themselves often perceive their actions as related to the death. In the end, you have to deal with the behavior, regardless of its source, and work on the grief component separately. When your child acts out, you can be understanding without being lenient; you can be compassionate without being an enabler. You have to create limits and keep structure, just like you do with any child, but you also have to find a way to support that child's grief, both at home and at school. This is a delicate balancing act, and it requires a patience you might not have right now; but your children need it. They have just lost an essential part of themselves, and they don't know how to respond.

THE CHILD'S VIEW: WHAT IT MEANS TO LOSE A SIBLING

What does a child lose when a sibling dies? The sibling relationship is typically the longest one you have with anyone, even longer than that with your parents. A sibling is part of your life, your being, your sense of who you are and where you fit into the world: losing a sibling is like losing a part of yourself.

Sibling relationships color and enrich childhood; they're dynamic, changing, and busy. Growing up in the same household, siblings share memories and learn similar family values. They provide each other with companionship and affection. Siblings fight, they play, they share, they disagree. They lean on each other, pull away, and then lean back again as they navigate their places in the family and in the world. Each sibling has a unique experience in the family, depending on his or her age, sex, and birth order, and each has a special way of interacting with parents and other siblings.

When children lose a sibling they also, literally, lose their place in the family. Josh's father considers how his relationship with five-year-old Kenneth would be different if Josh had won his battle with cancer and been able to teach by example:

> A lot of what I do would be done by Josh as the big brother. Kenneth would be the middle child. The whole dynamic in the family would be different. It defies our imagination. We have no concept.

This death is probably the first loss your children have experienced, and for it to happen to someone so close to their own age not only disrupts their world but it shows them their own vulnerability in a deeply personal way. Your children will need your help to learn to cope with all of this.

How Children Respond

Like all mourners, children feel shock and disbelief when their sibling dies. Even when they knew death was imminent, they find it hard to believe that their sibling is really dead. When the death is sudden, the level of shock is deeper. Kayla was injured in the accident that killed her mother and sister. She was sixteen. Numbness, and her own struggle to survive, made her almost blind to what had happened:

> I actually had a sense of peace. Reality didn't hit me until I was out in the real world. The first time I really cried was in a grief group of other kids my age, about three months later.

Jocelyn was seventeen when her older brother was killed in action in the military. Now an adult, she remembers chasing after the Navy chaplain who came to tell the family about the death:

> I just couldn't believe it. He told my mother and made sure she called another adult to be with her and left. I needed to hear it myself. I wanted him to say it wasn't true. Of course he couldn't.

When a sibling commits suicide, the shock has an additional dimension as the family struggles to accept this act. This child describes his reaction:

> It was almost impossible to believe that my brother chose to kill himself. I knew he was unhappy, but I couldn't imagine he would do this. My mind raced with all sorts of questions about what I could have done. I was so angry. Then I just sort of shut off. Otherwise, I don't know how I would have gotten through the funeral.

Recognizing Your Children as Mourners

Involving your children in the rituals surrounding a death is the crucial first step in the grieving process. Your children need to be recognized fully as mourners in their own right; they need to be told what all these mysterious rituals mean and what roles they will play. Three-year-old Teddy was killed in a farming accident fifteen years ago. His parents knew instinctively to keep their three other children informed and involved in what was happening. Alan was eleven at the time:

> We are farmers; we see death all the time, see animals die. But I don't think we even had a clue that we weren't going to get to see Teddy again. One thing about kids and death, you can see death, but it's nothing until you experience it.

Teddy's brother Mark was five:

> I didn't remember having anyone close to me die. I was pretty good for a couple of days because I thought after a few days he was coming back to life. I remember thinking, Jesus came back to life after a few days, so I thought Teddy would. I looked everywhere for him. I didn't really understand. Now I am glad Mom and Dad explained everything about what was going on and they took me to the wake and the funeral.

The expectation that the dead can come alive again is not unusual in communities where that is a deep-seated part of the religious tradition. Resurrection is a powerful idea that appeals to children who are struggling with the reality and finality of death. Family members or clergy can help by explaining the concept and gently reminding your children that in their religious construct, even Jesus didn't stay on earth after his resurrection. Similarly, if your tradition includes a belief in reincarnation, you might remind your children that in that construct, the soul does not return to the same body, the same family, the same life. These concepts are not the same kinds of magical thoughts that lead children to fantasize about their loved ones really still being alive; these are childish misinterpretations of religious or cultural beliefs. For that reason, clarifying your beliefs is not about challenging the magical thinking that may help them cope; it's about helping your children understand the meaning behind the ritual words so they're not stricken anew when their sister or brother fails to rise from the dead.

If your religious practice is to view the body and if it's in a condition that allows for a viewing, seeing the body can help children understand more fully that their sibling is really gone. It helped Eric, who was nine when Teddy died:

> I remember going into the funeral home and it seemed like we were in there forever. I had some anxiety about seeing him. I didn't want to. But I think it was a good experience— make sure everyone does it. In a way, it helped make it real, even though I kept looking for him for a long time afterward. We saw a rainbow after he was buried, and we decided that was him going to heaven.

If you don't have an open casket or if you prefer that your children not see the body, don't worry that you will be making it harder for them to accept the death. It might take a little longer for it to sink in, but even children who do see their sibling's remains continue to struggle with the concept that death is forever. Grief doesn't care about logic.

It will take a good long while before your children truly recognize that there is no returning from the grave. You can't rush that reality for them—they may know the truth intellectually, but emotionally, accepting it will take a long time. The best you can do right now is to recognize your children as mourners, respect their pain, involve them in your traditions and rituals, and help them honor and remember their brother or sister.

FRIENDS AND BULLIES

Starting in the first days after the death, interactions with friends and peers will play a big part in your children's journey through grief. In the best-case scenario, your children's friends will be a source of care and connection, confidants to turn to when family stability feels uncertain. It can be very helpful to have friends to talk to who are not as personally touched by the death as family members are. Your children need to be reminded right now that life can and does go on, and this is something that friends, whose lives have not been shattered in such a personal way, can do for them. Jocelyn says:

> The thing that helped me most was friends. They didn't know what to do, but they would come and include me. Sometimes they would just come and sit. That was the support I had. Things they would do normally, they just kept on doing—being normal with me.

Your children might not be that fortunate. Some of their friends might shy away or treat them differently. That happened with Kayla's friends after the accident that left her injured and her mother and sister dead. Like many who have lost a loved one, she finds her relationships shifting in the aftermath:

> My friends—either they didn't know what to say so they avoided me, or they were very supportive. Two people who I wasn't close to became very close. They were just there. They came to visit in the hospital. They just accepted me throughout all the stages. After the accident, I told my friends, if you have any questions, ask me, it is open. It helped me to talk about it.

Surviving children can also find it difficult when they come in contact with friends of their dead sibling. These friends are themselves mourning and often unsure of how to behave. Priscilla found this stressful after her brother, Peter, died from an aneurysm.

> It was really hard to go back to school. I started to see some of my brother's friends. We didn't know what to say to each other. A few came around some after the death, but it was too hard for them.

Some potential friends may distance themselves because they don't know how to deal with your children's grief. The same thing might be happening to you, because many adults are also uncomfortable with the subject of death. It may help your children make sense of what's happening if you talk to them about your own reactions when friends don't respond the way you'd like them to. You can also explain that even when you understand the reasons your friends act this way, it can still hurt. Priscilla describes that pain:

> They feel sorry for us. Some friends ask how it feels to lose a brother. I say it is horrible. Sometimes when we meet kids who don't know me, if they ask how many brothers and sisters I have, if I say I had two brothers and one died, then they sort of step back. So it makes it hard to tell them.

Like Priscilla, and like you, Kayla also finds it hard to know when to tell people about family members who died:

> If I don't say I had a sister, it's like denying her existence and that's not fair to both of us. But sometimes I hold back because it is hard for some people. I find if I do talk about it, after a while people do get more comfortable. If I'm comfortable, then they become comfortable. Maybe it's part of growing up.

Something much worse than the lack of social support is also affecting the lives of too many bereaved children. It's not unusual for them to report that people at school are saying mean things or making fun of them. Nobody understands why this is so. It could be that these bullies are trying to handle their own anxiety and get some control over a situation that makes them anxious, but whatever the reason, their actions can really hurt your children. If this happens in your family, it can be extremely challenging to find ways to help your children deal with the meanness of others. Despite all that has been written about how to deal with bullying, it still exists, and there's no single response that will invariably defuse a bully. You might have to call the bully's family or involve the school. You might also suggest that your children consider that something else could be going on in this bully's life to make him or her behave in such a hurtful and disrespectful way. It can help your children just to know that it's not their fault that they're getting picked on and that the bullies are responsible for their own actions. Armed with this understanding, your children might be able to come up with their own ways to ignore the bullying or defend themselves against it. Kayla found one way to deal with a group of bullies at school. The result was empowering:

> I just felt different. My hair was just growing back after the accident. I remember one of my first days back to school, some boys started throwing spit balls at me. I saw one of these boys in the hall later, and for some reason, I felt I had to talk to him. If I was going to survive, I couldn't let them get away with this. I said, "Take one good look; this is the closest you will ever get to me, and pray that you are not the one in the back seat who walked away." I walked away feeling really proud of myself. What I did sort of said "this is who I am and it's OK!" No one ever said another word again.

COLLAPSE OF THEIR WORLD: A LOST WAY OF LIFE

In many ways, children's grief and the feelings they experience after the death of a sibling are similar to those of a child who has lost a parent. But of course the two relationships are very different, and the implications of the loss are, in turn, quite different. Kayla understands the distinction, having lost her mother and sister at the same time:

> Individually there are different roles: with my mother, I lost the nurturing and the guidance. With my sister, I lost the unconditional love of a sister and a friend, no matter what phase she was in.

The perception of what is lost depends on the ages of your surviving children and how they characterize their connections to the person who died. Younger children see the loss in terms of their lack of a playmate or a competitor. Sam's younger brother, Barry, lost someone who shared and enlivened his days:

> The worst part about my brother's death is that it is so quiet in the house and there is no one to fight with now.

Barry uses the word "fight" to characterize the relationship because he has not yet developed a vocabulary to describe all the various ways in which he and his brother related to each other. From his perspective, with Sam's death, he lost someone who filled his life with noise and action, without which his daily life now seems empty. Barry also lost a protector, someone who watched out for him:

> Since my brother was a year and a half older than me, he was tall, so he stood up for me. If I got into a fight, he stopped people from bugging me. Now I have to learn to do that myself. He kicked butt. He was a good kid, very bright.

Older children recognize that when their sibling died they lost a teacher, a student, a role model, a protector, someone to protect, a companion, a sparring partner, and a friend. Jocelyn's brother helped her develop constructive behaviors and to value herself. Years after his death, the lessons remain, and the loss still stings:

> I was seventeen when my brother died at the age of nineteen. He was the one who always looked out for me, took care of me. He kept me from using drugs. Part of the reason I

never used drugs was how hard he had worked to keep me away. His death was a terrible loss—there was no one who could ever fill that bill for me, even though I am married with children of my own now.

Your children's place in the birth order also plays a part in how they experience the loss. If it was the older sibling who died, your younger ones can feel adrift after the loss of a protector. Darrell's sister remembers him reading to her and playing with her. Now she sees him continuing his role as big brother by serving as her guardian angel. Justine was sixteen when her older sister died in a motorcycle accident. She recalls:

I lost someone who really took care of me. Sometimes it seemed like she was the only one who paid attention. I felt like I didn't have any direction after she was gone.

When it's the younger sibling who dies, the older children don't talk about losing a caretaker but rather the person they took care of. Kayla was two years older than her sister. When she died, Kayla lost her role as the big sister who led the way:

I lost a best friend. She went through a period where we would fight. Then something changed. She was always doing what I did, like a little sister, I guess. I would play cello— she played. I played softball, and she would play softball. Then, just before she died, we really became friends.

Upsetting the birth order can leave surviving children in unfamiliar roles, as when the child in the middle of three suddenly becomes the older or younger of two. Eight-year-old Dan lives in a single-parent family. His younger brother died suddenly at the age of three, leaving him an only child. Now Dan's the only male in a house with just two people:

What did I lose? Another boy in the family.

Your children don't have to be raised in the same house as the child who died to be profoundly affected by the death. Kayla has a half-brother who was raised by his biological mother, her father's first wife. Their relationship gives Kayla someone else with whom she can share memories of her mother and sister:

We didn't see each other but once a year. He really liked my mother, and he thought my sister was neat. He used to tease me, in particular, a lot. After my mother and sister died, he reached out. He was very upset. It has become important to both of us that we can share our feelings about this—and some of our own lives now as well.

No matter what your children's ages, in losing a sibling, they've lost someone to be with, talk to, and play with; ultimately, they've lost a lifelong companion. You can't make up for that: you can't fill the shoes of the child who died, and neither can your surviving children. It's important that you don't try to remake anyone in the lost child's role and that you make sure your surviving children know that. If they're willing to talk about it, your children might also benefit from conversations about what they have lost with their sibling's death, in both a concrete and an abstract sense; it will do them good to know that you understand and respect what they're feeling and what they're missing.

THE LOST WORLD

When their sibling died, your surviving children lost their shared past as well as the shared future of the lives they would have led together. They can't know how those relationships would have unfolded in time because death disrupted a relationship in process.

Your children are grieving not just for their sibling but for the world in which that sibling existed. In many ways, that world has crumbled. Their relationships with you and their other siblings will change; their sense of self will change, and so will their relationship with the sibling who died. Peter's younger brother Greg thinks about his family:

Our whole life as a family has changed. We were once three and now just two. So many things remind me of my brother; I hear a favorite song on the radio, I see the kind of clothes that he wore. I feel so confused and so sad.

Your surviving children will experience strong new feelings as they deal with the changes in themselves and in their world resulting from the death. They may feel lonely; the house is very quiet and they can't quite get used to it. Eleven-year-old Greg complains about how boring things are now. Mark describes how alone he felt after his brother Teddy died in a farming accident:

I think I was kind of lost because Teddy and I used to do everything together, and then after he died, he wasn't there any more. I had to do things by myself. I couldn't do the things we used to do. My mother tells me that I came to her in tears, maybe two or three weeks after Teddy died, wanting to know what I had done that God would take my best friend away. She tried to tell me that I didn't do anything. We still talk about it every once in a while. She had not understood what it meant to me because he was my best friend. I remember she started to do some things with me we had never done before. As I think about it, it wasn't the same.

This ten-year-old girl is struggling, too. She doesn't know what to do with her feelings:

I'm like my father. I don't cry. I am very bothered when I see my mother cry. I want to run away from the pain. Sometimes I go visit a friend.

Your children's sense of helplessness may pervade all aspects of their lives. Losing a sibling makes them aware of the reality of death and that it can happen to anyone, at any time. Peter's brother, Greg, is very specific about his fear:

I am scared that someone else will die in my family. I drew a picture of my mom going to work and I am sad because I am not with her and I don't know if she will die or not.

You can help ease some of those fears by addressing them directly, even if your children don't bring them up, and by being sensitive to the need that many grieving children have to stay close to you. They are looking for comfort in their newly unstable world and trying to make sense of this incomprehensible blow. Dan's brother died three years ago. Now eight years old, Dan still can't figure out how to respond:

I'm mad and sad at the same time, even now sometimes. What do I do with this anger? You can't go around banging cars or people. I keep a lump in my throat. Sometimes I can even swallow it, but it comes back, two or three times a day.

Anger can be an outlet for anxiety, a way to release some emotion by blowing off steam. Even so, it's usually not very productive—it doesn't make any situation better and sometimes makes it worse. It's hard to find constructive ways to deal with anger. You can try talking to your children about their feelings and ask them to consider the corrosive aspect of anger—how it can take up so much space that it gets in the way of making the most of their lives. These approaches might help, but it will still take a long time for the anger to dissipate.

But most of the time, after a death, there isn't even anyone in particular to be mad at, no person to blame. For some children, like this boy, that leaves only one other option:

I'm angry at God for letting him die, and that it happened to me. So weird that it is happening to you, that your brother died. I think it was God's fault. Sometimes when I get angry with God, I feel guilty.

If your children are challenging their spiritual beliefs, try not to insist that they fall into lockstep with yours. Many children have only a cursory understanding of their religion's views of God's role in saving lives—or ending them; you might want to talk to your children about what you believe and what your faith allows, and you might try to help them come up with a construct of God that works for them.

With all these swirling emotions, children are looking not only for outlets for their grief but also for ways to escape it altogether. Justine found the pain after her sister's accidental death intolerable. She sought a way to numb it:

I started to use drugs. It made it easier. It didn't hurt as much. One of the counselors in school started talking to me. I realized what I was doing and I got help before I really lost it. I guess I was lucky.

Not everyone is lucky enough to have early interventions before things get out of hand, so you'll need to be on the lookout for substance abuse in your grieving children. Drugs and alcohol can be a tempting escape, and they're readily available in most communities, even for children of middle school age. All parents need to talk to their children about the potential dangers these substances pose, but a few extra warning conversations might be in order with your bereaved children. If you suspect that they're using drugs or alcohol, don't wait long to confront them with your concerns; it's important that they know you are paying attention and that you're looking out for their well-being.

Communicating with your children can be very tricky when they're in an emotional crisis and you are in such a precarious state yourself. It can be hard to recognize the difference between the way you need to approach your grief and loss and the way they do. Kayla remembers:

My father was grieving over my mother a lot more because that was his life partner. I felt my sister was getting gypped—no one was talking about her. He thought I was trying to deny their deaths. He wanted me to grieve like he did. The first few months he would sleep at the cemetery all the time. I didn't even want to visit there. I couldn't. And we argued a lot about that. I had my own understanding of it. I really had to wrestle with my feelings in my way. I was angry for a long time, but I would fluctuate between very angry, rageful, and depressed, in an instant. Most of that was directed at my father. I took all my aggression out on him. Nothing he could do was right.

Lose Yourself to Your Grief, and Your Children Lose, Too

It can be all too easy to let your grief get the better of you, leaving your surviving children to watch, agonized, as you struggle with your own loss. They may feel like you've become unrecognizable, almost overnight. Just as you are no longer certain of who you are at this moment, neither are they.

Having lost their accustomed place in the family, your surviving children might not know where they fit in with you, either. They worry that they come second to their dead sibling, who, in their absence, is remembered more fondly. If their sibling had been sick before dying, the other children might have hoped that your pain would end with the death, making you more available to the rest of the family again. When this does not happen, it may feel to them like another blow.

The catastrophic collapse of your surviving children's world, then, is a result of their sibling's death as well as your turning inward with grief, no longer in charge of your family. Shortly after Peter's sudden death, his siblings feared that the whole family had irreparably come apart. Twelve-year-old Priscilla says:

> I feel that our family is not whole and never will be until we all die. We don't go out as much or go camping. We're usually locked in our rooms. I feel confused, scared, and I always wonder what will happen to us or to me. I hope my family can become whole again.

In Dan's family, the pressure was on him to ignore his own feelings so as to not cause his parents further grief:

> My mother said I should listen and try to be good. I was having a hard time believing he was gone. I felt sad but I just knew not to talk about it to my mother. She would cry and I would feel bad that I upset her. Sometimes I would get angry and get into trouble at school, and then I would feel worse because my mother would get all angry with me.

At some point, you can get so caught up in your own despair that you fail to recognize that your other children still need you. In Steve's case, that's driving him away from his parents:

> My parents don't think about me anymore. All I hear about is my brother and all his accomplishments. I can't tell them why I don't come home more often or why I won't talk to them about my brother. They say I was jealous, but that wasn't how my brother and I saw it. It was OK while he was alive because we had each other, and we could laugh with each other about how lopsided their ideas were. But after he died, there was nothing there for me.

Your own loss is immense, and the demands on you are going to be nearly impossible to withstand. Your children see this, and in family after family touched by this tragedy, the remaining children describe their parents as being in distress. Six months after his brother Kevin's death, eight-year-old Jay drew a picture of himself crying, standing near his parents, with their hearts broken in two:

> The biggest change is that I am an only child now. The house feels very strange and my parents don't say much about all this. My folks cry a lot. I see mom crying and I don't know what to say or do, so I just hug her. Makes us feel a little bit better, but we don't talk to each other about it. Mom says sometimes her heart is taken right out of her.

Three years after her brother Carl's accidental death, Linda remembers a house in turmoil:

> I had never seen my parents out of control and when I saw that—that really scared me. My parents had always been able to fix things for my brother and me and they couldn't fix this—and I couldn't cope with that. That has always stuck with me. They went from parents who were in charge, fixed my bike, put a bandage on my cut, to parents who couldn't make a decision about what to wear tomorrow.

Your children's vision of you as out of control or unable to function is terrifying to them. They're used to a world where you provide comfort and support, and now you may be unable to give them emotional sustenance. Paradoxically, at the same time as they're learning that you can't keep them safe or make everything better, your children need you to do those very things. When you can't, it adds even more instability to the foundation of their lives.

Since your own foundation is so shaky right now, you might ask a close friend or relative to stay with you and help keep the family going for a while. If that's not possible, try to carve out a little time every day when you put aside your own great loss in order to attend to your surviving kids. Even a tiny gesture will reassure them that you're still there behind the mask of grief, and it will let them know you're trying, on their behalf, to get going again.

The coming days and months will be full of fits and starts, mixed messages and missed signals between you and your children. None of you knows what to do, what you want, or what you need. Responding to all of this conflict may be too much for you to assimilate at a time like this. There might not even be an effective way to respond; you will surely make mistakes and misinterpret clues along the way. In Linda's family, her parents expected her to continue along the path of independence she had followed before her brother's death. But that wasn't what Linda wanted:

> I was sixteen when my brother died. My parents kept saying that they would understand if I wanted to spend more time with my friends, as if nothing had happened. But whenever they would go anywhere, for about a year after he died, I always wanted to be with them. My parents were funny. They were always buying me something. If I said "Gee, isn't that nice," they would say, "Do you want it? We'll buy it." I finally realized that they were, in a way, bribing me to be with them. They finally caught on and I said I knew all along what they were doing. I told them I couldn't take advantage of them because I needed to be there with them. I didn't need the presents. I needed them as much as they needed me.

The desire to stay close can be healthy and restorative for both you and your children, but in some cases, fear, rather than a need for support, fuels that increase in proximity. Just as bereaved children worry about their other family members dying, your own fear for your surviving children can be so great that you become overprotective. In the words of a healthy seventeen-year-old whose two sisters died of a congenital disease:

> I can't wait to go to college. My mother is smothering me. She is so frightened that I will get into an accident that she won't let me drive, and if I am five minutes late she is a wreck. My father lets her do the talking, but he's no better. Sure I understand, but I need my life, too.

Now that you know what was formerly unimaginable—that you can lose a child—it's really hard not to panic at the thought of having another child in peril. But your other children need to live their lives. All too often, you may (intentionally or not) clip their wings out of fear of losing them and not let them out of the nest. Jocelyn was afraid to leave her parents alone after her brother's death:

> The most heartbreaking thing was watching my parents, because the whole thing was so unreal, just as unreal for me as for them. My father completely disintegrated. He started screaming and yelling. Those kinds of sounds, I don't think I'll ever forget. My mother was very stoic and so she didn't show it as much. I started to take care of my parents. How did I do that? First thing, I didn't apply to any college outside my home town. I stayed nearby. I always told them where I was and when I would be home, to be sure that they wouldn't be hurt again. I was not going to give them any more cause to worry. At the time, I didn't know that no matter what I did, they were going to be upset.

If you're unable to steer the family and unable to bring in outside help, you're putting a serious load on children who are already burdened with their loss. Allie was twelve when her big sister, Stephanie, was killed in that drive-by shooting. She describes what happened to her family:

> I thought it was my job to keep my little sister from bugging my parents. They seemed to imply that was what they needed when my older sister died. After a while, my sister got pretty angry with me. She would have temper tantrums and beat on me. Her teacher called and explained what she was hearing at school. My sister lost my parents and her big sister and she was blaming me. I learned that my parents had to get their act together. I wasn't helping anyone. I finally realized I was having my own troubles dealing with the fact that she died, and how she died. I noticed that after this crisis my parents started to wake up.

Pulling Yourself Together

It's important for you to try hard to "wake up" on your surviving children's behalf before you take even more away from them. You all need to adjust together to the altered landscape of loss. The pain will remain, but even if you were unable to function effectively for a period of time, you'll begin to reengage as a family. Realignments will take place between you and your children as well as between remaining siblings. Years after Teddy died, Alan describes one of the changes in his family:

Another thing that my kid brother's death did, it made my next younger brother and me best friends, and that hasn't changed over the years.

As your children move away in time from the death and reach different developmental plateaus, they will have new questions and new needs. But they may also be able to understand how much you have gone through. Linda says:

I guess the most important thing I learned over the years was that my parents were not crazy—that this is what happens to parents whose children die.

A NEW OUTLOOK, FOR YOU AND YOUR CHILDREN

As time passes and the horrendous early days become memory, you will realize that you are no longer the person you were before the death. Somewhere along the way in your journey of grief, for better and for worse, you have changed. Some of you began this metamorphosis earlier, when your child became ill. Dale's father remembers what he discovered when his son was diagnosed with cancer:

I soon learned that I couldn't control the world. I found out what was important. My whole attitude toward work and family changed. I think that this all started as soon as I found out how sick my son was. I was a changed man.

To deal with your loss, you have to surrender your sense of order and control in the universe. As you move through time with your grief, reestablishing some order and control becomes possible, but in a whole different way. Three years after Stephanie was killed, her mother says:

Only now can I see what it means. I was forced to grow. All of a sudden I did feel like a grownup. Until then I still felt in part like a teenager. It also forced my husband and me to be more introspective than we would have been otherwise.

You may find that you've developed a new voice. Bruce's mother began to speak out:

At church, I realized I was being told by my pastor that suicide was a sin and Bruce was doomed to hell. The old me would have sat there quietly and accepted what he said. The new me said, he can't be right, and I told my husband, I'm leaving this church. It was

OK with me if he stayed. I couldn't have done that before, either. I would have waited for
him or been upset if he didn't come along. As it turned out, he felt the same way.

You'll notice a change in the way you relate to other people, including your
children. After her son's death in a bicycle accident, Sam's mother participated
in a parent support group and spent a lot of time reflecting on her approach to
life. She describes the resulting change:

I was raised to understand that my parents were in charge and when I got to be a parent,
I would be in charge. That's what I did and I was just like my mother. You don't challenge
that order, and you don't think for yourself. I taught my children "You don't step outside
these boundaries and you listen to what I tell you." After my son died, I realized that's
not the way things are. Waiting for other people to tell you what to do doesn't help at
such times. I talk differently to Barry, my other son, now. I realize that I have to hear
him, too. If I let him, he has something to contribute. I don't feel so helpless, and neither
does he.

You can help your children find their way, and sometimes they can help you,
as they move into a place of growth and change. Kayla reflects:

I had two choices and one was not even a choice. I could sit in my room for the rest of
my life and cry "poor me." But I said no. I have to go on, in honor of them.

Kayla gradually became able to give voice to her sadness and anger about the
death to find more constructive ways of dealing with her feelings and to make
peace with her father:

During college, I started telling my father that we have to decide that we are either going
to fight for the rest of our lives or we have to come to some understanding. We both have
grown from this, even though it has been very painful. We are very different people and
now we are very close.

Teddy's seventeen-year-old aunt was living with the family when he died.
She realizes now what she has learned from that experience:

After Teddy died, what changed was not what death meant, but what life meant. I realized
that it doesn't matter how old you are, it matters what happens today— you might not be
here tomorrow. It is important to appreciate everyone, no matter who they are, because
they might not make it tomorrow. I try to help people see that we just don't know. His

death also made me believe that everyone has a purpose in their life, and when you are born, God knows your purpose and when you finish your purpose, then you die. The sadness is for people around you. We all have a mission and it affects how we interact with other people and who we touch. And when we finish touching other people, then we are able to die.

Children can grow in other directions, as well. Some will find new academic and professional pursuits. Jocelyn became involved in community work and politics, and she found a direction in life:

I asked, is there any way I can make something good come out of this? Maybe I can save someone else's brother from being killed in this way. I started to worry about everyone killed in the war—on both sides. I think that was part of my grief—trying to save everybody. I see a lot of people not paying attention to themselves and what they need. They focus on helping everyone else and that's what I found myself doing. I also found a church where I felt at home. That helped. I then began to work with hospice, because I really needed to understand dying. This was about eight years later. I went back to school and did my dissertation on sibling death. After that I found I was able to put things together and I could live with a new perspective on my grief.

Kayla began studying philosophy and religion, areas she would not otherwise have considered. Six years later, she thinks back on what she's learned from her sister's death:

I think part of the mourning process has been accepting that I'm not going to have a sister. What I realized was that it makes me feel sad to think about that. But I don't feel like I've run away from it. I don't feel like I fight it so much anymore. It's like, that's who I am. And yeah, it really changed my life.

Your grieving children may appear to grow up before their time in the years following the death of their sibling. They become more sensitive to other people's needs and more grateful for what they have. They know that life is precious. They discover new aspects of themselves, new philosophies, and new appreciation for what matters. All of these are wonderful and valuable lessons, although they are learned at great cost.

7

After a Friend's Death: Invisible Mourners

The words come easier now. I can express what I lost. I have lost the validation that Mara provided—the voice that confirmed me to myself, that told me I could; I have lost her presence, her ideas, the new things she brought into my life; I have lost my belief in plans, in our ability to control our lives; I have lost the confidence that we could do anything, that we could conquer the world, change it, make it ours.

A teenage girl, one year after her friend committed suicide

The death of a friend is a little-explored and little-explained loss. Unlike the families of the dead, friends who grieve are often forgotten mourners, rarely receiving much support and guidance. For the young, in particular, a friend's death is a challenge to their developing sense of self. It is through friendships that children expand beyond the family and begin to create a world of their own on their journey toward maturity. When a friend dies, they lose control of that world. Gila reflects on how Mara's suicide destroyed her expectation that friendship is forever:

I have lost the security that no matter how rarely we saw each other, she would be there, and the knowledge that our futures would somehow, sometimes overlap.

If your children's friend has died, you may think that there's not much you can actively do to help. But at least attempting to understand what your children are going through may make it possible for you to be there with them, to help them sort out their feelings and guide them through this difficult time. Just by recognizing your children's pain and confusion, you will send a message that they are not alone and that what they feel is significant. Finding ways to help your bereaved child might not always be easy or obvious, but even if you don't think you know the best thing for them to say or do, remember that your advice and presence is very important to your children at this critical time in their lives.

As your children grow, their friendships take different forms and different shapes. Younger children may develop rituals of loyalty to each other; they are given to such dramatics as blood bonds and life pledges. The older the children, the more easily they can reflect on the relationship and its meaning in their lives. After a friend died, this high school junior tried to define what friendship really means:

> A friend is someone who is there through thick and thin, always there, regardless of who or what you are or what your sexual orientation may be. A friend is going to be there when you need help, and when you don't need help. A friend is someone you dare to be yourself with.

Adolescence is typically portrayed as a time of storm and stress, but this is really not the case for the majority of teenagers. Many will go through occasional periods of turmoil, but these years are primarily a time of growth and exploration in which friends play an active role, helping each other negotiate all the changes in their lives, emotional, hormonal, and physical. They are years of learning, of recognizing similarities and differences between themselves and others, and of developing skills for living in a more complex world, in more complex relationships. In short, friends help children navigate the world. Friendships can also be fragile. They may last despite distance and differences, simply because the participants wish them to. Or they may fade and even disappear as people change, as interests change, as children grow and mature, or as physical distance makes it difficult to maintain personal contact.

In many ways, your children's sense of themselves is connected to their ability to negotiate this world of friendship. It is in the realm of their peers that they are introduced to new kinds of interests and interactions and begin to hone the framework for the adults they will grow up to be.

Lauren, a seventeen-year-old high school student, reflects on her friend who was killed in a drunk-driving crash. He was a passenger in the car:

> He was the first boy I knew who said it was OK to be me.

Your children feel a different kind of intimacy with their friends than they do with family members. Friendships are chosen; friends are not held together by societal obligation or by blood ties. Ruth, now twenty, compares her relationship with her siblings to that with her friend Jessica, who died of cancer three years earlier:

> When I was fifteen, a friend meant more. I couldn't talk to my older sisters. I was just the kid sister to them. My older brother was not even living at home any more. You go out with friends, you do everything together. You tell all your secrets to friends, not to your brother or sister.

Sometimes a friendship grows within a family relationship. Now eighteen, Donna had both ties to her cousin Tina, who shot herself three years ago:

> When she killed herself, I lost a friend. Yes, we were cousins, but we really liked each other and we chose to spend a good deal of our free time together. I used to think that we talked about everything, only now I realize that there was a part of her I knew nothing about.

Family members, in a perfect world, love each other unconditionally, under any circumstances. Friends choose each other, and together, they often develop new attitudes and new approaches to life. Anna, another of Jessica's friends, remembers:

> We felt there wasn't anything we couldn't do. We encouraged, we suggested, and we helped each other try new things. We always made each other feel good about ourselves. One of us was always there if someone was in a bad mood, upset about something, or sick.

Friendships are based on shared dreams and shared desires, enveloped in trust. Sean's friend Corey had Duchenne muscular dystrophy:

> Corey was my closest friend, my confidant, someone who I truly connected with, even when we first met in fourth grade. We just understood each other, and as we got older it didn't change. He was someone I could talk to about girls, my parents' divorce, the struggles of being an adolescent. We knew we could trust each other, we had no secrets, and we could really work at solving problems in ways that worked. It took a long time before I found anything like that again.

Friendships can also develop and flourish within the little pockets of difference between two people. Deborah's friend Klara was killed in a random act of violence at the age of fifteen. Deborah remembers:

> We always fought about little things, but I think best friends should always fight—it makes it more interesting. That's what makes it a real friendship. Sometimes we would get so angry we wouldn't talk to each other and after a while when we saw each other we

would start to laugh and see how silly we were, and everything was OK. It never mattered
if one of us was right or wrong. We tried to learn from our differences. We both always
felt if you agreed about everything it wasn't as interesting.

The loss of a friend disrupts a crucial part of your child's development; the
persona that was developing inside that friendship is now unmoored. Clarisse is
a high school sophomore:

You lose a piece of yourself when a friend dies, like a piece of a puzzle. If you have only
one friend and that person dies, then you ask: who can I be myself with?

Your children might not know that you understand the potency of
their friendships and what they lost with the death. You can help them
grieve by encouraging them to reflect on the relationship—what they did
together, what they liked or disliked, where they agreed or disagreed. If
you've ever had a friend die, talk about what that felt like, and how it
feels now, but try not to make your loss and your feelings the center of
the discussion. Encourage your children to summon up old memories and
anecdotes and record them somewhere. They'll be grateful for them in the
future.

Anna can remember Jessica before she had cancer—and after:

I have pictures of her in my mind when she was beautiful and healthy, but I also have
some memories when she wasn't. I think if I hadn't been there at those times, I would
be very angry with myself. I think that if you're really a good friend, you have to be there
even at the most difficult times—that's when friendship is really tested.

It can be hard for children to talk about friendships, and even harder to
talk about death. The adolescent and teenage years are full of expectations of
how to behave, how to talk, and what to say, and they often divide up along
stereotypical male/female lines. Girls, for the most part, are given more lati-
tude in expressing their feelings directly and in finding comfort in talking about
them. Donna describes how her group of friends coped after another classmate
committed suicide:

We talked, we felt closer, we weren't ever really alone. If someone wanted or needed to
talk about it, we did.

Boys, for the most part, try to deal with death in what they think is a ratio-
nal, logical manner. Boys think they're expected to contain their feelings. Sean's

friendship with Corey was based on their special ability to communicate with each other about their feelings and various personal experiences. Nevertheless, Sean says it was hard to navigate between his perception of how society wanted him to express himself and how he really felt, after Corey died:

> Maybe it is a boy thing. I was uncomfortable crying. I worried people would think I was weak, that I shouldn't let this get to me. I think Corey's family helped a lot. They were never embarrassed by my sadness or tearfulness. At least there I could let it out. I began to learn that I wasn't less of a man if I let myself feel. He was my friend for a long time and I felt very lost.

Sean was able to spend time with Corey's family after the death because he was comfortable with them, as they were with him. Whether your children should pay condolence calls to a friend's family is a decision that depends on their relationship with the family, the depth of the friendship, and whether the parents seem open to the contact. Some bereaved parents are touched by the contact; others may find it too painful to bear. You can help your children parse this territory by contacting the parents, or a trusted friend who is helping them out, to see what would be best for them.

Different Ways to Cope

Discussing how their friend's family is dealing with the death is a good opportunity to show your children that everyone—boy or girl, child or adult—mourns in a unique way. There are many different grieving styles, and none of them is the "right" one for everyone. Some people are open with their feelings and want to talk about them. Others are more self-contained, and the pressure to talk makes them uncomfortable. It goes against their personal style. Jon reflects on how he reacted to his friend Ethan's suicide:

> I'm a more introverted type. I cried when I heard, but for me the best thing was to just get on with things. I was glad I was performing in the college theater. There was no one to replace me and that kept me very busy and involved. I needed that distraction. People kept asking me how I was doing. They seemed to expect that I would want to talk, but that's not my way.

Your children might feel angry or dislocated from their school or community in the period immediately after the death if they don't feel that sufficient attention is being paid to their loss. They can feel alone and misunderstood, questioning their own reactions and behaviors when people who don't appreciate the meaning of the loss wonder why they don't get over the death more quickly. Outsiders often feel that because of their youth, and because the deceased was not "family," friends should be able to move on. Schools might be similarly dismissive, perhaps giving time off for the funeral but then expecting everything to return to normal. Joseph was sixteen when his friend was killed while a passenger in a car driven by another friend who was drinking:

> It was hard to get back into studying. I couldn't concentrate. I kept seeing him in school, all the places where we were together. I kept thinking it could only be a dream, but I knew it wasn't. Everyone kept saying you have to get on with your life, you can't let it bother you so much. I was confused—was something wrong with me that I was so upset?

Of course nothing is wrong with being upset. Friendships are among the most important and defining relationships in life, so it's natural that when one comes to an untimely end, those who are left behind will feel the pain and lasting ache of loss, just as they do when anyone they love dies.

DEATH AND FUNERALS

Friends can die from medical conditions or diseases like cancer or muscular dystrophy, but more commonly, adolescents and young adults die sudden and violent deaths from accidents, homicide, or suicide. All too often, for older teens, alcohol or drugs are involved. In the inner cities of America, more teenagers die of gunshot wounds than from all natural causes combined.

The cause of a friend's death does play some part in the ways your children will react. If the friend's actions or behaviors contributed to the death—if the friend took his or her own life, for example, or was involved in gang activities or got in an accident while driving when drunk—your child's frustration and anger will be aimed, in part, at the friend. If the friend died of an illness or was the innocent victim of an accident or a crime, the frustration is more toward a universe that would allow something like this to happen. Still, regardless of the cause of death, your children will experience great sadness that their friend is no longer there, and disbelief that he or she could really be gone.

Just as family members are still taken by surprise when a loved one dies after a long illness, friends also find themselves unprepared. Since they aren't part of the family and in constant touch with the sick person, it can be easier for them to keep up the illusion that things might get better. That was the case for Anna, even though her friend, Jessica, had been sick with cancer for a long time:

> I don't think that I realized what she was going through until she died. It was unexpected in a way. I think that I was denying what she had. Even up to the very last days when it was clear that she was dying—I remember even then that I thought, okay, so she doesn't feel so good. I had heard of people who died of cancer but it wasn't anyone I knew. I was just going along as usual. I didn't realize how difficult it was for her—we kept including her and she did what she could. She even managed to organize a birthday party for me a month before she died.

Although they were aware of the possibility of death, their focus was on continuing to live. Death was not dominating the picture. Such was also the case just before Corey's death from muscular dystrophy, as his friend Sean remembers:

> I don't recall any specific conversations about dying. It was something we both knew. I always knew he had a limited life expectancy. He was already in a wheelchair when I first met him. The only time it did come up was when we talked about dating. He was interested in girls, just like I was. There were several women who would have been interested but they were afraid of losing him. I think my role as a friend was to facilitate his living. We didn't think about the future or the past, we just tried to do things in life.

The expectation of imminent death is more foreign for young people than for adults. You can help prepare your children by explaining what might be happening to their friend, and what might happen after the death. You can prepare them for what they might see and hear and feel. After consulting with the sick child's family, you can advise how much time can be spent together, and then encourage your children to make an effort to be there through the last days, painful as that may be. Even when all that is done, your children will probably still be surprised when the end comes. It was made clear to Sean that Corey was about to die, but he says it still didn't seem real:

> The night before, his mother called me to come over. He was out of the wheel chair and in a regular chair which was very rare. He seemed so alive. How could I think that in a couple of days he would be gone? When it happened I couldn't take it in.

With a sudden, unexpected death, the sense of disbelief has a different hue. Weeks after her friend's death in a car crash, Lauren says,

> It is still hard to have in my brain that he is actually dead. I think about it almost every day.

When hearing about the death, when they feel their world is falling apart, children of all ages seek reassurance and comfort from their parents. Jon was away at college when Ethan killed himself. Jon remembers that the first thing he did after hearing the news was to call home:

> I'm not sure why, but I found out that everyone in the house did the same thing after they found out. We needed to touch base, to let our families know, and in a way, to be sure that everything was okay with them. In fact, it was very comforting.

Lauren found out about her friend's death when she was visiting her aunt in another city. Her aunt recalls:

> She could hardly tell us what she was reading on her e-mail. She simply froze. When we realized what happened, we told her to get in touch with her friends. Use the phone, use e-mail, and call her brother who knew her friend. We saw her relax a bit when she did this; then we arranged for her to go home as quickly as possible. I'm not sure she was aware of what we did. We got her through the day until she could fly home. We were sure that it wasn't a good idea to try to make her feel better.

This is how Lauren remembers it:

> On the plane home I kept saying "Jim is dead" in my mind. I couldn't get it out of my head. That wasn't helpful, but that's how it was.

Deborah describes a similar sense of disbelief after her friend Klara's murder:

> We had just seen each other at school that morning. It didn't sink in. She was so alive, so many plans. Funny, what I thought about was that I wouldn't hear her laughter any more. She had a wonderful laugh. I couldn't believe she was gone. Even now—it's been six months—it's still hard to believe. Even at the funeral, I could not believe it was her in the coffin.

Attending a Friend's Funeral

Going to the funeral can be a reality check for your children—no more denying that their friend is really gone. That was too much reality for Clarissa when her friend died:

> I couldn't go. My teacher had just died, and then my great-aunt and a cousin were killed in a car accident. I don't regret not going. Now I am beginning to find my way. My mother took me to visit her mother and I could handle that.

Deborah thought about what to do and talked to her mother about it, before deciding to go to Klara's funeral:

> Going to a friend's funeral, it's not something you expect or are prepared for. My mother wasn't sure about my going to the funeral but my whole class was going, so she decided it was okay. At the funeral, I thought I could see Klara standing next to me like she always did.

You might be unsure about how to advise your children about attending the funeral. Some things to consider are whether your children have been to funerals before and know what to expect; how your children deal with stress; how open you and they are to talking about whatever emotions the funeral stirs up; and how they feel about going, or not going. Lauren's mother thought about all of that before making up her mind:

> I grew up knowing that when someone died I went to the funeral. My parents were very open about these things and we've been the same way so I had no problem letting Lauren go to her friend's funeral. I didn't want her to go alone. Her brother and good friend went with her. I was worried about an open casket—that was not part of our tradition. I don't think she has ever seen a human body and if she got upset, I wanted to be sure there was someone there to support her. I know that she has always been very sensitive to things dying, whether it was a pet animal or an insect, and had funerals for them. She keeps a picture of her uncle who died in her room. She likes to look at the picture and think about him.

It helps if you tell your child what is likely to happen at a funeral or other kind of service. You might find out which of their friends are planning to attend, and see if you can coordinate with them or their parents to go together—it's a good idea to talk to other friends' parents anyway, so you can all work to help your children through this crisis. You should also try to find out from the parents of the person who died, or someone close to them, what the funeral service will be like. If that's not possible, you can prepare your children for the most likely possibilities. They need to know that it's possible that the body will be openly displayed, either before or during the funeral, in accordance with some religious traditions. This can be too much for some children to take, but if they are prepared, or if those around them are comfortable with this tradition, it is not necessarily upsetting. In fact, seeing the body helps make death real for some children. Donna wishes she could have seen her cousin after her suicide, but it wasn't possible:

> You never want to believe that anyone you know would deliberately kill themselves. She shot herself in the face. The coroner said if I was a relative I wouldn't want to look. So it was really hard to believe. It would be easier if I could say that I saw that she was not breathing any more.

The funeral or memorial service may be one of the most emotional experiences your children will ever have. Jon says humor helped him and their other friends get through Ethan's funeral. On the way to the cemetery, they were laughing in the car:

> Ethan would have appreciated the jokes. The last remark someone made when I got out of the car at the cemetery to be a pallbearer was "Don't drop him!" A lot of people probably wouldn't understand that. I actually mentioned this to someone—he was sort of aghast, but it helped us get through.

It was the kind of gallows humor that was typical of their group. This type of continuity with the life they had before the death was comforting for them, just as it had been for them to call home.

Never having experienced such situations before, your children may not be sure how to give expression to all of their feelings at this time. It's more acceptable to show emotions at a funeral than in most other public places, yet even there, tears may not come easily. Sally, another of Ethan's housemates, says that only as they began to recite the mourners' prayer at the cemetery did she give in to her tears. Donna describes her reaction to Tina's funeral:

> I know now that I tried to be real tough. Her brother and I said, no one will see us cry. We were going to put up this front that we could handle this. I don't know why we thought

that's what we should do. Then we got to the funeral. My aunt had asked me to help pick
out some of the music that they played. It was the music that really set us off and then
it was like we couldn't stop crying.

Self-control is particularly important to teenagers, and your children may
not want to be in a situation where their emotions could get the better of them.
They might feel the impulse to get away from all those feelings, as if that would
somehow make them go away or change the situation. Ruth talks about Jessica's
funeral:

The first time I saw Jess's father crying was at the cemetery. Suddenly I felt all the pain.
I felt like running, but I controlled myself.

If your children are invited to participate in the funeral, it helps them feel
respected as mourners. They welcome this opportunity to share their grief. Sean
read a poem he had written, at Corey's funeral:

When we were young, that seems so long ago,
I just never thought you would really have to go...
When he was here he taught me to live every day
As if it were the last...
Because before you know it
Your present is your past...
I hope I made your stay here more enjoyable and free.
When we were young, not so long ago,
I guess I really knew that you would have to go.

Whether in person, in letters, cards, or e-mail, your children can share some
memories and tributes with their friend's family. Families of the dead often have
an intense need to hear that their child has touched others and will be remembered, despite his or her shortened life. In turn, your children will be able to
gather and organize their own thoughts as well as reflect on what this means to
them. Gila recalls how important this sharing was for both Mara's parents and
friends:

We exchanged stories with her parents. They told us of her illness, we told them stories
from better days. Together we wove a portrait of this woman who had left us and the
tremendous impact she had on our lives.

TRYING TO MAKE SENSE OF IT ALL

Most adolescents have never experienced death close up before, and its reality will leave them feeling lost and dazed. Jon describes his behavior during the first days after he learned of Ethan's suicide:

> It is difficult to explain what I felt. It was like a leaden feeling, a numbness, so it was very hard to do anything, to even talk. There were things to do, and we did them because we had to. It was very hard to interact with anyone who didn't know Ethan and didn't have some of the same feelings.

The word "denial" is often used in a negative way, but within reason, denial is not a bad thing as it helps mourners function despite their pain. If they give in to their grief and just sit at home, immersed in sadness, the mourning can become circular and unproductive. Your children will find some relief from their immediate situation by keeping busy, often throwing themselves into activities, their bodies working in a way that gives their emotions time to catch up. Sally remembers having a lot to do, such as making arrangements to go to Ethan's funeral, calling others on campus to tell them about his suicide, and being involved in planning a campus memorial. These concrete tasks provided a framework to guide her days at a time she was "in a fog." Ruth and Anna both say that getting back to college and a life they had not shared with Jessica helped them cope. Sean recalls how he felt for many months after Corey's death:

> People say that at the beginning, you don't feel it, you don't believe it, and then little by little, the feelings come out. That was true for me. The sadness was always there. I would watch TV or try to read something that would bring me up, or go see my friends. On some occasions when it was more overwhelming, I would stay alone and be sad. At the beginning, I couldn't talk much to others. I found it mattered to me if people knew Corey or not. Then again, sometimes it is easier to kind of be in denial. Keeping my mind busy works at such times.

After the shock begins to abate, other feelings begin to emerge. There can be a sense of helplessness, of being lost in the world. Terrence's friend was killed in a drive-by shooting:

> We all knew about different gangs in the neighborhood, but we thought if we stayed away, kept our noses out of other people's business, we would be safe; but now we know that's not how it works. It makes you want to go get a gun, but that's not the answer.

Anger and hurt are other emotions that friends experience as they try to understand the tragedy. Lauren describes her anger after Jim's death:

> It was so awful. Two lives were ruined. Jim's best friend was drinking and driving and is being charged with vehicular homicide. He may go to jail. I started to worry about how Jim would manage without his friend and then I remembered he was dead. Then I got so angry—such a waste.

Sally began to feel unsure of the world and her place in it when Ethan died. Even though he chose to end his own life, it made her realize people her own age can die:

> I found myself being scared. It started right after he died and lasted for about five months. I was scared even crossing the street. I had never lost anyone close to me before. I was frightened in the sense that this thing that had taken over Ethan so fast; could it take me over just as suddenly? I felt so vulnerable. Things are so fragile. I wasn't one to hurt myself, but a car could come along and hit me. I was at my folks' that summer and one of my favorite movies, *The Big Chill*, was on TV. I used to have this fantasy that all of us would be like the people in that movie. I forgot it was about a suicide. I just started to cry and cry and after that I didn't seem to have the same fear.

Struggling to Make Sense of Suicide

Donna experienced two suicides within months of each other. Shortly after her cousin's death, a classmate, Ken, killed himself. She and her friends felt a pervasive anxiety that another disaster could happen at any time. School officials were heavy-handed in their concern that people who had been close to Ken, who were having trouble dealing with his death, might try to harm themselves. Donna says that all the attention and worry about copycat suicides just scared her and her friends more. She describes how they coped:

> We went everywhere together. Nobody went anywhere by themselves. We never left Ken's former girlfriend alone. She never ate alone; if she went to the mall someone went with her. We were frightened for her that she might do something. There was no real danger, but at that point everything worried us.

After a suicide, your children may become angry with their friend for choosing to cause others so much pain. Ethan's friend Sally remembers:

> We were angry. We said, what a stupid thing to do, and asked, why did you do this? It would have been easier if we knew that he didn't see any alternative.

Donna describes her anger when her cousin, Tina, committed suicide:

Oh, I was angry. I would talk to her and say you didn't have the right to take that away from me. Why should you be able to do that? It is not fair and of course it is sad. It is not fair to my Mom, to me, to her family, that she didn't let us say good-bye to her. Even her Mom is angry because she didn't let her see what she was feeling—like she had no faith that anyone could help her.

Your children might ask themselves if they could have done anything to prevent the suicide from happening. Donna recalls:

Ken wasn't in school that day. I was in a class with him, and he wasn't there. So we all asked, what if someone had forced him to go (to school); what if someone had happened to call at the moment this happened?

It's hard, after a suicide, to reconcile the mode of death with the friend they knew. Sally says:

Just think, one day your best friend is standing next to you and the next day he's not. And you thought you knew him, inside and out. Obviously you didn't know anything. There is the sense that I should have known my friend and I really didn't. In a sense there is a feeling of betrayal.

Like most young mourners, Donna asks herself why she wasn't aware of what was going on with Ken, why she didn't see the real danger signs. She tries to get inside his head to understand what happened to the friend she thought she knew. Donna knows all the questions, but not the answers:

Of course I keep asking WHY? I can't find a good reason for why he wanted to die. I have never been at a place where I felt I wanted to be dead, so it is hard to understand. I don't know why I feel I should have an answer. If it had been a car wreck, it would have been different.

For Sally, learning to separate the Ethan she knew from the Ethan who killed himself lets her see his actions as the result of an illness that consumed him:

I said to myself, that person wasn't really Ethan. After he died, I learned that in high school he had been diagnosed with clinical depression. I prefer to see it in medical terms.

Sometimes, signs of that depression had been present but went misread or overlooked. Donna says that her cousin, Tina, talked to some friends about her plans, but they didn't believe what they were being told:

> We found out that she had confided in several of her friends that she was going to kill herself. She never let on to me; she knew I would tell my mother. Her friends should have known better, but they kept their promise to her not to tell. No one wanted to believe that she could really mean what she was saying. She kept promising them that she wouldn't do anything, and they believed her.

It's hard to imagine how terrible those friends felt when it turned out they were mistaken. Adolescents and adults alike need to be taught to be alert to suicide threats and know where to turn for appropriate help. The clarity of hindsight haunts Donna as well as her cousin's mother:

> Her mom is also angry with herself because she didn't understand the signs. Tina was spending a lot of time alone in her room and she gave away all her new clothes. We just didn't realize what it meant.

Donna says her experience with the suicides of her cousin and her friend has made her hyper-aware of the lengths people will go to escape their dark feelings of sadness, despair, and fear:

> Now that this has happened to me, I realize you have to take these things more seriously. Now even if someone just says, "I could kill myself," I ask more questions. I say, no that's not funny to me. I've become an expert on suicide prevention. I've learned a lot.

Often, the signs of depression were not at all clear to friends until after the death, when people put the pieces together. Donna saw that happen after her classmate's suicide:

> We learned that Ken had slit his wrists a while ago. He told them in the emergency room that he fell in the shower when he cut his wrists and they believed him. They sewed him up and sent him home. It's hard to believe they accepted his explanation. Then he wouldn't go to school. He wanted to be caught but no one picked it up. In the end you have to accept that it wasn't anyone else's fault. No one shot him but himself.

There are always people who find it easier to cope if they have someone to blame; they're looking for simple solutions to what are in fact very complex problems. Finding someone to blame may be a way to avoid their feelings and give a sense of control when in fact there is none. Donna describes some consequences of this kind of behavior:

> Ken and his girlfriend had broken up just before he died. It was easy for everyone to blame her. She was devastated. I told her that it was not her fault. I explained that it is easier to blame someone when this kind of thing happens. We kept those kids who wanted to point fingers away from her.

Ethan's friends also came to the realization that there was no one to blame, and there was nothing they could have done to prevent his suicide. Jon explains:

> We never felt that we could have done anything differently, although I think we all asked ourselves that question. He had talked to me about losing his sense of direction, but I would never have thought that his moping and withdrawing were signs of danger. I listened, I tried to understand, but I guess I couldn't. We were really relying on the professionals to help.

With their lives outside the home becoming nearly as important to them as their family life, young people who lose a friend feel that their world has fallen apart. As they cope with the death, your children and their other friends may join together to provide support and to protect each other when they are frightened or worried about their own ability to handle their loss. Donna describes how her friends worked to put things back together, after Ken's suicide:

> There is a kind of bond. We had kids leave class sobbing, even months afterward. They would sit in class and think he is not there, and start to cry. After class we would try to get together to talk. Me and my friends formed a support group from our high school and the other high school in town.

Staying close together and watching out for each other helps recreate a sense of community and safety. Donna goes on to describe how she and her friends were able to work through some of their torment after Ken's death:

> After this happened we just realized that it was very sad; but if everyone just sits here and says "what if?" it is going to kill you. We decided that we can't go through all the "what ifs." This did help and it brought a lot of us closer together. We had to just accept what he did.

Looking for Meaning in Life—and Death

Adolescence is a time for self-searching, a time to seek meaning in life. The death of a friend can bring new questions about the power and place of faith in your teenagers' lives. Donna finds great comfort in her religion. She finds that reading religious poetry makes her feel more comfortable about what has happened. Anna, now doing graduate work in biology, knows that faith helps some people, but she does not find comfort there:

> I think religious people accept it because they believe in life after death. I'm not sure about that. I think that we become—this is my biology perspective—organic garbage. I don't know how much we have souls. Maybe because of that it's hard for me to accept that something happens after we die.

When death occurs at an age when children and adolescents are questioning so many things, it is understandable that those who have lost a friend would ask how God could let this happen. Ruth describes how Jessica's death from cancer made her wonder:

> If he is a good God, and really cares, how could he have allowed Jess to suffer so and to die so young? I was pretty angry with him, for a while.

Try not to get too upset if grieving children challenge your family's religious views or traditions. You can talk to them about your beliefs and ask about theirs, but you can't tell them what to think. They're working through this, and they need your understanding and support as they tackle these major philosophical and ideological ideas.

Regardless of their faith, these mourning adolescents begin searching their own lives, looking for meaning. This may be their first encounter with their own vulnerability. In the words of sixteen-year-old Terrence, whose friend was killed:

> When you lose someone close who is your own age, it shows you your own mortality, that you are not going to live forever. This is someone who is your friend, someone you were cool with. Just like that, you're never going to see that person again. You could die.

Not only are your children now more conscious of the fragility of life but they also develop a new appreciation for what they have. Ruth reflects on what Jessica's death has meant to her:

I think I was younger then. I looked at life much more drastically—everything in extremes. Then you see someone dying in front of you, it makes you see how much you have. You say to yourself—wow, how lucky I am that I'm living, that I can go on with things. I think her death gave me a lot. I started to look at life with a different perspective. I sort of grew up fast. Before, every little thing—like being fat, doing bad on a test—was the end of the world for me. After Jess died, these things seemed so small. I tell myself: think about Jess, she's not here any more. Her life stopped. There were so many things she didn't manage to do. I don't have to be perfect.

Sean says Corey's death gave him the push to try new things and find a new place for himself in the world:

I think that I started several different journeys that I would not have gone on before or would have started much later in life. I didn't have a lot of friends. I started seeking out people who I thought could really support me. I had to learn to be more social.

Corey's death also helped Sean to be less fearful of his own death:

To see his strength. To say, this is the deal and he didn't flip out. He had a presence, he knew what it was all about—he was ready—he didn't appear to be outwardly afraid. That gave me the calmness to say that I'm not going to be afraid of this. I think I was afraid of death. I don't know if I ever expressed that to Corey. I think that I have a greater peace about it since I went through this with him. I am very different now than I was before.

CONSTRUCTING A RELATIONSHIP WITH THE PERSON WHO DIED

Death does not end the connection your children had with the person who died. As Deborah describes, the relationship carries on in memory:

It's not something you choose. You don't choose to remember; you just always carry it with you.

Your children might carry the sensation that their friend visits them in spirit. Sean feels Corey's presence and influence on things that are happening in his life:

At the funeral, there was this balloon, his favorite color, and it separated from the other balloons and floated away. I thought that that would be Corey doing that. Things like that happened in several situations. I don't know if they happened or I wanted them to.

Now it is more like a thought or feeling, almost as if he came to visit. I have a sense of his presence. It is a synchronistic thing. His mother is part of this. For example, I begin thinking about Corey and then his mother will call.

Your teenagers may find comfort by keeping in touch with their friend's parents—a contact that gives both sides a way to keep the memories alive. Most likely, this independent relationship with a friend's parents is not something that would have happened if the friend had lived, yet this bond now provides meaning and support to both. Deborah sees Klara's parents regularly:

I go visit a lot. I don't want them to be alone, because then they think about what happened. They need people around. I'm her age, and we laugh, we talk about her, we cry. We feel like she is here but she can't speak. That feels good.

Helping sort out a friend's belongings, and sometimes keeping some of them, can be another opportunity to remember and to maintain a bond with the deceased. Gila remembers that during "shiva," the Jewish week of mourning, Mara's mother wanted Gila and her friends to have some of her things:

We took turns trying on her clothes, remembering when she bought each thing and how she looked in it. I wasn't ready to accept that she really wasn't coming back and would not need these things any more. Now I'm glad her mother insisted. It made her parents happy to know her things went to people she loved and I always have something of her with me.

Not all parents are comfortable seeing their child's friends because it can be a painful reminder of what their child will never be. It may be hard for your children to understand this in their own time of need, but if this is how their friend's parents feel, they will need to look elsewhere for connections to what they've lost. Sometimes, that's found through contact with mutual friends, although, as Anna warns, those relationships can also be altered by death:

We were always together; we went everywhere together. Things changed after Jessica's death. I think she was the catalyst that brought us together and kept us together. When we finished high school, and Jess died, we went in different directions. We don't see each other as often. The connection is still there, but it is different.

As time goes on, your children will remember their friends less constantly, but memories will resurface in different ways, at different times. Anna welcomes those memories, in spite of the pain they can bring:

There's a song that reminds me of her. Every time I hear it, I think that it's her song and I remember—then you feel the pain. When I wrote something for the memorial at the first anniversary of her death it was hard. I realized then that crying can also be comforting.

Some, like Sally, find religious rituals an important framework for remembering:

I said Kaddish [the Jewish mourner's prayer] the first year during the memorial service on Yom Kippur. If I am in synagogue on the anniversary of his death, I also say Kaddish. I did it this year. This ritual has a lot of meaning to me. It affects me to say it in his memory—it feels good.

Encourage your children to attend and participate in public rituals that remember their lost friend. Jessica's friends were invited to talk at a service on the first anniversary of her death, and they were grateful for the opportunity. Anna found that speaking there gave her an opportunity to remember. She wrote:

You are gone. You withered away before my eyes, and at nineteen we buried you. You became my hero, even though you were only human, with good and bad sides. You taught me to feel, to experience life in the moment, and to appreciate the life I've been given.

Even though their friend is no longer a part of the world that they created together, there are other ways to keep their friend in their lives. Sean includes Corey in many things he does:

I still use him when I meditate, and when I pray, I talk to him. He is still very much a part of my life.

Deborah talks to her departed friend:

Every night I talk to her. I look up at the sky. I say "Hi, Klara!" I also write to her in my diary. I write that you are in heaven with others where you belong and I am sorry that I didn't get to say good-bye. I tell her things I want her to know.

Ruth often thinks about Jessica during times they would have shared:

> Only with time, did I begin to understand that at the holidays or when I see something that reminds me of her I will remember. Sometimes it's a shock to realize that she's not here. When I went to Europe last year, I said this is for Jess. She wanted to travel so much. Thinking of her wasn't easy but it felt good to think she was seeing Europe through my eyes.

Sally thinks about Ethan a good deal and about how she has lost the potential they had to grow together. In some ways she feels he is still guiding her:

> When I think about him, I think of where would he be now. I am in New York and I am sure that's where he would be. I keep expecting to see him out of the corner of my eye. He was my conscience, my role model, my alter ego, not on personal matters but on philosophical and social issues. He would be the person asking, if you are still thinking of doing that, why aren't you? No one has taken that place; I do it in part for myself. I just recently got in touch with someone who worked with him on a project in college. It felt good to know how much she missed him, too.

Jon likes to reminisce about the friend he's lost:

> A lot of people I know knew Ethan. When we get together, we talk about him, things that happened during the year that might have interested him. We don't talk about his suicide. We often recall things we did together. We don't talk about his having been depressed or go over what anyone should have or could have done. Sometimes we talk about how hard it is to believe that he is gone and not someplace where we can call him up.

Your children may like to tell new acquaintances about the friend they've lost, as part of a kind of mourner's biography that describes the person, the death, and the friend's importance in your children's lives. It can be meaningful for them to share this information, not only because they want others to know about their experience but also because it becomes a sort of litmus test for choosing new friends. If people cannot appreciate the loss or find room for understanding, the bereaved child might back away. Sally recognizes that Ethan's death will always be with her, and new people need to know this:

> It got to the point where anyone who knew me had to hear about it. I felt I needed to tell people even if it didn't come up—people who I thought I might be interested in getting

close to. Partly this was so if they should ever be some place with me, if *The Big Chill* came on, or something reminded me, they should know that I might break down, that I had this vulnerability, that I might need them more than normal.

Don't be surprised if the friend's death inspires your children to take some sort of action in the friend's memory—a new direction emerging from the loss. Lauren needed to do something active after what happened to Jim. Her goal may not be all that feasible, but its intention is from the heart:

I sent out an e-mail to all my friends; I was very clear. Don't drink and drive. Call me wherever you are. If you are drinking, I will come get you.

In a sense, part of a friend's living legacy is created by what happens after the death. Donna is going to study psychology in college:

I found that helping others was a good way to help myself. If I learned anything from Ken's and Tina's deaths, maybe I can help so other suicides can be prevented. Becoming a psychologist is a good way to keep their memory alive and a way of honoring their lives. My aunt still can't talk much about what happened, but she does like to hear what I'm doing, my work with suicide prevention, and she encourages me.

As your teenagers move on with their lives in the shadow of the death, you'll see how this loss has changed them. They carry with them a new appreciation and sensitivity for life, yet their friend remains an important part of who they are. They learn to live with the paradox that their friends are gone, yet they still live on in memory. Gila describes how this works:

It is never really over. She is never really gone. In life and in death, she is so much a part of who I have become. A piece of her will live on, and a piece of me will always be missing. Mara, I have let you go, but I will always miss you.

8

Help of All Kinds

I don't know what I would have done without my friends and family those first months. We were in a total daze, operating on autopilot just to get out of bed and off to school and work. They took care of so many things, starting at the funeral and moving on from there. I don't know how they knew what we needed, because I didn't even know myself. I sure couldn't have asked for it. Now I'm in a bereavement group and I hear from widows and widowers who don't get much help, and I wonder how they manage.

A widowed mother of two

After a death in the family, you and your children find yourselves in a frightening and surreal situation, almost like waking up in an altered universe. Even if the death was anticipated, that element of surprise is still there. The life you were leading has collapsed, and now you have to dig yourselves out of the rubble. Overwhelmed by events, and lacking knowledge and perspective, you will need all the help you can get to feel supported and whole, to cope more effectively, and to deal with your changed and changing world. Help is out there, but too often, you won't know what you need, or how to get it.

The goal and the nature of what is truly helpful will change as *you* change over time, depending on where you are in the grieving process. As you adjust to the all-pervasive rearrangement of your lives, you will need different kinds of assistance. In the best case, this help is offered and accessible, but you might have to go out looking for people and organizations to help you manage. Nobody likes to have to ask for help, but it may be a little easier to do so if you know what's out there, and what works.

THE EARLY PERIOD AFTER THE DEATH

Friends and relatives might not realize just how much practical assistance is needed after a death to help you survive the first, worst days. While you may be feeling numb and having difficulty functioning, your family's needs cannot be put on hold. Close friends or relatives can set up a telephone chain to call others with the terrible news and manage some of the arrangements for funeral and burial. You need to eat, but you won't be able to stay on top of cooking and mealtimes. Gifts of finger food and home-cooked meals are not only greatly appreciated, they're essential. Offers to hang out with and play with your children, take them somewhere, or babysit, can be very helpful. A "gofer" can also be useful to take care of many of the questions, chores, and problems that come up. Often, one close friend will take the lead, coordinating the meals and other offers of assistance, and acting as go-between, so you don't have to pay attention to these details. One widow remembers:

> Friends in town set up a dinner chain where a different person sent over a family meal every night. One of them was in charge of the schedule, so food just appeared. Sometimes I didn't even know the person who had sent it; they just wanted to help. I don't even know if I ever thanked them, but they saved us.

During this early period when you and your family are still quite numb, you may inadvertently give others the impression that you are managing well. Since at this time you really do not, in fact, feel very coherent, appearances are deceiving. The most meaningful help is likely to come from those who can look beyond this surface impression and understand that your family has ongoing daily needs.

Helping Mourning Children Cope in the First Days

Friends and relatives should be told that meeting those needs does not mean protecting your children from reality. Your children will appreciate distraction, playing games or spending time with others, but they may also ask a lot of questions and need to have their sadness and other feelings legitimated. They may be confused about all the adult commotion that follows a death in the family and need to be told what everyone is doing there. Helpers have to be able to answer questions with sensitivity to the special fears of grieving children.

They need to know, for example, that children who have lost one parent are often concerned about where the surviving parent is at all times, and that this concern needs to be respected and addressed as forthrightly as possible. Even telling them that a parent is arranging the funeral is reassuring to children; this is an activity that, once explained to them, keeps the reality of the loss in focus. Helpers should be advised to follow your children's leads in conversations. They don't need to push your children into talking about the death if they don't want to or try to tell them how to feel, think, or behave.

Having familiar faces around your house serves a dual purpose: it takes some of the pressure and responsibility off you and gives your children support and continuity. Andrew was twelve when his father died. His mother describes the help she got afterward:

> My sixteen-year-old nephew came over whenever I needed some relief. Andrew had company when he wanted it. It was good to know there was someone else he could count on besides me. I know they talked a lot about his father's death. For me, it was like putting a knife in me when I talked about my husband, so I was glad he had someone else to talk with and it was someone who knew and loved my husband and missed him very much as well.

Andrew found it easier and more consoling to talk about memories of his father, to "remember when" rather than talk about his emotions:

> People kept coming up to me to ask how I felt. What could I say? I tried to be polite but I didn't know what they wanted to hear. They could see how I felt. I was so glad when my cousin came over. We would just talk about things we did with my father.

Your children need help coping with the sudden cataclysm in their lives—not only the death but the change in how other family members are behaving. They're desperate for any signs that their familiar world has not entirely vanished and are grateful for just about anything you can do to signal that you're still aware of their needs. Sixteen-year-old Linda recalls the period immediately after her brother's accidental death:

> My best friend Arlene went with me to the wake. I remember telling her everything I knew about what happened. We kept going over it to try to understand. Maybe three years later, my parents and I were talking about what happened. They told me they

couldn't remember much about that period, but they remembered calling Arlene to be with me. It makes me feel better even now, to know that they were thinking of me then.

Meeting Day-to-Day Needs

Help from family and friends can be informal and spontaneous, often responding on the spot to what is happening. Out of these informal helping networks rises a community that makes it possible for your family to get through the first months. One widow says this support helped her identify and articulate her most pressing concerns:

> My sister called every day the first month. She and a friend would come by occasionally and take me out for coffee and just let me talk. We talked about my fears of making it alone without my husband, we talked about the kids, and we talked about my husband. I needed to work and they helped me work out how I could manage a job, a home, and have some energy left over for my children. They were surprised after a while at my own ideas about what to do. I didn't know this part of me existed.

Colleagues at work, friends from clubs and organizations you're involved with, and members of religious communities often provide help. At this early stage, these groups tend to focus on very concrete needs, like funds to help defray some of the family's medical or funeral expenses, making hotel arrangements and travel plans for relatives coming to the funeral, or keeping food on your table. The "casserole brigade" was a very real source of support to this new widow:

> The women's group from our church arranged for someone to bring a casserole every day for about a week after the funeral. I found out later that they deliberately brought the food in a good dish that they wanted back. This gave them an excuse to come visit some time later, to get back their dish. It really was an excuse to talk and I appreciated that.

Some congregations have organized groups that provide information and coordinate assistance. Billy's mother describes how this helped after her husband died:

> Our synagogue has a bereavement committee. We had prayer services every night here at our house during the week of mourning. They brought food. It made such a difference to know we weren't alone. Billy's Hebrew School class came. It meant so much to him.

> When I first heard of this committee I could not imagine why it was needed. I couldn't
> imagine anyone being as out of it as I was, even though I knew he was dying.

Sometimes You Have to Ask

Unfortunately, there are many of you who won't get this kind of organized assistance, and no one will step forward to take control. It's not that people don't want to help but they just don't know what to offer. You may get offers of "anything I can do" but be loath to call and ask for food or babysitting or grocery shopping or just someone to talk to. In families where someone had been ill for a while, you might feel like you've already used up your friends' and families' goodwill—or they might feel that they've already done enough. Hard as it is, you might have to make the first move—calling someone who offered vague assistance and asking that person to do a particular thing for you, whether it's picking up the dry cleaning or addressing thank you notes for sympathy cards or helping you get your children to bed. If they don't respond, you'll know their offer was shallow. But many people *will* respond and be grateful to know how to help a friend in such dire, personal, need. This widow explains one thing she asked friends to do:

> People would tell me funny or nice things they remembered about my husband, or sometimes tell me about surviving their own parent's death, so I asked them to write the stories down and send them to my kids in letters they could keep. I collected the letters in a scrapbook for the children to read when they're older.

This woman who was trying to help a grieving family came up with another way for them to hold on to their memories. She thought about what she had needed as a child when her own father died:

> Just recently, my cousin was killed in Iraq, leaving behind a wife and three children. His older brother seemed so lost, so I suggested that he put together a collection of pictures and stories for the kids, since they will probably spend the rest of their lives craving scraps of information about their dad. More than anything, I told him, he can give them the gift of sharing pieces of their dad with them. For my cousin, this was a revelation and a lifeline. Now he had something tangible he could DO. I always wanted people to talk about my father, but they were pretty silent. I think people aren't sure what to say, but I felt it added to the loss to lose even the stories of my father.

Your friends and family won't know automatically how best to help you grieve. Some of you prefer to be alone with your private thoughts, while others want an intimate friend to sit with you when you cry. Tell them what you need. Let people play to their strengths—from the organizational marvel who figures out how to manage child care and after-school schedules, to the neighborhood mom who takes control of the carpool, to the teenager next door who takes your children out for pizza night. These people won't take away your grief, but they will make it easier to manage.

FINDING HELP AT SCHOOL

Children spend nearly half their waking hours at school, so figuring out how to make that work for your bereaved children is of great importance. Teachers and school personnel are an essential part of a child's helping network. Some schools have plans for dealing with family crises that you might not even have known about before; other schools respond to situations as they arise.

One of the first steps at your school has to be figuring out how to welcome your grieving children back into the classroom. Some children appreciate peer recognition of what happened. Eight-year-old Seth describes his first day at school after his father's sudden death:

> My teacher told my class that my father died. The class decided to write me letters about how sorry they were. Some kids made pictures for me and they said welcome back. They were all on my desk when I came back to school. I was scared about what the other kids would say. Sometimes kids can be mean. It turned out everyone really tried to be nice.

His sister, two years older, cried when she talked about returning to school. Her teacher had thought it would be best to give her some space, so she had advised her class to not talk about the death. But the girl had liked it when her classmates had come to her house to visit during the week after her father's death, and she wanted attention in the classroom like her brother received. Without it, she felt abandoned and alone.

Other children do prefer to be given that space, as they're not comfortable with getting extra attention in class. A high school student talks about what did and didn't work for him:

I didn't like it when they were solicitous, like saying, if you need to talk I am here. If I wasn't close to the teacher, why would I want to talk to them? Sometimes I had the feeling they wouldn't hear me anyhow. One teacher said her father had died when she was my age. She wanted me to know that she understood. I appreciated that. If I ever wanted to talk, I knew she would listen.

Varied reactions like these show that there is no one right response or action that works for everyone, and that it is impossible to always know what a child wants or how to match the response to a given child's needs. Your children might not even know themselves how they want their teachers and classmates to respond after a death, but you can talk to them in advance about whether they lean more toward silence or sympathy, and then have a conversation with the principal, guidance counselor, or homeroom teacher before your children go back to school.

You can't expect your schools to provide significant, long-term therapy, but they need to know that this is not a short-term crisis. They'll need to remain sensitive to your children's ongoing special needs for as long as they're in that school. As the initial shock wears off, the next wave of school-related issues may set in—difficulty in focusing, feelings of loneliness and alienation, moments of extreme sadness. You might need to talk to the school many times over the years about how to deal with these issues and to remind them that grieving is a long-term experience. Most teachers and principals would like to help and will appreciate your guidance as to what's appropriate.

HELP WITH FINANCIAL AND LEGAL ISSUES

After the death of a spouse, you may need assistance in financial planning and learning to manage your money. First, there is a probate or an estate to settle—dozens of questions you may never have considered. If you and your spouse split up the household duties, death might have left you without the knowledge of the password for online bill payments, details of a mutual fund or a debt, or the name of the person who mows the lawn. It now all falls on your shoulders in a heap of things to do. All these decisions, all these forms, all these new things to learn—all fraught with the reality of what brought you here. You won't want to do anything of substance for a long time. You need help.

No matter how limited your financial resources are, you need to make long-term plans for your family's economic needs. For many of you, the economic structure of your family has to be revamped; you may have lost the sole wage earner or a second income that the family depended on. On the other hand, there may be a life insurance payment coming, and you and your children may be entitled to Social Security payments and other benefits. One widower says this income makes a difference in his ability to manage:

> I found out I was covered under my wife's benefits. That gave me money to help pay the babysitter I needed after school.

If your health insurance was part of your spouse's benefit package, the family may lose coverage after the death or after a short extension period that you might have to contribute to. This forces many who did not work outside the home to consider finding jobs that will provide some benefits to the family. Options vary from state to state; friends can help here by rounding up the pertinent information for you to look at when you are able to pay attention to the details. If you have contact with other widows, widowers, or single parents in your community or through bereavement groups or your place of work or worship, you may also find that they are founts of information on this subject, as it is a major issue faced by just about everyone.

Take advantage of all the help that's offered. Hospitals and hospices often have staff available to help you work through the medical bills that amass from efforts to save a life or from an illness that preceded the death. Your employer, or your late spouse's, may have a benefits coordinator who can discuss pension and retirement fund rollovers. Local banks have financial advisers available to help, sometimes at no cost, no matter how small an account is. Continuing education programs at the local high school or community college commonly offer excellent courses in money management. Friends and relatives can help find these resources, organize your papers, and make lists of questions to ask a professional when you address your overall financial picture. Your circumstances will change over time, so whatever you decide now doesn't have to be irrevocable, but you at least need to do what's necessary to stay afloat.

Economic and Legal Issues Can Overlap Your Children's Concerns

One of the hardest things to balance at this time is your financial reality and your bereaved children's need for as much stability as possible in the period after the death of a parent. Children are frightened and disturbed by the erasure of their loved one from their physical space—when pictures come down or clothing is given away or put out of sight. It is that much harder for them if you have to move away from the house where they lived with that parent. If you need to move for financial or other reasons, it is important that you share those reasons with your children. Explain that you will bring physical reminders of the person who died, but that, most importantly, their memories will keep their loved one in their hearts forever. Even with that explanation, you can expect children to be upset by the move—a further sign that the world, as they know it, is lost.

Out of the turmoil of emotions your children experience after the death of a parent arises another potent issue: who will take care of them if something happens to you? Some children prompt this discussion by asking you directly, with the anxiety that comes from knowing that now there is only one person standing between them and orphanhood. This means that you need appropriate legal advice to help you prepare a will and make sure that your wishes will be followed. This is not an easy undertaking, and it may take some time before you feel ready to act on these issues. Friends can help by getting names of local attorneys who can get you started more quickly, at least to get your custodial plan documented. Children become more relaxed when you talk to them about what would happen if you got sick or died; often, simply hearing that they'll be taken care of leaves them surprisingly calm and accessible during the conversation. It may also reassure them if you tell them that even though you are very sad right now and maybe not acting the way you normally do, you will still do your best to stay healthy and take very good care of yourself. Of course, by now, you and they know that this cannot be guaranteed, but speaking to their deepest fear lets them know that your grief will not carry you away from them.

TIME MOVES FORWARD, BUT HELP IS STILL NEEDED

Whatever the source of help, your family will find its way during the early period after the death. You will manage to keep your heads above water and get some sense that there is a future out there, with a place for you in it. But grieving takes time; you won't finish mourning and tie it all into a neat package. As the process goes on, the nature of help needs to evolve as well. Help and understanding will be needed for a long time, but not always in the same form.

It may take a year or more, but eventually the numbness lifts and feelings became clearer. The pain remains great, though not quite as constant. Most family and friends return to their own lives. While they may still be available, they probably don't understand how long this grief is going to last—and, in fact, they might already be telling you it's time to "get over it" and reclaim your life. This woman's husband died less than a year ago:

> I'm going out with some friends this weekend. I didn't want to go, but they said I have to "get back into the game."

Like many mourners, she feels guilty and inappropriate for not being "ready." She hasn't yet learned to challenge the assumptions of those who tell her what to feel. The reality is that the pain is not going away, you are not going to get over this, and it is not possible to just resume your normal way of life. Your concept of normal has changed, anyway, and there can be no going back. Your former life is gone forever, and you'll need help in charting this new direction.

Some Friends and Family Won't Be There to Help You

It is important to identify those friends and relatives who are willing and able to remain a significant part of your lives. This doesn't have to mean a significant amount of time—most people's days are so busy that they barely have a moment to themselves. They can still help, though, by giving emotional support and encouragement as you find concrete ways to deal with your pain. This mother sees the need for someone to fill in the gaps for her son:

> I worried that he was living in a woman's world. He needed a man to be a role model. My brother was pretty good about including my son in things he did with his son. They seemed to get along real well and they understood what he had lost.

Another widow has not had such good fortune with male role models:

> I have three brothers-in-law—two married to my sisters, one married to my husband's sister—and I wish I could say they've stepped up to the plate for my boy, but they haven't. They'll come and help me with handyman kind of things, but when it comes to

just taking my son out to do something—anything—they're pretty lame. The few times
they've done anything with my son and theirs, they always pay a lot more attention to
theirs. I've tried hinting to their wives but they don't get it, either.

There are things you can do to help yourself and your family without assistance from others. Music, writing, painting, or poetry can be great sources of comfort, outlets for expressing your grief and the turmoil of your emotions. One mother, an artist, said:

I spent most of the first year after my son died in my studio. I painted out all my pain
and anger. My art kept me sane.

Kayla, whose mother and sister both died in the same accident, describes what she found consoling:

Basically I would just write in my diary and listen to the *Dying Young* sound track. Now
when I listen I realize how sad that music was. At that time, it was comforting.

You might try writing letters to your loved one who died, or keep a journal about this journey through loss. Exercise, yoga, or other physical activities are good ways to release tension. Meditation, chanting, and prayer can help you relax and renew your soul. These parents find comfort in their faith:

If anything good could have come from my daughter's death, it is that we found Jesus.
This has been enormously consoling to us.

Friends can go with you to a spirituality group, look through your sketchbook, sign up for a yoga class you can attend together (or alone), pick out some music they think might be soothing, or otherwise help you to find and engage in an activity that brings you some relief. Anything that captures your attention and harnesses your energy and resourcefulness can be helpful.

You may also find some direction when you weren't even looking. A bereaved mother describes how she discovered new resources:

I went to the library one day with my son who was doing a project for school. I never
talk about these things to people I don't know, but one of the librarians saw me waiting.
I guess I looked like I felt. She asked if I needed help. I laughed and said what I need
you don't have. She took me to the computer and said I would be surprised, people don't

appreciate what you can find in a library. She asked for a subject. I said "death." The first title I noticed was *The Bereaved Parent*, by Harriet Schiff. I said, that's me. It was an old book but her message was never outdated. This got me going. I found all kinds of books and then I realized there were books for my kids also. My husband started to read too. Things started to make sense. We didn't feel so odd. I began to feel that there were things we could do.

Like the library, the Internet can be an invaluable clearinghouse of information, leading you to Web sites and chat rooms for people who share your experience. You may also be able to find help through hospices, which are mandated to provide bereavement services to families they have served for a year following a death but which often expand that support to the larger community of the bereaved. Some hospices simply send out information packets about grief, while others offer support groups and even individual counseling.

The trick is finding your way to the type of assistance you need: help is out there, in some form that will work for you. There are many options available and it may take a while to find the kind of support that fits. But this is a crucial task because you have to get the support and care you need in order to give your children the support and care *they* need.

INDIVIDUAL COUNSELING FOR CHILDREN AND ADULTS

There's another kind of assistance that can be vital in helping you navigate this new universe you inhabit after the death of a loved one. It has nothing to do with external realities, such as getting food on the table; instead it's about your internal realities. You and your children need someone to talk to about what's happening in your lives, and that might lead you to seek individual counseling. This child appreciated having a safe place to go:

My mom took me to see this shrink she is seeing. He was nice and I didn't have to worry about upsetting him if I cried.

The idea of being able to talk to someone about your feelings of guilt, anger, and despair—someone who is not affected by the death themselves—is very appealing. Several months after her daughter's death, this mother consulted the social worker at hospice:

> I needed a professional to listen to me. I didn't want anyone who would try to make me feel better like my family did. Knowing she could accept my pain was what I wanted. I wasn't sure but I think this is what I needed to learn as well.

If it was your spouse who died, that can lead you to a fundamental self-examination of who you are now, and who you used to be. You are a different person from the one you were before you got married, and you have now lost the future you anticipated. These kinds of issues can stir up all sorts of questions about your identity that are well raised in a therapeutic situation.

Your children have other needs in therapy, like finding out who they are without this person in their lives and figuring out how to deal with feeling different from their peers. Counseling can also help them decipher some of their feelings about you. Four years after her husband's death, this woman suggested that her preteen daughter go see a therapist:

> I told her that since I was her only parent there may be times when she is not able to tell me what is on her mind. I want her to have someone she could talk to besides me. She went a few times. She liked this woman and she said it was good to know she was there, but she thought she didn't really need her now.

In addition to helping you cope with the loss, counseling can also focus on issues that may have existed prior to the death but were exacerbated and brought to the surface by the loss. Bruce's suicide made his parents confront their problems in a new way:

> My husband and I had a lot of serious differences. He always said therapy had nothing to offer him. After our son killed himself, my husband realized that our problems could have contributed to our son's unhappiness. My husband agreed that to save our family we should go for help. A group couldn't help us. We found a good marriage counselor who had worked with other families where child had committed suicide. It is taking a long time, but we are in a much better place.

You may have to shop around for a therapist who works for you. Your family doctor may have referrals and friends may have advice, but you won't know if the person's right for you until you meet. In a therapeutic relationship, individual styles are crucial—what's good for your closest friend might be all wrong for you. It's important to be sure you are comfortable with whoever you go to see and that the therapist can really listen to you and not be focused on trying to make everything better. It helps if the person has training in grief counseling or is at least aware that mourning is a process, not a disease to be treated, and that there's no timetable for mourning and no getting over the loss. Even years after the death, there will be times when you and your children feel sad, confused, and disjointed. There's absolutely nothing wrong with you for feeling that way, and absolutely nothing wrong with needing to talk to someone about those feelings.

BEREAVEMENT GROUPS FOR CHILDREN AND ADULTS

By reading this book, you are getting a taste of what we consider the most beneficial assistance out there—the advice and comfort of others who share your experience. Unlike individual therapy, which concentrates on your emotional well-being, bereavement groups focus on understanding and managing your life after loss. When so much of the "outside" world is struggling to relate, you may find yourself startled by how relieved you are to be among your new peer group of the bereaved. Mutual help programs can make a huge difference, and they can be found, in some form, in many communities.

You can find out about grief programs from employers, clergy, doctors, or therapists. You'll learn about programs from the Internet, newspaper articles, community bulletin boards, or from friends. Funeral directors are a first line of help for many people, as was the case for this man, whose daughter was killed by a drunk driver:

> I didn't expect to hear from the funeral director but he called about two months later. He wanted to find out how we were and to tell us about the Mothers Against Drunk Driving Organization. It took a few more months but my wife and I went to a meeting. Suddenly I didn't feel so alone. This organization was doing things that might prevent other parents from going through this hell. After a while I found my wife needed to go on talking but I wanted to get involved and see some results. I joined the committee on legislation.

Reinforcement from other bereaved people can be especially important when the expectations of family and friends do not coincide with your own experience. That was the experience of this grieving mother:

> I thought I was crazy because I wasn't getting over it. Our family liked to remember Bobby. We talked a lot about him. My friends told me that, it's six months, we should be getting over it. Here I was, at a Compassionate Friends meeting, in a room full of parents who all were doing the same thing and many of their children had been dead for a long time. For the first time in a long time I felt normal.

Groups exist for bereaved parents, for children, and for both, offering a supportive environment and the opportunity to learn from others in a similar situation. Some organizations, like Compassionate Friends, have groups all over the country. Others spring up independently, at hospitals, hospices, churches or temples, or at centers designed just for this purpose. Teachers or guidance counselors can also be a resource for help in your community. As this widow describes, some schools have their own programs:

> The high school guidance counselor set up a group for children who had a death that year. Kids could come when they felt like it. My son went reluctantly. He had a friend who was killed in a drunk-driving accident that year too, in addition to his father dying. He said it helped to just shoot the breeze for a while. He wouldn't say much about it, only that he liked the guidance counselor, who had also lost her father when she was a kid. He felt she could understand.

You're Not Alone

We can't overstate what a difference this support and understanding can make. Kayla was seventeen when her mother and sister were killed in an automobile accident. A few weeks later, her father saw an ad in the local newspaper about a bereavement program for children. Four years later, she remembers her first days there:

> It met in a local church. I found myself in a room with kids my age, more or less. I was very nervous. It felt safe to talk and I started to cry. It was the first time I was really talking about it. I didn't feel as alone.

The feeling that they are the only ones who experienced such a loss can leave your children feeling isolated, vulnerable, and different from their peers. Participating in a group for the bereaved can help them feel less alone, more accepted, and safe. A ten-year-old girl contrasts her experience at the bereavement center with her experience at school:

I have only one friend in school who doesn't tease me. They pick on me and say, you don't have a father, and they laugh. No one teases me here and that feels good.

A nine-year-old boy says:

I wish they had special schools for kids who've lost a parent. It could be like the group I go to, where I don't always feel different or have to explain myself.

In bereavement groups, children learn to talk about the death and to be less fearful of its consequences in their lives. As a result, they feel more in charge. This seven-year-old can see the connection between what he did in his group and how he feels now:

I liked the volcano room where I could jump around and throw things and no one could get hurt when I was angry. I wasn't so angry after that. I liked the art room where I could get messy, paint on my face, like a clown. I learned from the talking circle that it was good to talk about what I remember about my dad. We made Father's Day cards and I put mine on my father's grave.

Often these programs help children correct superstitions and misconceptions about the death. Some children are shunned by people in their school or community who fear that the cause of death or even death itself is "catching." This can be especially painful when the death was a violent one. Karin, eleven years old, reflects on how a group helped after her father was killed:

I never knew anyone in the same situation. I used to think my father had done something wrong that he was murdered. I began to understand that he was in the wrong place at the wrong time. Then I could compare my feelings—sad feelings and glad feelings. The leaders really understood my feelings and they didn't make faces. My friend doesn't understand my feelings that much. She always feels bad and she has a sad face and that makes me feel bad and I don't like that. I don't like people feeling sad for me. It shouldn't be a big deal; people shouldn't feel bad if I want to cry in school. That should be OK.

When the person who died committed suicide, there is another kind of burden on the survivors. Some children learn that it is not always safe to talk about how their parent or sibling died. This sixteen-year-old attends a group for children whose parent or sibling committed suicide. While the group is composed primarily of teenagers, there are children as young as eight involved. He reflects on what he's learned:

> At first I hated coming here. I was very angry and in lots of trouble. I learned a lot in the two years I've been coming and I really appreciate that my Mom and school made me come. I can now understand why my father killed himself. I don't feel so alone. I met lots of other kids who this happened to. I know that I both love and hate my father and that's OK. Now I want to help start a group in my school for children who had a death in the family. My guidance counselor is going to help me.

You can't always find groups just for children who've had a suicide in the family. After this teenager's older brother killed himself, the only suicide group in his area was for adults:

> My mother found this group. I wanted to go with her. She took me, but I found that after one meeting I was bored. My mother still talks about it as a lifesaver for her but I needed kids my own age.

It may not be possible to find a group in which all the members have a loved one who died the same way, but it's usually not necessary, either. Bereavement groups that encompass various causes of death can be helpful to all the members. One eight-year-old attended a group with other children whose parents had died. He came to group meetings regularly and he would listen, but he would never talk about his own situation. That was fine with the group leaders, who didn't push him or insist that he speak. Finally, after about a year, he took the talking stick as the group began and said, simply, *my father killed himself,* and then passed the stick to the next child who wanted to talk. From then on, he had no problem talking about his father's death. The group's quiet acceptance gave him the support he needed to talk about his father, and the space he needed to get there.

Whether their family members died suddenly or died slowly, were innocent bystanders or had lifestyles that played a part in their deaths, these children come together to realize and recognize their shared loss and their terrible knowledge about the fragility of life. For this reason, and for the comfort it brings, attending a group can become a very important part of a child's life. A mother describes her children's reactions to their bereavement center:

> The kids were so excited. There is a quietness and safety about this place. The longer we have been coming, the more they seem to talk about their father. I had to find some of his things they wanted to put in a memory box. That helped me, too.

Bereavement groups are designed to help you through this ongoing crisis as you learn how to manage your lives; they aren't therapy in the conventional sense. Many people choose to attend a group in addition to individual therapy. This seventeen-year-old girl compares the two experiences:

> I like my therapist and I like talking to her. I know I have her full attention. But at the bereavement center I feel safe. It is very comfortable, and I am understood in a very special way.

If your community only has bereavement groups available for adults, not children, don't let this deter you: helping yourself will help your children as well. You'll discover how useful it is to talk to other parents who have had similar experiences, and you'll learn from each other new ways of coping, including new ways to parent. You may even find a way to involve your children. One mother recalls:

> Here were other young widows. We talked about how to deal with lonely evenings. They understood and we began to share ideas. We exchanged phone numbers and now there was someone to talk with when I thought I was going to blow my stack. We arranged to do an outing with our children. That was very successful. We went bowling—that made it easier for the kids to get to know each other.

There's a social and emotional benefit to meeting people who share your experience, as well as information to be obtained. This widower says his group gave him both:

> I wasn't so sure this group was for me. I'm not a big talker, but once I got myself there I was glad I came. I was feeling so helpless and I learned that most widowers have the same difficulty when faced with trying to care for their children and hold down a job. The women got a kick out of teaching us. I was dating. They said to remember I had to learn a whole new way of doing things, and to tell the kids that they weren't in any danger

of losing me. No one would take their mother's place. It never occurred to me that they would worry about that. It made sense. Maybe that's why they never like anyone I date.

Programs that involve both grieving children and the parents who are struggling to raise them offer the kinds of insight you can't get elsewhere because it's coming right from the horse's mouth—other people who have been there, and who are still there. One father describes how his group helped him understand how his daughter's age and stage of development affects how she deals with her grief:

In the group, as we talked, we came to realize that we didn't always understand our children's behavior. My daughter was only eight. Sometimes I would find her crying; other times she would just get so angry and then she would cling. I needed to learn that eight-year-olds can't always keep things together. In some ways, she was so grown up, and that's how I wanted her to be. But in fact she is still a little girl.

Consider how hard it is to understand and cope with your own grief. And then think of your children, who have so much less experience in dealing with crises than you do. And yet, you are all expected to manage this catastrophe in your lives—keeping up with work, school, chores, and friends—while changing the course of your lives. Grief groups can be a lifeline, showing you the way, helping you not only to manage, but to flourish.

NOT ALL HELP IS HELPFUL

Sometimes the help people provide will not meet your expectations. You may feel disappointed or let down when help is not forthcoming from people you thought would understand. Other times, people volunteer help and advice that is not appropriate. They might mean well, but that's not enough. In the words of a father whose child died:

What we didn't need to hear was that we were spoiling our other children. We let them sleep in our room when they needed to. They needed to be reassured that we were there.

A new widow experienced similar disapproval from those who were supposed to be there to help:

I found my daughter coming into my bed at night, saying she was afraid to be alone. I understood that feeling. Then my son came. I finally decided that they could take turns sleeping in my bed. I began to appreciate that I had the same discomfort about being alone in the bed. I stopped telling my family. They all had opinions about it—mostly that it wasn't a good idea. When I talked to other widows, I found my children were like lots of others and my needs were the same as theirs. We did this for about six months, and gradually they began to stay in their own beds. It was as if it was time!

It goes without saying that help needs to be helpful to the person on the receiving end—you. If friends or family members disapprove of the way you're responding to this crisis in your life and you feel otherwise, have faith in yourself. You know your family best. As long as you are attending to your children and to their loss in some fashion, you're doing what needs to be done.

Well-Meaning but Misguided Words That Hurt

Bad help often comes from people who are trying to make you feel better but who have the wrong ideas. One mother recalls a teacher's comments:

My son was devastated. He's only eight years old and is having a real hard time. His teacher told him that it was time to be over his grief, his sister was already dead three months. She wanted him not to show his tears in the classroom or to not use the death as an excuse for not doing well on a test. I would have thought she'd know better.

Teachers often don't know better. If they are unaccustomed to death, they may need to be prepared to deal with the continuing grief of their students that can intrude on the class. It may fall on you to intervene and to educate the teacher. Sometimes, even this is not enough, and a change of teacher or school is needed to get the appropriate support.

Physicians may also need to be educated. It's not at all uncommon for doctors to automatically recommend sedatives or antidepressant drugs to help you cope with the physical tension, anxiety, and pain that you are experiencing from grief. While these drugs can be enormously helpful, they are not always needed. Sometimes grief is just grief. It's not a syndrome or a condition or something to cure. One mother describes her experience with her family doctor:

After a while I realized that it wasn't drugs I needed. I found out about this parents' group and I began to learn about other things I could do to help myself. I brought my doctor their literature. At first he was annoyed with me for questioning his medical judgment, but after a while, as he saw me change, he began to listen. Now he keeps the group's literature in his waiting room.

If they're inexperienced or untrained in grief counseling, some therapists may not understand the need for a different approach from the one they take with other clients. If the help is simply focused on the expression of feelings, it may not be enough. Working with the bereaved in individual counseling may require the counselor to be more active and ready to educate about bereavement as well as to listen. After her friend Ethan committed suicide, Sally decided to go to her university's counseling service that had advertised its availability to help students deal with a death. She did not find it as helpful as she had hoped:

> The counselor was too passive. She just sat and waited for me to talk. She didn't seem to connect to where I was at. I had no experience in counseling so I didn't know what to expect. I didn't go back. I'm not sure what was wrong; part of me said she didn't know enough about bereavement. She needed to direct my thinking with some questions. I wanted more information to help me understand what I was experiencing.

Too many mental health professionals adhere to the idea that letting go of the person who died is an essential step in successful grieving. That kind of thinking didn't work for this bereaved mother:

> I found a psychiatrist about a month after my son's sudden death. I was in such pain. I was overwhelmed and looking for some relief. I had heard of Compassionate Friends, but I didn't think I could deal with a group at this point. My family was upset because I would console myself by watching a family video taken a few days before my son died. This therapist told me that I should not be looking at this video, that I had to start letting go. This only made me feel worse. Finally I stopped going. Then someone suggested I call the local hospice—they would know some therapists who had experience with grief. I found another psychologist and she could hear me. She said it was OK to watch the video. That I would be the judge when it might not be helpful any more. Later I was ready to consider attending a Compassionate Friends meeting. By that time, I was ready and it was very helpful.

The concept of "letting go" is quite pervasive. One divinity student tells of an assignment he was given in his psychology class the year before. Asked to write a paper on the experience that most influenced his life, he wrote about his mother's death five years earlier, when he was a teenager. His professor thought that his description of the death was too vivid, given the time that had passed. He said the student should have let this go a long time ago and suggested that this young man see a therapist as soon as possible. The student was stunned and dropped the course. His school adviser supported his decision, but the student remains disturbed about how some clergy are taught about grief.

Many spiritual leaders have thought a great deal about death and the meaning of life and are experienced in sharing their wisdom with others. But some are uncomfortable about grappling with the deeper aspects of death or are simply overwhelmed by the demands of a large congregation. Just as there are neighbors or friends who seem to stay away from you or avoid conversations about the person who died, so might your clergy. When that happened to this mother, she felt rejected and hurt:

> We continued to go to church every Sunday. Our minister was always very glad to see us. We told him we wanted to talk. He said he would call and make a time to visit. He never followed up. I finally realized it wasn't us—it was him!

Only you can know if something is helping you or not. A minister, a therapist, a book, or a group that worked for a friend or relative might not work for you, and vice versa. If you go somewhere that seems like a waste of time or makes you and your family feel worse, there's nothing wrong with walking away. This widow made it through only one session at a hospice bereavement group:

> This group was only for kids. The parents sat in a waiting room until the kids got out. We went one day, and while my kids were in the group, I sat in the waiting room, and sat, and sat. It was completely silent. I was writing thank you notes for condolence cards and just to break the silence, I said something about how the Catholic Mass cards people had sent were lovely, and now nice people were to write. This unleashed some fury in the room I completely didn't expect—anger at the church, anger at God, anger at people who wrote the wrong thing or didn't write at all—a lot of free-floating anger in that room, with no place to focus it. And I thought, this might be OK for my kids, but I'll go crazy here. The next day, I went looking for a bereavement center where both kids and parents had a place to talk, and learn.

You don't need more stress in your life; you need some relief. Don't feel like you have to fit in somewhere. It may take a bit of searching and a few false starts, but you can find someplace that works for you and your family.

A REORDERED UNIVERSE

You will feel powerless and exhausted, and you may even want to give up hope along the way, but you and your family can and will survive this. This boy's father died when he was two years old. Now seventeen, he describes how his family managed:

> I don't remember ever thinking about not having a father. I always knew about his death. I was surrounded by relatives who cared for me and did things with me and for me. My father's best friend took me out on a regular basis and my mother was always there for me. I never think of her as someone who dwelt on what she didn't have, but on what she did have. In the world as I knew it, I never felt cheated or deprived because I didn't have a father. I guess you can say I felt supported all along the way.

You and your children can feel whole again. In fact, you might even find, in time, that coping with death is in some way transforming, opening you up to new experiences and parts of yourself that you didn't know existed. Your growing awareness and acceptance of these changes is, in part, what is meant by making an accommodation to the death. Some of this transformation comes from the realization that you have survived; you can look ahead and see the sun shining again. There's a feeling of accomplishment from finding a new way for your family, and for making it work. One mother describes how much she changed:

> I was always waiting for someone to give me permission and here I am very much in charge. Even how I treat my other kids has changed. I've learned to listen better. Sometimes when I see how much I've changed I almost don't recognize myself.

This is not to say that you feel like you're better off without the person who died or that you have even fully accepted the death, but you've grown from the experience. A group of widows nodded in agreement when one woman said:

> Sometimes after I've done something I don't think I could have managed before, I find myself saying to my husband, "OK, I proved I can do it. Now come back."

It takes a lot of hard work and a lot of help to reach the point where you feel whole again. For Bruce's mother, finding a voice made the difference:

I joined the Compassionate Friends' group for parents whose children committed suicide. I started to learn about what leads to suicide, to deal with my own guilt. We live in a small town. I met someone from the local newspaper and I started to tell her what I was learning. She wanted to write about it in the local paper. I said if it would help someone else, go ahead. Then a couple of days after the article appeared, I got a call from a minister in town who had a congregant whose daughter had just killed herself. He wanted to know if I would call her. The next thing I knew, I was the town resource and I was invited to talk at the high school about suicide prevention. It wasn't my intention but here I am. Me, who could never open her mouth in a group, talking loud and clear. If I can prevent even one death, or help one parent, then I feel as if my son's death will have some meaning.

Darrell's mother finds some peace through helping others, reaching out to mothers whose children have been murdered in her community. Instead of letting her sense of futility get to her, she became a community activist, reaching out to newly bereaved families and, if they are willing, going to visit. She wears a button with her son's picture on it. She also organizes a community vigil every Mother's Day in memory of the children who were murdered there:

I heard so many families blaming themselves or trying to convince themselves that their children were killed because of the color of their skin. You feel helpless because you could not prevent it. I could have become part of the problem or part of the solution. I wasn't going to be trapped in helplessness so I created a way of being part of the solution.

No matter what the cause of your loved one's death, you have something special to offer the newly bereaved. You'll likely be called on when some family in your community or office or church suffers a loss; you'll find yourself the face of what's to come, as new families enter your bereavement group. Many people find strength in helping in this way—and not only adults. Kayla passed the help forward when she went away to college:

I felt that if I needed something, then there must be others, so I put up a notice and five people responded. I started a group similar to the grief group that I was in before. It actually helped me see how far I had come. I realized that now I was dealing with my issues by helping others deal with theirs.

The need for help does not end, even as you achieve some kind of accommodation for your grief. The help you'll need in the years ahead will look very different from the way it did at the beginning, but it's still important and necessary. In many ways, this is part of a lifetime process of helping and being helped. You will grow from this terrible experience, and you will nurture others through theirs.

9

Continuing Bonds

I think about him and the good times we had. I like to talk about him to my mother.
I sure wish he was here to see how we're doing. I don't dream about him or talk to
him in the way I used to, but he is in my mind all the time. In some ways I am like
him. I like to do things for other people.

A fifteen-year-old boy, two years after the death of his father

In life, we carry our relationships both within ourselves and without. We talk on the phone, e-mail, and spend time with loved ones near and far, but our connections live inside us at the same time whenever we think of the other person, take pleasure (or sometimes pain) in the knowledge that they're in our lives, or ruminate about a conversation or a disagreement or a shared experience. When someone you love dies, you have to find a way to hold on to that internal relationship, to keep that person in your life, even in their physical absence. In death, as in life, relationships change shape and form as time passes, but they do not end.

All too often, the bereaved are admonished for not letting go of the past and told that they must put it behind them and go on with their lives. The more we talk to people who are grieving, the more we learn that this does not happen, nor do they want it to happen. You, too, will find that keeping a connection to your loved one doesn't only honor the dead; it provides guidance, comfort, and solace to the living as you develop a new sense of who you are and what you will become. It's been two years since this sixteen-year-old's mother died. He feels, and encourages, the bond between them:

I feel good that I remember my mother every day. You keep going, but it is important to
remember.

There are many ways in which children can connect to their dead loved ones. Your family might work to fashion some of these bonds together, but ultimately, you will all develop independent connections that will grow and change over time but always be there in some form. You won't necessarily know how your children are doing it, but they will find a place in their private world for the person who died, in a way that gives them comfort and frees them to go on with their lives. The past serves as prologue to the future. It gives it direction, and roots.

WHAT HAPPENS AFTER DEATH: FAITH, DREAMS, VISIONS, AND VISITS

In the days and weeks following the death, you and your children will try to make some sense of what could have happened to this person who was so important to you, who was just here, and is now gone. Thoughts, questions, and ideas about what follows death have come down through the ages, across societies and cultures, and numerous concepts of some sort of afterlife coexist in melting-pot America. Children learn about these concepts in churches, temples, and mosques; through books and movies; and from their communities.

Thoughts of an Afterlife

Most of all, your children's beliefs develop out of what you teach them. This bereaved father finds the teachings of his faith and family to be sustaining in this time of need, and he's passing those beliefs along to his son:

> I am glad that I believe in an afterlife. My religion is very helpful. I believe my wife is in heaven and I talk with her all the time. I can reassure my boy when he asks about heaven.

This is a time when you will reassess your own previously held beliefs about what happens after a death. This newly bereaved father says his wife's death has strengthened those beliefs:

> I have never shaken in my faith that God will take care of us when we die. I don't believe in a God who chooses who to take and who to leave behind, but I do believe that God is

with us to help us with our happiness and our suffering in life, and that He's still with us when we die.

You might find faith, keep faith, or lose faith now that you are confronted with having to reconcile your beliefs with your huge loss. One widow's story shows that you can't always tell where that reexamination might lead you.

All my life, I wished I could believe in heaven, but I just couldn't. Now that my husband died, I find that I simply can't believe that he could be gone. He was so much here, how could that go away? There must be some spark of him that remains. It's not the heaven I wished for, but it's something.

Even if you still don't believe in heaven or an afterlife, you will likely continue to relate to the person who died in some fashion. You'll find that you can't cut off your link to someone you love, just like that.

Whether or not they connect their beliefs to faith, most children say they believe that the person who died remains in spirit. They describe their loved one as living on somehow, even if they don't call their vision of an afterlife "heaven." Rachel thinks of her mother, in death, resembling her mother in life:

I think of my mother in heaven—at the beach with all her relatives who have died. My mother loved the beach.

Even though they can distinguish between the body that ends at death and a spirit that may go on, children still tend to think of the dead as having some attributes of a living person: that is, that they can see and hear what's going on below. A sixteen-year-old boy says:

I think heaven is not a definite place. I know I'm not imagining him—it's not as if I actually see him standing there, but I feel him and, like, in my mind I hear his voice.

While older children know that the dead cannot do these things corporeally in our world, they still speak of a place where their loved one has gone (a place that cannot be seen from here), where such possibilities exist. A fifteen-year-old girl created a vision of heaven, at least in part, to match what she wants to think:

I want my father to see me perform. If I said a dead person can't see, then I would not be able to have my wish that he sees what I am doing. I believe that the dead see, hear, move. Don't ask me how, I just believe it. Heaven is a mysterious place. My father is with all the other relatives that died.

Feeling Their Presence

Many children say they actually sense their loved one's presence. After their deaths in an accident that left her injured, Kayla experiences her sister and mother as still being with her:

> I feel that they are here. I just feel them. Every time I feel something wonderful or something bad, I feel them. Is it inside me or are they present? I don't know, yet I feel as if they are here—they make a difference in what happens to me.

These ideas, however unlikely they may sound, are children's attempts to put the person who died in a place where he or she can continue to communicate and connect. If your children's ideas of an afterlife are outside of your tradition or otherwise don't jibe with yours, you might be tempted to try talking them out of their beliefs. Telling them what you believe can be useful, but trying to convince children that their sense of things is wrong can create conflict in your relationship, and it doesn't usually work, anyway. This teenager feels betrayed by her mother, who doesn't agree with the way she envisions the father who died when she was eleven:

> The dead can see and hear. It's what I would like to think, so he could hear comforting words. Maybe he can see significant events in my life. My mother says this is not what happens but I need to believe this.

Feeling and believing in her mother's presence is what makes it possible for this eleven-year-old girl to manage the pain:

> This Christmas was hard, but I got through it because I got used to it. Just looking at her picture is hard because I miss her. I think about whether or not she can see me and she can hear me. Is she happy? I hear her voice in my head telling me it's OK. I talk to my friends I can trust and to my Dad, because he loved her, too, and understands what I am going through.

You don't have to believe in heaven to have a concept of a life after death. This boy's mother was from Japan and raised the family in a Buddhist tradition. He thinks of her as a spirit who remains present in his life:

> When she first died I had a dream in which she told me she didn't die. It felt good. Now I think she is probably in Japan, helping my Japanese grandmother get over my

grandfather's death. Sometimes it is really hard, but I know that her spirit will be there to help us get through. In the spirit life she can make herself available to people having a hard time.

Children often perceive their father or mother as still taking on a parental role in death, supporting them, cajoling them, encouraging them, urging them to keep on with their lives. This seventeen-year-old feels her father helping her through the sadness of loss:

He talks to me. He said, "Just get yourself together." He said, "I know you miss me. I know it is hard. I miss you too. But I care for you. I am waiting for you, and just try to get yourself back together as much as you can." I know I am not imagining him, consciously imagining him. I just see him. I don't see him standing on the lawn or anything, I feel his presence.

I'll See You in My Dreams

That feeling of a loved one's presence by day is often experienced as actual visits by night. One girl learned this from her mother:

My mother believes the dead can come to you, they can come in dreams and can help. She says my father comes when she asks him to.

Another widow describes a visit from her dead husband that gave her strength when she needed it most:

I dreamed that he came to visit me. He was dead. He told me that everything would be all right. He was safe and OK and he was sure we would do fine. When I woke up, I felt more hopeful than I had in a long time. He wants us to carry on, and we will make it.

You can talk to your children about your dreams and what they mean to you, and encourage them to talk about their own dreams, if they have them. This child explains that his dreams bring him a little more precious time with his mother:

Dreams feel good because I see her. I feel like she is watching over me.

Some dreams are escapes, some are visits, and some, like the one this seventeen-year-old describes, are wishful attempts to change history:

One time I had a dream that Dad made a deal with the doctor that mom could come back, and she walked in the house with luggage and everything. That was strange.

Dreams can return children to a favorite fantasy: that the person isn't really dead, after all; they're just away for a while. A teenage girl remembers:

I dreamed he would be with us for a few days and then leave, that he had come back and had to leave again. He had this suitcase and he'd pick it up and leave again. I'd wake up in the morning and think he'd been there. It made me feel good, but it stopped after two weeks though.

In the dream of this eight-year-old, it seems like the sleeping mind is trying to catch up with reality:

I used to have a dream about him coming toward me and then when I got to him he'd just disappear. He was living; I thought he was alive. It's not scary. It's just sad.

Dreams can be opportunities to interact with and experience the person who died as well as to receive reassuring messages. One girl recalls:

I dreamed we met on my way home from school. He hugged me. I kept some of that warmth after I woke up.

Not all children have these sorts of dreams, and if yours don't, there's nothing to worry about. There's no relationship between whether you have dreams like these and how well you deal with the death of a loved one. If your children don't dream, it doesn't mean that they'll have a harder time keeping a connection to the person who died. The main difference will be that they will miss the solace found in these nocturnal visits. This boy doesn't even remember what he dreams, but as long as his father is in them, it doesn't matter:

I forget right away when I wake up. But the dreams make me kind of happy because I get to see him, but sad when I wake up because he is not there.

Friendly Ghosts

The sense of a visit from beyond is not limited to the dream world. Some children also experience visits of a more spectral variety, visits that reassure them that the person they loved is still with them, still watching them, still loving them. One teenage girl perceives her mother's presence through unexplained happenings at work:

> I waitress at the same place where my mother worked before she got sick. Sometimes when the door blows shut everyone jokes and says, "That's your mother's ghost visiting." We talk a lot about her and we all like thinking of her spirit being here.

While it can be tempting to try to get your children to "face facts" and to tell them that these sorts of spirit visits aren't possible, it's more helpful to let children work through these thoughts on their own. Shortly after his mother's death, Russell saw flashing colored dots in his bedroom at night. He said he liked to think that it was his mother trying to be in touch with him. When he asked his father if that was possible, Russell's father said it might be and did not try to rationalize away the experience. While it might feel awkward to let these kinds of ideas pass without challenge, this kind of magical, emotional thinking is part of the process of integrating the person who died into your children's lives.

The way children experience their parent in death often reflects the parent's nature in life: nurturing or distant, organized or unpredictable, calming or explosive, approving or disapproving. This eleven-year-old boy's father was the family disciplinarian:

> I sometimes think he is watching me. It scares me because sometime he might see me do something he wouldn't like. Like, it's weird. It's not scary. Like if you are doing something, like if someone is watching, you don't do it, if it's bad. You don't do it if someone is watching.

Rachel also thinks the idea of being observed helps to keep her from going down the wrong path. Good grades were important to her mother, she says:

> I can imagine her yelling in heaven if I didn't do well in school.

But the feeling that someone's observing you isn't always comforting or positive; it can be disturbing to feel you don't have any privacy. Sometimes the concern is related to specific things, like the idea of being watched while you're in the bathroom, slacking off in school, or sneaking a cigarette. One little boy admits:

> Every time I pick my nose, I think about my mom seeing me. She always told me to stop doing that!

The idea of being watched can be particularly uncomfortable when it grows out of a larger, preexisting issue in the relationship. This girl's father was an alcoholic. Shortly after his death, she found that the idea of his remaining near her was an unwelcome intrusion:

> Me and my brother think about him. We get nervous. What if he is watching? That's scary. Sometimes I think I shouldn't take a shower. I don't dream and I don't like to talk about him. I guess I do talk to my mother. I like to remember when he would give me a piggyback ride.

In the longer term, her fears abated. As their life became more settled and they were no longer dealing with the consequences of their father's excessive drinking, those children began to focus more on the positive aspects of their relationship with him and to put the negatives into some perspective. You can help your children do this by talking to them about their parent's foibles and struggles in addition to the triumphs, and by humanizing, instead of demonizing, the person who died. Ultimately, your children will need to make some sort of connection, even with a troubled parent, and it will be easier if they have some context in which to do so.

There's Nothing Wrong with You if You Don't Have These Experiences

Everyone struggles after a loss to make sense of this hole in their lives, but no two people experience things the same way. You may have one child who makes a regular personal connection to the person who died and another who can't make contact. Not all children have visions, feel a presence, or dream about their loved ones, and when they hear that others do, it can leave them feeling sad and alone, frightened, and even unworthy because they are unable to summon their loved one. Ten-year-old Julia says:

> I almost never dream about my dad. I wish I would. It makes me feel bad that he doesn't visit me.

Some of Julia's relatives dream about her father frequently and consider those nighttime visits full of portent. Julia's mother gets exasperated:

> I feel like saying to my sister-in-law, if he were going to visit, it wouldn't be to tell you what color to paint your living room. It would be to help his daughter!

Julia's mother reassures her daughter that dreams are not necessarily reliable indicators of her father's whereabouts. She tells her that she doesn't really know what happens after someone dies, but that she feels her husband looking after them from above and that they might feel his presence differently from each other, but that that's all right. Older children and adolescents can accept this sort of ambiguity because they can understand that nobody really knows the answers. Just as you don't want to try to talk your children *out* of believing something that brings them comfort at this time, you don't want to try to force them *into* a belief or a construct, either. Over time, they will develop their own ideas about what happens after death as well as their own techniques to maintain a connection with the person who died.

However you and your children make that connection, you will all find solace and support there, as well as a continued sense of your loved one's presence. Still, as comforting as these experiences might be, they're no substitute for the real thing. Drew sums it all up eloquently:

> I think of him in heaven, but that doesn't help because right now I miss him!

CONNECTIONS OVER TIME

As time goes on, the nascent connections you've made to the person who died begin to develop into a long-term relationship. Your children feel less sad and more optimistic that things are getting better. Your lives seem back on track, and it seems less like you're going through the motions. But while you have, in that sense, gotten on with your life, you have not left your loved one behind; the connection is moving inward, where it will take hold and thrive. This widow gets direction and hope from thinking about what her husband wanted:

> He would want us to carry on in spite of the pain and the sadness. It somehow makes it easier when I think that's what he would want.

As the weeks turn to months and years, the frequency might decrease, but you'll still talk to your loved one and feel him or her nearby. Children often describe a benevolent, loving presence, watching over them. Chris's father has been dead for years, but he's still present:

> When I am taking a test, I think of my father as right next to me, giving me encouragement.

Teddy died in a farming accident. Even years later, his brothers feel him helping them:

> He always liked cows and that's where he got killed. Sometimes when I am chasing cows, trying to get them together and nothing is going right, I ask him for help, and usually, about five minutes later, the cows start going in the right direction, just like someone shows up and turns them. Sometimes I think he is around like a guardian angel or something—keeps a guy out of trouble. If I go out at night when it's snowing, you have to think that he is sitting there, keeping his eye on things. Sometimes when you need a little extra help, it's always nice to have him up there with you.

Visits and memories can wash over you at any time—while doing activities you used to share, watching a television show you enjoyed together, in the kitchen, on vacation, and especially during special celebrations. Over time, instead of bringing fresh pangs of pain, you might find the feeling of a loved one's presence to be a comfort. A woman whose husband died six years ago describes her experience:

> I was really expecting to be a wreck at my daughter's middle school graduation this year. We've always had a hard time at events like these, but this year, we both felt like he was there with us, watching proudly.

Another widow finds that the cemetery is the best place for her to go to feel her husband's presence:

> I often go to his grave. I sit and talk. I tell him about how the children are doing. I talk about my problems. I don't know where the answer comes from, but I always get one.

While there are children, and adults, who find cemeteries or other memorial settings too painful a reminder of what's been lost, others find them a place of contemplation and connection. This mother brings her twelve-year-old daughter:

> I always invite her to go to the cemetery with me. We go on holidays and put flowers on the grave. We live near the cemetery. I know she goes by herself. She used to skate near there with her father. I think it is good.

This widow also helps her children connect to their father at the cemetery:

For several years now, we go to the cemetery on his birthday. We bring a cake and some balloons. After we sing Happy Birthday and eat some cake, we go to his favorite ice cream parlor and have sundaes that he always liked. It feels good. It's like we created good memories, and that is important.

These rituals can serve you well for years to come. But if this sort of formal remembrance feels artificial or brings you or your children pain, it may not be right for you, at least not right now. The idea isn't to do one particular thing to make a connection but to identify what works for you at any given time. Finding ways to feel close to the person who died is the goal—and the challenge.

You'll have to experiment a bit to see what methods work for you. Reminiscing about good times, funny events, and even times of conflict can be a long-term, comforting way for your family to feel close to the person who died. An eleven-year-old boy puts it nicely:

It feels good to remember, to feel that he is still part of the family.

A sudden memory of a shared experience can bring a burst of bittersweet emotion, as this boy describes:

Everything reminds me of him, when I see a pennant or fly my kite. My father was smart. You could talk about food, sports. We played cards, watched documentaries. We got along well, even when we disagreed sometimes about baseball. He would have been proud of us. We did the Thanksgiving dinner just the way he would have liked it.

Over time, memories can fade and lose their potency. It can be disconcerting and downright scary for children when they think they are starting to forget their lost loved one. One boy, whose father has been dead more than half his life, says:

I have to find other ways to feel close to him because I don't really have many memories from when I was three.

Keepsakes and Mementos

You can help children keep what memories they have by talking about the person who died, reminding them of events and times together, and filling in the details. You can create a memory box or choose a special location in which to put mementos and artifacts from times you shared. You can also create new memories by telling stories and showing pictures that give a sense of who their loved one was.

For some children, it helps to literally hold on to something that belonged to the person they loved. Chris took his father's Navy commander cap right after he died. Two years later, it remains a touchstone:

> I still have it. I keep it in the closet now. I used to wear it more often but now I don't. Now when I think about him I guess I just feel him by me when I need encouragement or support like on a test or a hockey game.

Eight-year-old Patrick has his father's pocket watch, which his mother is keeping for him until he is older. Sandy wears her father's school ring around her neck. David describes how his mother divided things up after his father died:

> We all share the tools that were his. I asked Mom for them and she said no, they are for the whole family. But she gave me his favorite blanket; it makes me feel close to him.

For Chris, the way to feel closest to his father is through regular visits to the cemetery on his way home from school:

> I tell him about my day, what we are doing in school, and I reminisce with my friend who my father liked.

Your children can write letters to keep their sibling or parent up to date on their lives. Jay writes to his brother Kevin:

> I told him how I miss him, things about school, and that I changed schools so I could be with my best friends.

Talismans, visits to the cemetery, dreams, and visions—whatever the method, the objective is always the same: finding a way to communicate with someone who is no longer present. Some children will make and keep the bonds on their own. Others will need your guidance and advice. The mother of this ten-year-old boy helps him find a way to connect:

> She says we'll pray every night for Daddy and that he'll be able to see me. She says we have to remember Daddy outside in the sunshine laughing, not like he looked when he died. I asked if Daddy can help me now, if he'll always be with me. Mom said yes.

Living Legacies

In a sense, the bereaved carry the dead within themselves and look for ways to keep their loved one's spirit alive. If it was a sibling or a friend who died, your children may see themselves as carrying on in that child's memory and honor. If it was their mother or father who died, your children may see themselves as repositories of that parent's looks, talents, hopes, and expectations for the family. They'll search for the qualities they share. And the older they are, the more deliberate they'll be in trying to emulate the best parts of the person who died. Listen to how this eleven-year-old describes himself:

> I'm like my father in almost every way. I like fishing, I look like him, I say things like him, I tell jokes, people remember him by looking at me. I want to become a scientist like my father.

This boy thinks about his big brother:

> It feels good to look at his picture. I feel as if he is with me. As I get older I realize that I look like him more and more. We are alike also and that makes me feel good when someone says "you remind me of Sam."

Those children are describing their emerging sense of themselves in relation to the person they've lost. They represent a sort of living legacy, where the deceased lives on through them. This works well when children come to this themselves, seeing their parent or sibling as part of who they are. But if they are pressured to follow in someone else's footsteps or to embody somebody else's role in the family, this can become a problem, turning talk of similarities into something to resent. You and other adults in their lives have to be careful not to make children live in a dead parent's image or have surviving children replace a lost sibling in any way. Drew, who looks very much like his dead older brother, feels the need to remind people:

> I am ME, not Ronald.

It's a delicate balance to keep the memories alive without taking over. One widow deals with this by using comparisons as praise:

> I always proudly tell them, "That sounds like something Dad would say." They like to know that.

Helping Your Children Build Memories

In all this, once again, much of the burden may fall on you. You have the challenge of helping your child create a continuing connection at the same time as you are doing this yourself. Caught up in your own grief and overwhelmed by all that's been thrown on you, you might ignore this aspect of the journey through mourning. You might justify this by telling yourself that your children would be better off not focusing on a person they barely remember. In reality, though, your children want you to help them remember. No matter what their age, your children will eventually want to know about the person who died. Without your help, it will be harder for them to do that. You are the repository of memory, of family history, and of continuity.

You don't have to turn this into heavy-handed discussions or interject the person who died into all your daily activities. Simple mentions at appropriate times can make a big difference. The mother of eleven-year-old Jane describes some occasions when she talks to her children about their father:

> There are things that will remind us of him. When the family is together, we'll say, "Dad would have liked that." I'll come up with that myself or one of the older children brings it up. Jane is more ready to talk. When she had the last operation [for back problems] I had her sleep with me. We would be in bed and we'd be talking about him—he had always been there when she needed surgery—and how she missed him. And then we would start laughing and then she would fall asleep.

Your children will be comforted by these sorts of reminders. Some appreciate a concrete conversation; others, like this fourteen-year-old, prefer the indirect approach:

> It makes me feel good when I hear my mother talking to someone about how nice my father was.

Children will also seek out family friends and relatives to help fill gaps in their memories. Grandparents, aunts, and uncles can be a great help here; one of their biggest concerns is that the person they loved, too, not be forgotten. A twelve-year-old describes how this helps her:

> When I went to my grandparents', they talked about my father. They had pictures and it was good to know what he was like as a child and the things he liked to do. I liked when they said I reminded them of him.

Your children's own siblings can also help keep memories alive. Participating in that way gave this child a role to be proud of:

> I'm lucky. I had a longer time with my father than my brother did. I have to help him remember.

Some Memories Are Unpleasant Reminders of a Painful Relationship

If you had significant problems in your own relationship with the person who died, you may be more focused on forgetting than on remembering. If your spouse was abusive to you but not to the children, you wonder if you should tell them about it. If there were criminal activities, you think about protecting your children from that knowledge. If your spouse had a drug or alcohol problem, you worry about how much to tell your children about how their parent lived and died. Helping your children construct a strong connection in situations like these might seem impossible.

But time and again, it's been shown that honesty and openness are essential. You don't have to—and you shouldn't—share all the details with your children, but you don't want to lie, either, and put yourself in a position where your children can't trust you. Whatever you say should be age-appropriate and compassionate, helping your children to see the person behind the problem. Children may find it easier when they have words for the problem, like "my father was an alcoholic," and when they understand how the behavior affected the family—"when he had too much to drink, he got angry, and that was scary." Several years after her mother died of an overdose of prescription drugs, an eighteen-year-old describes her thought process:

> I used to be furious with the doctor for giving her all those pills. Then I was furious with my father because he took her off life support. I was confused because my mother told my father in front of us that it was his fault he gave her so many children. But now I realize she was responsible for taking the pills, and for taking too many. It was an illness no one would talk about. How would we kids know? As I get older I also realize that it is a lot easier not living with someone who was always depressed. I miss her very much. I try to remember the good times, when she was feeling good.

These are deaths that ended troubled lives and unhappy marriages, and they can lead to the awkward situation where the person is missed but the traumatic relationship is not. This father of two girls and a boy explains the dilemma:

> My wife was a good person but she had serious anger problems. One time she broke all the dishes in the cabinet and she was always screaming about the smallest things. Sometimes the kids would run to their rooms and hide. My sister said maybe she was a borderline personality but my wife wouldn't even hear about going to a psychiatrist. I was thinking about leaving her, but I didn't know what to do about the kids. When she died of a stroke, I was relieved, to be honest.

The challenge, if your family has a difficult history, is to acknowledge the pain while also celebrating the positive things about the person who died. That's the message this child was given:

> My mother said my father was two people. When he was drinking he was difficult and always in trouble. When he was sober, he was bright and funny and really nice. Sometimes it was hard to believe it was the same person and what I like to remember about him was when he was sober.

This sort of understanding and acceptance can be a long time coming, no matter what the relationship was like. Your children will make these connections bit by bit, in communication with you and in private reflection.

Finding Ways to Talk

You can encourage your children along the way, but sometimes, despite your best intentions to help keep strong bonds between your children and the person who died, you may come up against a wall of resistance. You need to be prepared if you are eager to talk and your children are not. You also have to allow for time to bring changes. Shortly after his mother died, a boy said:

> I know my father would listen but I don't want to talk.

One year later, the same boy sees things differently:

> Talking makes me sad but it is better than thinking about it alone. My father listens and it really helps.

It's a difficult balancing act for the grieving and for those who love them to know when to draw connections, when to bring up the person who died, and when to give voice to the loss that's always there. You might find it awkward to talk about the person in everyday conversation or you might talk too much. One widow tries to find a happy medium:

> I think it's easier to just mention my husband casually, like saying that he liked this recipe or bought that clock. My kids like to know things like that. But if I try to engage them in a serious conversation about him—forget it.

You also have to be aware of how your own feelings and behaviors affect your children. In the words of the father of an eleven-year-old boy:

> I knew my son's silence was an effort on his part to protect me. In the first year I would cry every time he tried to talk about his mother. Now, it's been two years and it is becoming easier for me to talk about her at home. I wait for my boy to bring it up. But I do initiate some conversation. I try to bring it up in a natural way. I just try to bring it up in a similar situation as when my wife was alive, or I ask, "What do you think mom would have done if this happened?" I'll ask him if he's thinking about his mother. At a particular time of the year I ask if there is something special that he used to do with Mama that he wants to do now.

It helps to give your children the language to express their feelings. One mother of two boys, eleven and thirteen, recognized that her older boy never talked to her about his father. She tries to find ways of encouraging him:

> Sometimes I try to explain how other people feel. I ask if that applies to him. I figure maybe if I give him some words that would help.

Keeping Your Focus on Who Your Children Are and What They Need

As always, no advice is one-size-fits-all. What works for one child might not work for another. It takes time to find the right path to conversation with your children. This father knows that it is important to talk to his daughters about their mother, but it doesn't always work out:

> Any mention of her is brief, but it is on a happy note. At the beginning it trailed off to sadness. Then I did not try to keep the conversation going. Now if we are close to something about her, I'll always bring it up, although I worry about Janice. She doesn't seem to like to talk.

Despite the father's efforts, the family's wires are crossed. Daughter Janice knows what she wants, but she isn't getting it:

> I don't like to talk about my mother in the family or with my friends. I am a private person. I sometimes go to the cemetery and sit there and think. But I wish we had had a big get-together on the anniversary of her death. We didn't do anything. It would have been nice to think about memories and to be there for each other.

Janice wants to keep a sense of her mother alive and she sees the value of ritual, but she rejects her father's attempts to communicate. She doesn't see the discrepancy between her unwillingness to engage in one situation and her desire to connect in another. Her inability to share her confusion with her father leaves them both spinning in circles around each other: he wants her to tell him what she needs and she wants him to know without being told. And if she won't tell him what she needs, he can't know to give it to her.

In another family, the father is having a hard time knowing where to keep his feelings for his dead wife now that he's in a new relationship, so he's having trouble guiding his children to make their own connections to their mother:

> My father remarried and he won't let me talk about my mother in the house. I don't think that is right. I need to do that. My older sister said she would help me. She remembers more than I do and she helped me put together a scrapbook with family pictures.

You can easily see how these kinds of communication breakdowns can happen, especially when you have situations when both you and your children are feeling several different things all at once. You might have to ask yourself every once in a while if your actions might play a part in your children's behavior. While they probably can't, or won't, tell you themselves, being aware of some of these typical stress points may help guide your way.

Your Children Need Your Help

Sometimes the reason you can't help your children connect isn't because of emotional conflict but because you don't believe in the value of continuing the link. The need to maintain connections to the dead isn't something that most people talk about or are aware of. Like those well-meaning friends who tell you to put the photographs and mementos away so you can move on, Christine's mother feels strongly that stirring up old memories would leave the family stuck in the past. Christine, now twelve, feels her needs are very different:

> My mother won't talk about my father. She said it is not good to dwell on his death. I don't agree. I need to remember him. We don't talk about it. I decided to keep a diary so I won't forget. I go see my grandparents. They like to talk about him.

Your children will have to make their way through this process of connecting and remembering with or without you. It's just a lot harder for them without you. Their relationship with you depends, in part, on your ability to accompany them in their struggle. It's been a decades-long challenge for this woman to keep up a connection to her living mother and her dead father:

> My mother spent years actively drinking, which alienated her both from her in-laws and us, her children. In the early years after his death, my mother's reminiscences were shadowed by her drinking. My siblings and I had very different relationships with my father, since the older ones were angry he had not protected them from her drinking by willing us away to someone else when he died. Talk about magical thinking. The way I remained connected to him was through my grandmother and through research I've done about his family. I still feel his love, even thirty years later.

Connections Made, Connections Continue

Through talk, through research, through remembering, through prayer, children will be continually constructing and reconstructing an attachment to the person who died. For one young woman, one of the most helpful things in maintaining her connection to her brother is making sure he's still in people's thoughts:

> On the anniversaries, it's important for people to remember and to call, or for me to feel comfortable to be able to call a person and say, well I'm thinking of my brother today; do you remember that day?

As special moments and life cycle events come and go, there's often a need or desire to include those who can be there only in spirit. One mother found a way to keep her husband involved:

> When my daughter was sixteen, we had a big party. I sent out invitations calling myself Mrs. John Jones. I never use that form. I knew I wanted her father to be at the party

and this was my way of letting people know who he was and bringing him into the festivities.

In another family, it was the child who figured out how to involve her father in a special way on her special day. Her mother tells the story:

> My daughter was a teenager when her father died. At her wedding, her brother gave her away. What I didn't know was that she had two bouquets. I learned this much later on. One she threw out to the bridesmaids at the wedding. Then she went to the cemetery to put the other one on her father's grave and to tell him about her husband and what a great day it was.

Kayla writes to her sister to keep her up to date on what is happening. She keeps the letters in a diary. Four years after the death, Kayla wrote:

> I was talking about you with Joe today and I started to reminisce about how we used to fight and protect each other too. Here's my news: I am facing new things every day. I'm off to graduate school. Since your deaths I have come to appreciate the gifts I received from you and Mom. You loved life and appreciated it like no one I have ever met since. Dad has trouble because I don't want to visit your graves. That's not where I want to think of you.

No matter what the approach or how strong the connection, something will always be missing when you've lost someone you loved. There's no getting around that pain, because it is as strong as the love you had and the shared life you have lost. Mark still thinks about how his brother Teddy would have grown and been involved in his life. He cries as he talks about what he and Teddy missed:

> It's whenever I see a rainbow, whenever I win a big basketball game, a big football game. I think it's because he wasn't there like he should have been. I know he would have been the best of any of us in sports.

It is a loss and a bond that goes on forever. This woman was a toddler when her mother died. Forty years later, she says:

> When I had my first child I really missed my mother. I visualized my mother, that same comfort of her hands. I remember her hands as if they were right in front of me. I woke up crying, wanting her arms around me. It was interesting—I felt cheated, I felt sad, but

thinking about her and talking about her made me feel good. I had to believe that she could see her first grandchild.

You can never be sure of what life would have been like had your loved one lived. All you can do is move forward, keeping hold of the memories and the love. This is a lifelong process, shifting and reinventing itself as your life changes. It takes patience, support, courage, and a lot of work to make and hold a relationship like this, but it is well worth it because in these connections, the person you loved is never truly gone. As this eight-year-old has learned, sometimes the most fragile bonds are the only ones you can hold on to:

My connection is in my heart, sort of. I don't remember my dad that well. I was only three. I'm like him in some ways. The only time I see him is in my dreams.

10

Looking Back, Looking Ahead

For me it's like we are no longer a family minus one. We are now a unit that operates
and functions as a threesome. That's how we act, but it's not necessarily how it feels
for everyone. I think one of the sad things I've found is that parents can come to
terms with the death, where the children really never do. It's not that I don't miss
him. I do, every day; but it's not entirely who I am. I had a sense of who I was before
I met him, and I know I am still mostly that same person now. My kids, on the
other hand, will live the rest of their lives with a part of them missing. It's like there
was an earthquake in an essential part of their formation. And while the first tremors
were the worst, there are aftershocks of reprocessing the death, and the loss, as they
grow. It breaks my heart, sometimes, to think about all that sadness at their core.

A widow, five years after her husband's death

In the years after the death of a loved one, you learn to accommodate your pain
and loss as you and your children adjust to your new reality. Sometimes it might
even be hard to remember what it was like before the death when you were all
together. Over time, feelings become clearer and the pain, while still real, is not
as intense as before. You have not "recovered," you have not "gotten over it," but
you are rebuilding a life. Ten years after Dale's death, his father tries to describe
this delicate balance:

> If the pain went away, then it would be a real loss, a greater loss. The pain that stays
> with me is to honor him. I keep the pain at a level that is tolerable, but it is important to
> me that it is there, and it's for the same reason that we like to talk about him. We also
> think that our zest for life is a tribute to him. Life can be exciting. How would it honor
> him—and all that he lost—if we didn't go on?

You can not return to life as it once was; there will be a different rhythm, with new priorities and altered relationships, especially with

those who don't understand that you are forever changed. One parent explains:

> It gets easier but it never goes away. Sympathy cards that say it will pass, you quickly learn that this is simply not true. People who haven't experienced a death think it will pass. When people stop showing sympathy—they think you are OK, but it's not OK. And then when you bring it up they say, "But that was five years ago. You should be OK." But I'm not OK. It still hurts. It did not go away. But I am enjoying life again and finding my way in a new world.

THE NEW WORLD

Several years out from the cataclysm of loss, the repercussions continue, leaving a terrain that at times barely resembles its original form. You may feel that you are worlds away from the person you were and the life you lived before your loved one died. In the words of one widow:

> My friends find it hard to believe how much I've changed since my husband died. I expect different things from people. I say things I never said before. I decide what is best for the family. If I was going to survive, that's what I had to do.

Two years after her husband's death, this mother of two school-age children also sees that she's changing:

> I'm becoming more independent. I'm less afraid of doing things, and I'm a conscientious, hard worker. I like my home and my kids. I like being home with them and caring about them, sometimes too much. Before, I was less independent, more afraid of doing things by myself and of trusting my own decisions.

It can be hard to find people who understand what you're feeling. Some friends seem to want to pretend that nothing ever happened or that everything's back to normal, or they may be so aware of your loss that they shy away from talking about their own relationships to avoid bringing up a subject that might be painful. This widow of three years says that kind of behavior just makes conversations awkward:

> Sometimes when I'm with my friends, I make the mistake of sharing an anecdote about my husband that's relevant to the conversation. Almost immediately, people take on that

look of sympathy that I hate, and it all comes to a screeching halt. I just want to be
able to add to the conversation or at least not be sitting there silently. And then I end up
changing the whole tone of things.

Paradoxically, the same people urging you to move past your loss often can't
get past the difference between your life and theirs. That's one reason that you
might continue to participate in groups with others who've had a loss, long after
the acute grief has passed. This mother finds strength in numbers:

I joined a support group for young widows. I was not sure why. It seemed to me important
to talk to other single parents. I was suddenly in a place where people understood what
I was talking about. When someone asked if we could get a baby sitter and go to the
movies, I volunteered my fifteen-year-old daughter and I realized what I was missing,
someone to spend an evening with, to see a movie.

Your children are also in need of continued comfort and understanding,
which may be even harder to come by in their daily lives than it is in yours.
Their friends can't begin to contemplate what it's like to lose a loved one or
how to help someone who has; their teachers can't devote their attention to the
personal problems of each student; and their fundamental support system—the
family—is at the center of the very upheaval they're experiencing. This mother
knows that her own progress depends in large part on making sure her children
get the support they need:

I felt strongly about my kids getting counseling. I needed to hear that my kids were not
off the wall. I could see that they weren't but I needed to hear it from the counselor. It
built my confidence. I was getting more independent and comfortable moving out, but
that wasn't really enough yet.

Much of the way in which your children reconcile the death with their life
will depend on your ability to accompany them on this difficult journey. The
process of moving toward change requires patience, time, and a great deal of
unhappiness and pain.

Hard as that sounds, you're already well on your way—change has been part
of the life of your mourning family from the very beginning. Often, you don't
even realize how much has changed until you look back. Years after his wife's
death, this father realizes he's coping better than he thought he could:

I didn't expect that my children would grow up without a mother. But here we are, and in many ways she is still a very positive force in our lives. I'm doing things I never thought I could do, and we are managing.

There's almost a sense of empowerment when you realize you have survived. This widow appreciates that when she considers who she was before and who she is now:

I was always waiting for someone to give me permission and here I am very much in charge. Even how I treat my other kids has changed. I've learned to listen better. Sometimes when I see how much I've changed I almost don't recognize myself.

One of the things we hear over and over from bereaved adults is how their lives take on a new order, built around the space that death has left. This bereaved mother sees the change in her whole family now:

I have a different sense of strength and a clearer idea of where I want to go in my life. We all seem to be in a different place.

All these changes are dramatic and pervasive. Several years after her husband's death, this mother of two preteenagers has found an interesting way to describe herself:

I'm a "recovering widow." I'm very intense and quick to react. I'm somewhat judgmental, happier, more content, a capable mother trying to enjoy life—get back into it. Before his death, I was less intense and less judgmental. I was more social and extroverted then. Probably nothing about me is the same—not all bad, some ways are better.

Some ways are better, and some ways are not. You have learned things about yourself and others in this grieving process; you have reexamined your relationship with the person you lost; and you've reevaluated what really matters in life. These are important and good things to experience. But as one widow puts it:

My life is definitely different, and even better in some ways. But is it worth it? Definitely not. I'd trade every speck of self-improvement just to have him back.

DATING AND REMARRIAGE

The place you find yourself in, several years after the death of a spouse, may be a private one of internal thoughts and perspectives on yourself and your family, or it may lead you to a different outward place in the world, with new friends, new jobs, and new hobbies. For some, but by no means all of you, it may also include thoughts of new romantic relationships. There is no timetable for these thoughts. Some people can't bring themselves to consider another relationship for years, if ever, but the basic concept of another partner in your life may have begun floating around your mind from the early days after the death when you were grappling with the concept of being alone, without the person you married, without the future you had anticipated. As time passes, you might decide you want somebody else in your life or you might prefer to stay as you are. Neither decision is right or wrong. Despite the chorus of well-wishers urging you to "get back out there," feeling ready to date or remarry isn't a sign of emotional health or a measure of neediness. It's simply a direction that some of you will choose to go while others will choose not to. There's no shame in either choice.

There are no adequate statistics that indicate how many widows and widowers date or remarry, though there are indications that men are more likely to pursue new relationships, and to do so more quickly, than women are. These new relationships are not something most people enter into lightly, though. As one widower puts it, three years after his wife's death:

> I married the love of my life. Now she's gone, and while I date other people, I don't really let them into my heart.

Getting back into the romantic realm can stir up a lot of thoughts and feelings you thought you'd put to rest, for you and your family. Man or woman, one year out or ten, if or when you take the step toward a relationship, you should be aware of all that's involved.

You're Not the Same Person You Were

For many of you, the last time you dated was when you were young, perhaps less rooted to a town or to a job, and most importantly, you probably didn't have children. Now, you are quite a different package. This widow says she just can't see it working:

> I can't marry again because I know I'll never find someone who loves my children as much as a father should. For me, that's the deal breaker.

Another widow agrees. She ended a relationship with a man who didn't share her priorities:

> We enjoyed each other. My children were comfortable with him, and my seven-year-old son was very ready to let him into his life. But we were in a different place about raising children and eventually I had to break up with him before the children got too involved. I couldn't be with someone who couldn't put my children first.

It's not only the question of how prospective partners feel about your children, it's how your children feel about your prospective partners. Whatever you do now, you don't do it alone. Your children will have their own ideas about what feels right for them, and for you. This widower describes competing strands of thought and need in his house:

> I realized that we all move along in different ways, especially if there are children. There are different steps—I moved faster than my children did. Put us out of sync at various times. I am now at the place where I was asking what was I going to do with my life, and then I realized that I miss being with a woman and being able to go out with someone and talk. It was one year after my wife died. I was in some way ready to take these steps and the kids weren't.

Everything you have gone through after the death of your spouse plays into the decisions you make now. The soul-searching about who you are and who you were in the marriage can lead you in new directions. Five years after her husband died, this woman thinks about all the different perspectives involved in her remarriage:

> I know now this is a different relationship. I had changed and as I thought about it I wanted to be able to communicate better. When your children are young I think they seem to want a new parent. My oldest, when he was six, worried what would happen to them if something happened to me. Until recently both boys would panic if they couldn't find me for a minute. The oldest told me to remarry so there would be someone to take care of them if something happened to me. It was certainly different for my future step children, who were teenagers. They liked me as a date, but when they realized that we were going to get married, they objected very strongly.

This widow also met with resistance when she wanted to start dating. She took her son's feelings seriously enough to have her new relationship move at a pace that matched his needs:

It was a strange coincidence but a mutual friend put me in touch with my childhood sweetheart who was recently divorced. I kept him at a distance. There clearly was something between us but I had a sense that my fourteen–year-old son wouldn't be happy to have another man in my life as if it would be a substitute for his father. We talked on the phone, wrote e-mails and then went out to lunch. It was a year before I let him stop by the house. He was very patient and understood. As my son got to know him it was clear that he was by now comfortable with my going out.

You and Your Children Might Be in Very Different Emotional Places

You might not have the patience, sensitivity, or interest to let your children's concerns take center stage. It's hard to separate your own desire for a new relationship from the feelings this brings out in your children. It can be frustrating to have to deal with this kind of conflict when you are feeling ready, and vulnerable, too. This father is dating and rarely home, but he can't appreciate how that looks to his family:

The children wanted me home more often. I was going out more after I met my girlfriend. It was about a year after my wife died. Then they were unhappy when I had her come and cook for us on Thanksgiving, to be together as a family. They complained, they weren't ready to have someone take their mother's place. That wasn't my intention but I couldn't explain it to them. My girlfriend felt hurt because she felt that they were mean to her. I felt caught in the middle.

That father is caught in the middle of a mess he made himself because he isn't considering how threatened his children are by his new relationship. Even when they tell him, he can't honor their feelings; he's just focused on what he wants.

Putting your children's needs first is hard to do when it flies in the face of what you want. But you ignore them at your own risk. This twelve-year-old girl feels abandoned by her father's new direction, and she's pulling away:

My father offered to take me to the cemetery whenever I wanted to go. This was not long after my mother died. He took me once and now he feels that I should tell him if I want to go. I think he should offer to take me—in my mind, he has broken his promise. I was so upset my father forgot to take me to the cemetery on my mother's anniversary. I think it is because he is getting married and has that on his mind. He talks about his getting married and he won't talk to me about my mother. Now I am uncomfortable sharing my dreams or feelings with him. I cry by myself in my room. I made a scrapbook of pictures of my mother.

As these stories indicate, your decision to date and possibly remarry may happen on a very different schedule from your children's. Your children might be happy with your decision and even encourage you to pursue romantic interests, but even then, children rarely take this lightly, and they want you to take their feelings into consideration. As much as this decision is fraught with significance for you, it is of an entirely separate magnitude for them. While you might be compelled, in part, by the thought of giving your children a male or female role model in the house, or letting them be part of a two-parent family, a lot of children don't feel that this is what they're getting when you bring a new person into your life, and they make that very clear in interviews.

Replacing Part of Who They Are

Your children didn't "choose" the parent who died, like you did, and it may be incomprehensible to them that you can choose someone else to take on that role. It's not like the experiences they have had with making new friends, or, for teenagers, breaking up with one person and then going out with another. For them, this feels like you're replacing a part of themselves as well as emphasizing the finality of death. In the words of a sixteen-year-old:

> I encouraged my mother to date when I was ten. She started dating. After three years she broke up and then she signed up for a dating Web site, and she met someone. She came home one night on her birthday and he proposed to her. It was like what I feared. I tried to be so supportive of her but when she left I played loud music and started to cry. Then I went to a friend's. Dating was one thing, but to remarry makes death more real. When I get upset I come back to it. Makes death more final—as if at some level he could come back, in some way, yes. I call her husband by his first name so no one would think he is my father.

In many blended families, the question of what to call new parents can be a tricky one. This widow met and married a widower. Both of them have children from their first marriages:

> Names can be an issue. We decided to let the kids decide how they want to call us. First names are fine with us. My children's father knew that there was a chance I would

remarry. The children were so young—it saddened him but he knew they might call another man "Daddy."

Children's concerns can range from general feelings of abandonment to specific issues, like where you'll live. Sometimes children will talk to you about their concerns and other times you'll have to try to figure them out. This thirteen-year-old girl was reassured that remarriage means a different relationship, not a replacement.

I finally talked to my mother. When she talked about "we," I got very upset. After we talked, I felt better but I still think of him as my uncle or something like that.

It's not that your children don't want you to be happy or that they don't necessarily like the new person in their lives. But having that much change forced on them can be excruciating, especially after they've already gone through the anguish of the death of a parent. For this sixteen-year-old, remarriage feels like a violation:

My mother took down all of the pictures of my father when we moved. I felt connected to my father in the other house. Her husband is OK but he is not my father. They can't act as if my father didn't exist, and that's how it feels.

Your children's ages may affect their responses to your romantic plans. Older children may be more sympathetic to your desire to have a significant adult in your lives, but they might also resent that person for invading their dead parent's space. Younger children may seem to adapt more easily to a new marriage, at least on the surface. A twelve-year-old girl describes her response to her younger brother's reactions:

When my brother is excited about my mother's husband and the new baby (he says he has a brother now and calls my mother's husband Daddy), I get angry. He gets all excited about playing ball with my mother's husband. For me, it's like he is being disloyal to our father.

You can help your children by being sensitive to what they're thinking, feeling, and fearing, by really listening to them, and then by really talking to them, addressing all those issues head-on. They need to know that no one can take their dead parent's place, and that they, and you, can still honor that parent while having this new relationship at the same time. This boy was four when his father remarried. Now a teenager, he reveals what was reassuring for him:

> I was pretty young when my mother died. When my father got married again, he explained that I have two mothers. One who gave birth to me and one who takes care of me now. That felt OK as I think about it now too.

Your Former In-Laws Are Part of This, Too

There are other people who may share your children's concerns about your dating or remarriage and who have a vested interest in what happens: the family of your deceased spouse. While they, too, most often do want you to be happy, the prospect of your new life can be very unsettling. This grandmother describes her emotions:

> When my son-in-law remarried, of course we were there. She is a lovely woman and very respectful of us, but we were not happy. Our grandchild who is just two years will call her "mommy," and it was a final blow to us as we had to face that our daughter was really gone.

In-laws worry about losing contact with you and with your children, severing that living link to their loved one. They may be hesitant or scared to bring up those fears, and it may be left to you to reassure them. One widow who married a widower makes sure to keep those bonds strong, for the children, for herself, and for her in-laws:

> We involved them, we talked to them. We told them we knew how important the children were to them. They came to the wedding. They sometimes babysit or just take the boys out and the men enjoy golf together. They try to give some attention to the older children, my husband's from his first wife, who really appreciate that. Their mother's parents are around in the same way. It means we have a very big family and we like it.

Like that woman and her husband, this couple had each lost a spouse before they met each other. Having this experience in common helped them navigate some of the problems a new relationship can bring:

> When we met we hadn't thought about the fact that we were both widowed. But we both found that people who had not been in this situation couldn't quite figure out how to deal with the death. They were afraid to approach it when we brought it up. We don't

have that kind of barrier between us. In this new house, in the hallway downstairs are all the family pictures from years past. Clearly our deceased spouses are part of our lives. The kids know all about each of them and the teenagers are gradually becoming more at ease with the new family.

It's a different kind of relationship from the one you had before, when you blend all these people together—in-laws, children, stepchildren, and so on—but it can make a big difference to everyone when they feel that you respect their feelings and that you still honor the loved one who can no longer be there. If you remarry, it's important to let them all know that their loved one somehow remains present in your new relationship and in your hearts. This widow says her first husband would have wanted her to remarry and be happy, and would have approved of her choice:

I had a dream with a very awkward moment. I had to introduce my husbands to each other. Then I woke up. I do think they would have liked each other.

Within a new marriage are the roots of the old. You're raising, with someone new, the children you had with the spouse who died, a person who had a profound impact on your lives. Sometimes the reality of how you got here can be painful to reckon with. This recently remarried widow explains:

On bad days when missing Alan is acute and being a stepmother is dreadful, I feel miserable. Not like I made a bad choice in remarrying but just missing my old life with Alan and our children. It wasn't perfect, but it was good, and it was my first choice.

You have learned, through your terrible loss, that life can be short and that good times are not something to squander. New romances, like every other life event that happens after the death of a spouse, are almost entirely different from those that came before, because of the knowledge of what you once had, who you once were, and who you are now. Happy though it might be, a new relationship will also disrupt the face of your new family, the one that grew out of the death, and it will give your children something new to struggle with.

THE CHILD'S PATH

Children go down a much different path from the one adults do in the years after the death of a loved one. All children undergo vast developmental changes as they grow and mature, but there's an additional facet to grapple with when someone they love dies. Bereaved children continually revisit and reprocess the death as they move through the different levels of development. A widow whose husband died when their son was three describes his progress:

> He knew that there was a picture in the house of a man who I told him was his father and he took that for granted that his absence was the way it was. When he started kindergarten he paid more attention and realized that other children had two parents. He suddenly asked, "Do I have a father? Where is he?" I had to start from scratch about dying and what happened to his father. All the sadness and pain was there again and I realized that as he grew he would ask more questions and I had to be prepared to answer them if I wanted him to know who his father was.

Friends Don't Always Understand

This is not just the case for children too young to remember their parent; adolescents and teens also experience the ebb and flow of coming to terms with what has happened. This high school junior reflects on his hard times:

> After my mother died, I struggled with getting along with my friends. Most of the kids at school didn't seem to understand. I sometimes lost the ability to focus at school; I often felt very intense sadness. But now I think I have a wisdom and a sense of maturity that I think came from dealing with her death. But even now, three years later, I sometimes go back and forth between the hard times and how things got better.

This sixteen-year-old is having problems at school even six years after her father's death. She says her peers still treat her differently:

> They are afraid of how I would react so they would be guarded. Afraid you will cry or be upset. So you become more guarded. People do not want to upset you. They look at you as if you are fragile, somehow different. Yet you may be stronger than they are.

This issue of how people respond comes up quite often when talking to children about loss. As one fifteen-year-old puts it:

> I did not want people to see me as different from what I am. I did not want them to look at me and say "oh poor kid." Not that they tell you but they look at you different than they did before the death. It isn't something dramatic; it is just the way they look. They

do not know what to say. As if you became radically different. Not something they can really see. There are so many parts to you that they do not understand.

Friends don't understand because these sorts of losses are outside the normal path of childhood. Many people don't lose someone they love until they are well into adulthood. That's one reason people turn to support groups—so they can find the comfort of people who do understand. This high school junior reflects on the tragedy it took for his peers to be on the same psychological plane as he is:

There was a boy killed in a drinking accident. It hit everyone very hard. I was close to him and the boys in the group. They were the happiest group of people. Now I see them so sad, crying and looking to me for help because I have been through it. They were so vulnerable. I feel that I can talk to them as I couldn't before. Unfortunately it had to come from that.

A Lengthy Journey of Discovery

The road to your children's change and growth is long, bumpy, and full of potholes. This young man realizes that he hasn't dealt with his father's death in the way he'd hoped he would. Now, he's approaching his high school graduation, and he's not ready:

I used to think that I would prepare so much for it and know where I was going to go to college. And have everything in order. But I don't know what I want to do. I want time to figure things out. My mom understands but everyone keeps asking me why. There's not a simple answer. I don't even know how to explain it, but I want more time. It is related to my Dad's death and now I am older and it seems to mean something different!

There's no particular age at which a child is better able to grapple with the changes death will bring. Some children think it's easier when the person dies before you are old enough to remember them; others believe it's better to have been old enough to have memories. This sixteen-year-old was two when his mother died:

I don't know what my life would have been like had she lived. I think it was harder for my sister. I can hear what she says now. She remembers my mother and talks a lot about her and what it was like before. When I was younger I couldn't listen and I didn't understand what it meant to her.

In contrast, an eight-year-old envies his big brother's memories:

He can remember all sorts of things and he knows what our dad was like. I don't even know if he liked to watch TV.

Sometimes the question is not what your children remember but how willing they are to learn about the person they did not know. For a long time, this girl did not want to listen to her mother's stories:

All throughout high school she kept trying to talk with me about my father and the work he had done. She wanted to show me examples and I wasn't interested. I could not really deal with it. I got to college, away from home, and now I needed to know, who was I like and where did my talent come from? By now my mother had put away all his things and was wanting to talk to me about her plans to remarry. Our timing was all off. But she did talk to me about him then. She even shared some of the problems they had. And I found out that my interest in music came from him.

All adolescents struggle to discover who they are, to define themselves, and to figure out where they stand in relation to the rest of the world—most particularly, their family. Those who have lost a family member have a greater challenge to find that identity. It helps them when they create a sense of the person they've lost, and then try to see how and where they fit in with that person. This seventeen-year-old girl describes her father, and herself, two years after his death:

He was a very gifted, intelligent, loving person, liberal. He never tried to judge people. He was very open-minded. We were very close. We always knew what each other was thinking. I respected him very much; he taught me a lot. I really miss being able to share what I'm learning, his not seeing how I'm growing up.

This thirteen-year-old uses her image of who her father was to help find her own place:

He was smart, like a good person, tried everything and didn't give up anything, gave everyone a chance. I try to do what would please him and make him proud. I try out things at school and in sports. I'm not as smart as he was. I like sports just to please him. I want him to be proud of me.

Another seventeen-year-old girl searches her knowledge of her mother to find herself:

I'm like her. I have her ability to listen and reason things out. Actually, a lot like both of them, but I have my mother's self-discipline.

Sometimes, filling in the gaps in their lives may lead your children to idealize and idolize the parent who died. Compared to this icon, you, the surviving parent can only come up lacking. This girl feels like she's lost the only one who really knew her:

I think about the things my father and I used to do when I was younger. My father understood me. I could really talk to him about anything. I miss that very much. My mother is not as understanding. He had more patience than my mother and was more encouraging when I didn't do well in school.

Finding a Healthy Balance between Your Needs and Your Children's

Over time, your children will be able to look outside their own selves and realize what it must have been like for you to raise them, alone, while you are suffering yourself. They'll appreciate how hard you worked to make a new life for your family, centered around their needs.

The opposite approach to raising bereaved children just doesn't work out that well. Nelly's father died when she was a teenager. She talks to other bereaved teens and has heard about parents who let their own needs supersede those of their children:

She can "parentify" you, so you end up taking care of your mother. She can say your life is devoted to me and taking care of me. My mother isn't like that at all.

It can be hard to not do this "parentifying" to some extent when you're asking your children to do things around the house that the person who died might have done, or when the absence of a spouse leads you to tell your children too many details of your workday. The real trouble comes if you're looking to them to help you get over your problems. Of course, you need support, too, but you're going to have to find it from someone other than your children. In Nelly's case, her mother found the balance that worked for them:

My mother treated me as an equal. She didn't ask me to take care of her and she didn't try to run my life. We were very respectful of each other. Gave me space to find my way and do my thing.

That same relationship might not work in your family, where the personalities will be different. It's not Nelly's mother's solution that matters here; it's finding the healthy balance between letting your children have their space and giving them the support they need. Some of that challenge can be met by helping your children create and maintain their own bonds to the person who died, to remain open and available to talk, and perhaps most importantly, to let them know that it's OK to still be grieving, to still be missing, to still be remembering their loved one.

This will take time, effort, and patience. Your children may reject your overtures or seem like they're not paying attention. In the end, though, most children, as they look back at how they've grown and changed, indicate their appreciation for their parent's attempts to help them in their journey through grief.

No matter how much you help, unfortunately, that journey will be long and hard. Much of what transpires along the way gets established deep in your children's core, and it is hard for them to describe. These children live with a dark legacy of fears and anxieties about themselves and their loved ones. Like this high school sophomore, they know too well how tenuous a hold we have on life:

> I worry now, five years later. If my mother is late, first thing I think of is a traffic jam, then that she died. I worried a lot when it first happened but now it is still there. I don't fear my own death; I fear for those around me. If my friend didn't come to school for three days, I thought the worst. I even pictured the funeral and how I got through it. A lot of people, if they haven't experienced death, they think "it doesn't happen to me." But when it happens, you know it can happen. Then you are afraid, and yet you understand and accept it.

These fears can lead children to a more careful approach to life than most of their peers. A high school junior who was twelve when her brother was killed in a car accident says:

> I'm more grown up, more serious. It made me stronger. I had to grow up faster than other kids. I didn't understand it. I understood a car accident. I never understood why he had to die. I've learned a lot and I've grown from it. You can't take life for granted but you need to find a way of living. For example, it affects my driving.

Time does not diminish these thoughts; it just leads your children to new levels of self-discovery and awareness. A teenager whose mother died several years ago gets frustrated as she watches her friends interact with their families because she knows what they don't appreciate:

> I would see them talking about what they were doing, and at the same time complaining about dumb stuff, and I would get really sad. Sad because my family doesn't get to be together, because they're just not doing anything, and also sad for them, because they don't think about what they have. But it's not the type of thing that you can tell them. No one could have told me. It just comes with, you know, the experience, I guess. It just usually probably comes later for most people.

This is an uncommon maturity, born of a terrible knowledge. These adolescents see themselves as different from their peers—stronger and more determined—and they *are* different because they are exploring philosophical and foundational issues in a deeper way than most people their age do. This high school senior was fourteen when his mother died:

> I feel older than my classmates. I have lived through something they do not understand yet. I am different and it is OK.

Your children will talk about knowing what really matters, now that they've learned the hard way that life is short and can be taken from you at any moment. This is an important perspective that can lead them to embrace life and live it to its fullest, but it can also be somewhat isolating. A college freshman reflects on the seven years since her mother died:

> I was in seventh grade. I walked a little taller, because I knew what life was really about. When I got to high school I didn't always have patience for the other kids whose only worry was about little things, like what to wear to the prom. I saw myself as knowing what was really important. I soon learned to keep some things to myself since very few people wanted to hear that I didn't have a mother.

Try as they might, it isn't healthy to sustain that pressure to be meaningful all the time—everyone needs some escape, some downtime, some frivolous fun. It's important that your children do things just for the joy they bring and that they engage in life, not just philosophize about it. This high school junior is determined to still have good times without her mother, but it's hard:

> I had to admit that I did care about what I wore to my prom, but it didn't take up all my time and energy. I didn't worry about the fact that I had to look perfect. That didn't seem

important. It was just sad that she wasn't there to help me pick out the dress and to see me in it.

Profound and Lasting Changes

As the years go by, the sharpest pain fades, and a new person emerges from the ashes of the death, a person shaped by it forever but also moving forward with new experiences and new expectations. Claudia's mother worried that her daughter's zest for life would be buried under the circumstances of her father's death from AIDS. Instead of letting it influence her negatively, Claudia has found a way to go on and even to use some of the lessons of his death to do good. Looking at how much has changed over the past four years, her mother is optimistic:

> Her father's death was a tragedy, but her life is not tragic now. We had a lot of support. She is a great kid. She is very accomplished. She has friends, she plays the violin, she's involved in sports, she's going right along. She walks in the annual AIDS Walk in memory of her father and gets all her friends to sponsor her. That's all a part of who she is.

When asked what it means to come to terms with a loved one's death, one young woman answers:

> Like a hole, a scar, it will always be there; it heals but it will not heal. This is part of moving on.

Moving on can take many forms, and you and your children will go through numerous adaptations of your own before arriving somewhere close to peace. As described by this teenager who has worked through the pain, there is acceptance and accommodation, at last:

> I don't know how my life would have turned out if my father had lived. But it is good and I am content.

Childhood and adolescence is a time of searching: for identity, for philosophy, for perspective and truth. You can't quantify whether that search is significantly different for teenagers who have lost someone they love, but it feels as though it is different to them. Since we can never know what would have been had our loved one lived, we cannot know who *we* would have been with that person's presence. This widow tries to grapple with the concept of never knowing how her children's lives have been changed:

> When my husband died, I was so upset that there would forever be a shadow on my children's lives. Then my sister told me, everyone has a shadow. You just know what this one is. That comforts me a little. But not enough.

Everyone has a shadow, but this one casts its darkness forever. Even into adulthood, the absence of a loved one is still felt; the loss runs deep. Four decades after her mother's death, this woman has lived nearly her whole life trying to reconcile the loss:

> I have never been particularly good at forming attachments (think of the life-lesson in the mind of that three-year-old who loses her mother: "Don't love anyone because they might leave"). But reconnecting with my mother's family as an adult helped me know myself better so that I could fight the impulses that constantly warn me to remain aloof. I am happily married, have two great kids and several really good friends—all of whom put up with my quirks. But it has been a journey—one started in young adulthood and is still ongoing. Never underestimate the impact of the death of a parent on a child—even forty-four years later.

People seem to have a general optimism that carries them through their darkest days and lets them say "it was terrible yesterday, but today I'm OK," and then get up and say the same thing again the next day. And it was terrible yesterday, and today it will be better, and tomorrow too. You'll live again, you'll love again, you'll lead a wild and wonderful life. But underneath it all, beyond the reach of moods and attitudes and good or bad intentions, remains the never-ending knowledge that someone you loved so, so much is never coming back.

Behind every joy lies that pain. In times of celebration, the loved one is missed. In everyday life, the absence is felt. These are enormous weights to carry through life, and they shouldn't be dismissed as dwelling on the past or wallowing in self-pity. This is a loss that never ends, and a recovery that's never complete. And yet, with help, with patience, with care and understanding, little by little, piece by piece, you and children will make your places in the world.

Index